A WORLD OF DIVERSITY

A WORLD OF DIVERSITY

Multicultural Readings in the News

Faun Bernbach Evans

NTC Publishing Group
Lincolnwood, Illinois USA

Articles from the *International Herald Tribune* are republished by permission of the International Herald Tribune, 181 avenue Charles-de-Gaulle, 92200 Neuilly-sur-Seine, France; The New York Times; and The Washington Post, the copyright proprietors.

ISBN 0-8442-5918-7 (student text)
ISBN 0-8442-5919-5 (instructor's edition)

Library of Congress Cataloging-in-Publication Data

A world of diversity: multicultural readings in the news / [compiled by] Faun Bernbach Evans.
    p. cm.
  Includes articles reprinted from the International herald tribune, the New York times, and the Washington post.
  ISBN 0-8442-5918-7
  1. Readers—Social sciences. 2. Pluralism (Social sciences)—Problems, exercises, etc. 3. English language—Composition and exercises. 4. Current events—Problems, exercises, etc. 5. English language—Rhetoric. 6. Readers—Current events. 7. Readers (Secondary) 8. College readers. I. Evans, Faun Bernbach.
PE1127.S6W67 1996
428.6—dc20

96-18423
CIP

Contents

Preface / ix

■

Preface

A World of Diversity is a multicultural reader for writing students that offers an opportunity to explore in depth the important crosscultural issues we encounter daily. The varied readings for *A World of Diversity* have all been chosen from recent issues of the *International Herald Tribune*. Based in Paris and known as "The World's Daily Newspaper," the *International Herald Tribune* is very popular among people who are concerned about the latest developments in world news. The selections for this book have therefore been culled from a source rich with information on themes such as turns in our world economy, changes in the Earth's environment, the ramifications of technological advances, and the ravages of war.

We live in a world where boundaries of nationality, race, ethnicity, class, and gender sometimes prevent us from seeing the wealth of diversity as well as the common ground we share. Although these boundaries can be exclusionary, we may often find ourselves traversing them as we negotiate our daily lives. While some issues may appear at first to be contained within the borders of a particular nation or group of people, a closer examination often reveals more universal phenomena. The flooding of a particular region might be the result of a climatic trend that ignores national borders; the economic stability of one nation can have significant implications for the economies of many other nations; and the discovery of a cure for a disease can change lives around the world. Given this interrelatedness, the goal of *A World of Diversity* is to encourage you to recognize the web of common ties we possess within our diversity and, in so doing, to become more active participants in the care of our global village.

Organization of the Text

Of the hundreds of articles reviewed, fifty-three were chosen to be included in this text. The readings were selected on the basis of three criteria:

1. their interest level
2. their ability to spark engaged discussion about an issue
3. their crosscultural content

The text is divided thematically into ten chapters. Each chapter addresses a particular theme from a multicultural vista and includes five or six readings. Every effort was made to compile a diverse group of readings for each chapter. Editorials, news reports, and feature stories have all been included. This diversity also encompasses both the locale and the nature of the news events. For example, in Chapter Nine, "Understanding the World Economy," the selections range from "Russian Firm Learns to Navigate in a Free Market" to "The Third World Is Shrinking Fast."

These articles not only examine the ways in which world events affect individuals, communities, and nations, but they also explore connections among the issues themselves. For example, in "A Forgotten Ecological Disaster," Donatella Lorch reports on how the Rwandan civil war has led to the deforestation of the Kibira Forest in Burundi, Africa. And in "Europe's Floods of 'Sins and Failures,'" Rick Atkinson investigates the link between urbanization and the "superfloods" that devastated much of the Netherlands and Germany in 1995. Whenever possible, the readings were chosen in order to challenge you to make these types of connections; both the discussion questions and writing assignments that accompany the readings help to facilitate these associations.

Although each chapter deals with a distinct theme, you will probably find some overlap among the readings and chapters. For example, you might see a relationship between the article entitled "Courses in English Flourish in Vietnam," which has been placed in Chapter One, "Educating Our People," and a selection entitled "Twenty Years After, Vietnam Treads Softly," found in Chapter Nine, "Understanding the World Economy." The chapter designations, therefore, should not be viewed necessarily as discrete entities unto themselves but rather as avenues for exploration, and the intertextual nature of the themes and readings should encourage engaged discussion and analysis.

Features of the Text

The following features form a framework for the book and can be found in each of the ten chapters:

- **Chapter Introductions:** The chapter introductions provide context for the key issues presented in each chapter and make suggestions for ways to approach the readings. Along with background information about the particular theme for each chapter, the introductions offer an overview of the selections and preview questions for consideration.

- **Selection Headnotes:** Each reading selection is introduced with a brief headnote that previews the reading by giving necessary context and a few questions to consider while reading.

- **Discussion Questions:** Several discussion questions follow each reading. These questions are intended to stimulate critical analysis of the readings and are generally open-ended to encourage an exchange of varied responses.

- **Writing Assignments:** Each reading is also accompanied by three to five writing assignments that ask you to write in a variety of genres, including interviews, problem-solution papers, informative reports, causal analyses, and so on. Whenever possible, the assignments suggest a specific audience for you to address. Further, the assignments have been designed to facilitate a process-oriented approach to writing, with prewriting and brainstorming suggestions often accompanying the assignments.

- **Chapter Writing Assignments:** Several longer writing assignments are provided at the end of each chapter. These give you an opportunity to explore the issues raised in the chapter in greater depth and to synthesize your knowledge. In addition, these assignments often ask you to connect the readings in one chapter with readings in another chapter.

A World of Diversity provides a portal into a conversation about a variety of crosscultural concerns. Yet it is not intended to be an exhaustive collection on multiculturalism. Rather, the readings and assignments might be viewed as fodder for an intelligent, informed, and rigorous examination of some of the important issues we face within our immediate *and* global communities. As the Greek essayist Plutarch wrote, "The mind is not a vessel to be filled but a fire to be kindled." It is hoped that an exploration of *A World of Diversity* can help to kindle that fire.

Acknowledgments

I am indebted to the many people who helped bring this project to completion. I am especially grateful to my editor at NTC Publishing Group, Marisa L. L'Heureux, for her guidance, good humor, and infinite patience, and to John Nolan, Editorial Director at NTC, for the opportunity to work on the project. I thank Robert Schwegler for his introduction to NTC Publishing Group and for his support. To Maria Teresa and Rodrigo Garretón, I offer many, many thanks for their computer expertise so generously given and for their friendship.

I would also like to thank the friends and colleagues whose help has informed this work and whose ongoing encouragement and conversation continue to provide a support network of invaluable worth: Betty Bamberg, Kathryn Barrett-Gaines, Robin Benny, Rebecca Binks, Donna Brazas, Jack Blum, Deborah and Philip Burns, Irene Clark, John Edlund, Barbara Gleason, Ana Jiménez-Hami, John Holland, Bill Howard, Frank Liebenow, Genevieve Lopardo, Margie McInerney, Jim Nagle, Paul O'Connell, Madeleine Youmans, Carson Veach, Mark Wiley, Norma and W. Ross Winterowd, and the extended RLL/FWP/USC family.

Finally, I express my gratitude to my family for their faith in me and for their love.

Faun Bernbach Evans

Educating Our People

In the United States, education is a common topic of discussion and concern for many people—parents, students, taxpayers, and politicians. The discussions range from equal opportunities for all students and the need for parental involvement to multicultural curricula and bilingual education. These issues are important and deserve attention; however, the selections in this chapter place education in a broader, more global context. The five articles in this chapter examine education from an international perspective. Whether discussing reforms in the Swedish educational system, reporting on the demand for English instruction in Vietnam, or describing schools with curricula rooted in democracy and international peace, the selections in this chapter reflect a growing interest in education that reaches beyond the confines of individual nations.

The chapter begins with an article by Thomas Fuller entitled "When Peace Forms Part of the Curriculum." In this selection, Fuller reports on a unique international network of colleges called United World Colleges. With eight locations worldwide, these colleges have been designed to promote world peace and global cooperation in addition to teaching traditional courses such as math, science, and history.

Similarly, "Spanish School Offers a Place in the Sun for Learning" by Barry James explores the history of the Menéndez y Pelayo International University, an institution founded in Santander, Spain, in the 1930s in the midst of a growing fascination with totalitarian governments. Begun as an attempt to break away from intellectual isolation, the university sponsored a curriculum rooted in democratic and internationalist ideals. Falling prey to Franco's fascist regime, the university reestablished itself when Franco died and democracy returned.

Turning to the specific needs of one country, "Equality Means Progress, Says Swedish Minister" is an interview by Keith Foster with Carl Tham, the Swedish minister of education. Tham discusses the educational agenda of the Swedish government. In addition to gender equity, the minister views preparing students for work in a global economy as a top priority. Specifically, language education is one area he feels cannot be overlooked when preparing students for international exchange. Although most Swedish students can speak and write English (as well as Swedish) relatively well by the time they graduate from college, Tham believes that they should be fluent in languages such as German, French, and Spanish.

"Courses in English Flourish in Vietnam" by Kate Brown examines the rapid growth of English-language instruction in Vietnam. In response to reformed economic policies, Western corporations have flocked to Vietnam. The Vietnamese, who have been isolated from much of Western commerce since the Vietnam War, are eager to gain the English-language skills that they need to succeed in international business.

Finally, Lawrence Malkin in "Broader Horizons in MBA Programs" explores the efforts by administrators at prominent business schools in the United States to internationalize MBA programs in terms of both the curriculum and the students. This effort reflects the concern we see shown in all five selections that educational and intellectual pursuits can no longer remain within the boundaries of one particular nation or culture.

As you read these articles, try to relate the general themes of globalization and international exchange to your own educational experiences, whether they have been in the United States or elsewhere. Can you relate to any of the issues being explored in these articles? Can you make any connections or associations between these issues and educational policies now being debated in your community?

WHEN PEACE FORMS PART OF THE CURRICULUM

Thomas Fuller

International Herald Tribune

◼

In this article, Thomas Fuller describes a unique group of colleges designed to promote world peace. United World Colleges was founded during the Cold War by Kurt Hahn, an Austrian who emigrated to England after fleeing Nazi Germany. This international network of colleges (with eight campuses worldwide) teaches basic courses such as math, science, and history, but it also has courses that focus on world peace and cooperation. Because the UWC is not aligned with any one nation, the curriculum is free of nationalism, so students receive an education based on international cooperation and goodwill. As you read this article, consider to what extent there is a need for an institution such as United World Colleges.

◼

1   Think of the Cold War and images of missile factories, fallout shelters and spy agencies come to mind—but probably not a network of secondary schools designed to foster peace.

2   Yet both the United World Colleges, founded within months of the Cuban missile crisis, and the spies were products of the same era. The school was the vision of a man who had fled Hitler's Germany and was determined to create a world-wide educational network that would teach students as much about international cooperation and peace as it would about math, history and science.

3   And while today's spies are scrambling to adjust to a post–Cold War world, United World Colleges still sees plenty of areas where its work is unfinished.

4   "Of course we have worries," says Colin Jenkins, headmaster of College of the Atlantic in Wales, the oldest United World College.

"We are seeing in our world the rise of nationalism. We only have to look at Bosnia. We only have to look at refugee crises in Rwanda, Somalia, Ethiopia, Sudan. I think the world doesn't actually look too great," he says.

5 Today there are eight United World Colleges located in the United States, Canada, Wales, Italy, Singapore, Venezuela, Swaziland and Hong Kong. Each is independent financially but tied to a central office in London, which deals with alumni affairs and provides information about the colleges to prospective students. Headmasters from the eight schools meet several times a year to discuss issues of curriculum, fundraising and the possibility of opening new schools.

6 Each United World College holds an annual seminar called Global Concerns, where topics such as economic development, the environment and conflict resolution are discussed.

7 But administrators at the schools say that most of the international cooperation occurs outside the classroom and that these seminars do nothing more than "provide a laboratory for discussion," in the words of Mr. Jenkins.

8 Mark Hoffman, chairman of the school's International Board in London, explains the mission of the schools:

9 "The UWC was founded on the idea that young people between 16 and 19 in that very formative period just before they're conscripted into the military and called up to shoot each other, can make lasting friendships which transcend the typical national educational experience.

10 "Supranational may sound a bit grand, but it's not a program of studies that was dictated by any national curriculum body or educational authority—so that the students would be able to have a personal foundation for international understanding and goodwill that would last their lifetime."

11 The school was founded by Kurt Hahn, an Austrian educator who, after being imprisoned in Nazi Germany for his views on that regime, fled to England where he also started Outward Bound, a popular outdoor program designed to foster leadership and teamwork among participants.

12 Frustrated to see that the Cold War had started so soon after World War II had ended, Mr. Hahn wanted to create a school that would mix students from as many countries as possible and allow them to learn together, outside their national educational systems.

13 The idea enjoyed support from Lord Mountbatten—himself Anglo-German—and his great nephew, Prince Charles, who became president

of the organization in 1978. The school is in the process of finding a new president to replace Prince Charles, who after 17 years at the helm has decided to step down.

14   The school's administrators say they try to recruit students who have traveled little, perhaps never having left their home country.

15   "We are not catering for the international clientele who because their parents are diplomats or international businessmen or whatever are already circulating around the world," said David Sutcliff, headmaster of the United World College of the Adriatic based near Trieste, Italy.

16   "We are taking Poles from Poland and Africans from Africa. They are coming straight out of their national systems; they are very, very well regarded in their national systems and now they're being plunged into this international atmosphere with colleagues of the same ability and range. That generates dynamics within the college that are very unusual, very different from the dynamics you would get in a standard international school."

17   To ensure the diversity of the student body, the Adriatic school has strict quotas for the geographic distribution of its students: 25 percent are Italian; 25 percent Western European and North American; 25 percent are from developing countries in Africa and Latin America; and 25 percent are from Eastern Europe. These quotas differ for each school.

18   All students at the Adriatic college are on full scholarships.

19   "They either win the scholarship or they don't get in," said Mr. Sutcliff. Most of the funds for his school come from the Italian government.

20   Additional funding for the Adriatic school and the other schools come from national committees worldwide, which also select the students from their respective countries for admission. Not all of the schools provide full scholarships for their entire student bodies. The Armand Hammer United World College of the American West, named after the late American philanthropist and located in New Mexico, follows a more American approach, requiring a mix of tuition and scholarships.

21   "The underlying principle of the UWC across the board is entry on merit," said Mr. Sutcliff. "That's interpreted by us here and by our colleagues in Canada in the absolute sense. Otherwise money somehow creeps in."

22   The college plans to expand beyond its current eight schools soon. Projects include schools in India, Norway and South Africa.

5

23   Most of the schools use the International Baccalaureate testing organization based in Geneva to deliver degrees that are recognized by universities around the world.

DISCUSSION QUESTIONS

1. Do you think the terms *international cooperation* and *world peace* mean the same thing to everybody? What do they mean to you?

2. What do you think is meant by the United World Colleges administrator's statement "that most of the international cooperation occurs outside the classroom and that these seminars do nothing more than 'provide a laboratory for discussion'"?

3. In small groups, discuss what specific courses should be taught in a college such as the UWC. Be as specific as possible. List actual issues and topics you think would be important to address in a curriculum designed to promote world peace. You might also suggest projects designed to engage students in real-world experiences. Share your findings with the rest of the class.

4. Mark Hoffman, chair of the UWC's International Board in London, says, "The UWC was founded on the idea that young people between 16 and 19 in that very formative period just before they're conscripted into the military and called up to shoot each other, can make lasting friendships which transcend the typical national educational experience." Do you agree with Hoffman's statement? Why or why not?

5. Do you think that most people develop a sense of national allegiance before they reach their late teens? If so, to what extent can a college such as the UWC break the barriers of nationalism? Give specific reasons to support your opinion.

6. How lasting do you think the effects of a UWC education might be? In small groups, discuss what you think some specific effects might be of a UWC education for both the individual and the world community.

WRITING ASSIGNMENTS

1. Write an informative report that details the history of the United World Colleges. Be sure to include information about the reasons for

its founding as well as the school's plans for the future. You might also consider interviewing people affiliated with the school. Be prepared to present your report to the class.

2. You have decided that you would like to attend an international college such as the UWC. However, your parents are not entirely in favor of your request and need to be convinced. Write a letter to your parents arguing your position. Your letter should not only give specific reasons that support your viewpoint but should also anticipate your parents' objections and offer answers to their concerns.

3. Write an exploratory essay in which you discuss the specific ways a curriculum based upon principles of international cooperation could affect a person's worldview and future interaction with others. Before beginning your essay, you should brainstorm on what international cooperation might mean.

4. Write an essay that compares and contrasts the similarities and differences between the type of education with which you are most familiar and an education that promotes world peace and international cooperation.

SPANISH SCHOOL OFFERS A PLACE
IN THE SUN FOR LEARNING

Barry James

International Herald Tribune

■

In this selection, Barry James describes a unique summer university program in Santander, Spain. Founded in 1932 by Spain's Second Republic, the Menéndez y Pelayo International University was a haven for intellectual enlightenment. From 1932 through the Spanish Civil War (which began in 1936), the university provided an environment for personal enrichment with, as James writes, "a specific democratic and international ethos." The university was eventually forced to close during the Civil War and was later taken over by the Franco dictatorship. However, the return to democracy in recent years has allowed the university to resume its original role as an intellectual and cultural exchange. As you read this article, think about the reasons for establishing such a university and the potential impact that an institution such as the Menéndez y Pelayo International University might have.

■

1   As rival totalitarian systems cast a shadow over Europe in the early 1930s, a group of Spanish intellectuals launched an experiment in tolerance and international understanding that continues to benefit thousands of students today.

2   The Menéndez y Pelayo International University in Santander offers what its first rector, Ramón Menéndez Pidal, called a combination of "vacation and fruitfulness."

3   The university was founded in 1932 by the recently installed Second Republic with the aim of "organizing general courses and conferences on varied themes of general interest."

4   Its headquarters were established in the Magdalena Palace, the summer residence of the royal family in Santander. Alfonso XIII had abandoned the throne the previous year. The palace was taken over and is still owned by the city of Santander, which makes it available to the university every summer. The baroque building is set on a peninsula dominating the Cantabrian coast resort.

5   The university, which is partly funded by the Ministry of Education, has autonomous status. It has a permanent secretariat in Madrid and branches in the cities of La Coruña, Seville, Santa Cruz de Tenerife, Valencia, Cuenca, Barcelona and Jaca, but its symbolic home remains the palace in Santander.

6   Last year, about 16,000 people attended one- or two-week courses on a range of subjects from sociology to health reform. Apart from the more than 60 subjects of general interest, often taught by the leading specialists in their field, the university offers highly regarded courses on Spanish language, interpretation, literature and culture for foreign students at one of its two centers in Santander. About 1,300 foreign students, including particularly large contingents from Germany and Japan, are expected to attend the courses from July to September this year.

7   Most people attend the courses for personal enlightenment, and the university does not exist to issue diplomas or degrees. Nevertheless, its certificates of course completion are exchangeable for credits in the Spanish education system and at some foreign universities.

8   The language school is an integral part of the university's philosophy, for it is in this foreign outreach that it finds much of its raison d'être. Foreign students are integrated into the overall cultural context of the university, and are encouraged to take part in the general activities, including literary conferences given by distinguished writers each Tuesday evening.

9   The idea of a summer university actually began with an English university professor, E. Allison Peers, who in 1921 organized Spanish courses in Santander for his students in Liverpool. A couple of years later, Miguel Artigas, the director of the Menéndez y Pelayo library in Santander, contacted the Spanish Center for Historical Studies with the aim of setting up general courses in the city. From these beginnings came the idea of establishing a permanent university with a specific democratic and internationalist ethos.

10   Spain was then to a large extent detached geographically and mentally behind the Pyrenées, and the summer university was seen as a

means of breaking out of this intellectual isolation. It was supported by many of the most prestigious Spanish intellectuals and writers of the time, including Miguel de Unamuno, José Ortega y Gasset, Gregorio Marañón, Dámaso Alonso, Américo Castro, Salvador de Madariaga and Federico García Lorca.

11   It was a short-lived experiment, for in 1936 General Francisco Franco issued his famous manifesto against the Republic. In July, a right-wing uprising erupted on the mainland, and as Hugh Thomas described it, "there was to spread over Spain a great cloud of violence, in which all the quarrels and enmities of so many generations would find full outlet."

12   Although Santander held out through much of the Civil War as a Republican bastion, the university was forced to close. In 1945, Spain under the Falangist dictatorship of Franco was more isolated than ever, and it was therefore decided to recommence the courses for foreigners, which were held in a variety of buildings around Santander. A purpose-built school for foreign students, known as Las Llamas, was added in 1958.

13   With the return of democracy, the Menéndez y Pelayo university regained its soul and rediscovered its vocation as a bed of ideas and cultural exchanges in a vibrant society. Greatly expanded, it has become as its founders envisaged an important forum for debate. It stresses the idea that culture allied to concepts of pluralism and liberty can be an effective force for modernization and social change. At the same time, the organizers do not forget that people attend the university for fun as well as learning. Most of the courses coincide with a summer season of theatrical events, concerts and *tertulias* in Santander and the other cities.

14   The university engages particularly in subjects on the frontiers of knowledge, which are often too new or experimental to be on the curriculums of conventional universities. The present rector, Ernest Lluch, a former health minister, for example, has introduced courses on medicine and biotechnology, law, economics, communications, artificial intelligence and information technology.

15   The university invites prominent personalities from the worlds of politics, science, culture or philosophy to give lectures or take courses.

16   The university is an intellectual tribute to Santander's most famous native son. The critic, historian and writer Marcelino Menéndez y Pelayo held the chair of Spanish literature at the University of Madrid for many years and later became director of the National Library.

17   He died in 1912, after bequeathing his library of 40,000 volumes to Santander.

DISCUSSION QUESTIONS

1. In small groups, brainstorm about the reasons why people might want to attend a university such as the Menéndez y Pelayo International University. Do you think you might enjoy this sort of experience? If you attended this university, how do you think you might be affected? Be prepared to share your responses with the rest of the class.

2. Do you think the impact of a university such as the one described in this article reaches beyond personal growth and enlightenment? How? Be as specific as possible in your response.

3. Do you see any similarities between the Menéndez y Pelayo University and the United World Colleges, which was described in the preceding article? Do you see any differences? Do you think that their purposes are similar?

4. The article states that the university does not issue degrees or diplomas. If degrees and diplomas are not offered, why do you think people might want to attend this university?

5. The writer of this article points out that, in 1932, this university, rooted in a democratic ethos, was founded in spite of the increasing fascist element spreading across Europe during the 1930s. What effect do you think the development of more universities such as the Menéndez y Pelayo International University might have on politics and international affairs?

WRITING ASSIGNMENTS

1. The university described in this article was named after the writer, critic, and historian Marcelino Menéndez y Pelayo, who taught Spanish literature at the University of Madrid and was the director of the National Library. After doing some library research, write a biographical sketch of the life of Marcelino Menéndez y Pelayo. Your biography should include information about his philosophy of education as well as his impact on the Spanish educational system.

2.   The Menéndez y Pelayo International University was founded just prior to the outbreak of the Spanish Civil War and was a Republican stronghold throughout much of the Civil War. Write an informative report that explores the role this university played during the Spanish Civil War.

3.   Write a research paper that compares and contrasts the educational philosophies of the Menéndez y Pelayo International University and the United World Colleges. You might structure your essay so that people considering attending one of these universities would be able to make informed choices.

EQUALITY MEANS PROGRESS, SAYS SWEDISH MINISTER

Keith Foster

International Herald Tribune

■

In this interview, Carl Tham, the Swedish minister of education, discusses educational issues such as gender equality, raising standards, the need for retraining, and language education. All these issues are key components of an effort to improve Swedish education in order to limit unemployment and produce a competitive work force. While reading this selection, think about whether Sweden and the United States have similar or different concerns about education.

■

1   Carl Tham, minister of education in the new Swedish Social Democratic government, has held several public posts, including director general of the National Energy Administration and director general of the Swedish International Development Authority. In this interview, he discusses moves toward sexual equality, increased language instruction and other issues in Swedish higher education.

2   *The Swedish Social Democratic government has now been in power for almost half a year. What were your aims when you entered the Education Ministry, and how far have you come?*

3   One of our chief aims is to improve the mobilization of education, by which I mean raising the standards of education of the labor force, retraining, improving competence levels, etc. That is part of the strategy against the emergence of a large unemployable sector of the work force.

4   We are also concentrating on extending higher education. This fall will see 300,000 Swedes in university, which is an increase of 50 percent over the past 10 years.

5   We have also just introduced a gender bill, which will increase the number of female researchers and professors, traditionally a male-dominated field.

6   *More higher education, more retraining—are there no thoughts of moving toward a low-wage economy, as in some European countries?*

7   No, this is part of the strategy against the so-called "two-thirds" society. According to recent OECD figures, one job in five is being transformed, replaced or simply obliterated each year by the tremendous changes taking place in the way we work. This is particularly affecting management at the moment. Our education system needs to be able to cope with those changes, and there we are working together with business. Many companies are seeing the need—and the opportunity—for this retraining process and are allowing their employees the time to upgrade their competence and skills.

8   *You mentioned your "gender bill," and sexual equality in higher education is an issue you have made much of. Why? How can you improve the balance of the genders in traditional male areas like business or technology education?*

9   Obviously, the government cannot regulate how companies select management, even though the more enlightened ones are now looking to women to an increasing extent. What we can do is open the way for more women in research and tutorial positions, particularly in an area like technology. Then we can encourage more women to take up posts in the academic world by giving universities and colleges gender targets, etc. By its very nature, this means that as more women have someone of their own sex to look up to in the academic world, as more women study under women, eventually more of them will reach higher positions in management, business, engineering and other fields.

10   This is a tough move because it will mean changes in some institutions. It may mean for some the surrender of status that is guarded very jealously. People are not happy about losing their positions. Knowledge, as they say, is power.

11   *Sweden, along with its Nordic neighbor Finland, joined the European Union this year. What advantages do you see there?*

12   As you know, education is one area that is not regulated by the EU. Each member country wants to keep it on its own agenda. However, I think the most pleasing aspect is the increased mobility of students—more of our young people going abroad, more coming here. We will certainly cooperate fully with the various exchange programs such as Leonardo and Socrates.

14

13 *Do you think Swedish graduates are attractive to companies in Europe? Swedes have a good reputation for speaking English, for example, but is language good enough at the top level?*

14 Are our graduates attractive? I am afraid you will have to ask the companies that. What I do think is that we need to improve our language education. It is true that most people can speak relatively good English, but that is not enough. At a higher level, we need to be able to speak languages like German, French and Spanish with a good degree of skill.

15 That is why, despite all the spending cuts going on at the moment, we have proposed in our new bill the creation of a thousand new places at our universities for the teaching of foreign languages, particularly those I mentioned. We need to produce top-quality graduates, no doubt about it.

DISCUSSION QUESTIONS

1. This reading takes the form of an interview in which questions are asked and answered. Do you think the questions were adequately answered by Carl Tham? Are there any other questions the interviewer might have asked? If you were continuing this interview yourself, what questions would you ask Tham?

2. How are the educational issues discussed by the Swedish minister of education similar or different from educational topics discussed in the United States? Be specific in your response.

3. Tham argues that, in order to remain competitive, Swedish graduates must improve their foreign-language skills. Do you think this is a concern in the United States? Why or why not?

4. Tham says, "Knowledge, as they say, is power." What do you think he means by this statement? Can you give any specific examples that might help to illustrate this statement?

5. The title of this selection is "Equality Means Progress, Says Swedish Minister." Speculate about the phrase "equality means progress." What do you think this means? Why might equality mean progress? Specifically, how might equality affect progress?

WRITING ASSIGNMENTS

1. Using this selection as a model, interview someone in a leadership position at your school. Before you conduct your interview, be sure you know what your purpose is and what you want to find out. Then

make up questions to help guide your interview. After the interview, write up the results.

2.   Write a paper comparing and contrasting the role of women in education in Sweden and the United States. Have women walked a similar educational path in both countries? Your paper will probably require some outside research.

3.   Write a paper in which you explore the meaning of the statement "equality means progress." Be sure to use specific examples and details to support your general claims.

Courses in English Flourish in Vietnam

Kate Brown

International Herald Tribune

■

The following article describes the dramatic increase in the need for English-language proficiency in Vietnam. This need comes as the result of major market reforms that were introduced in the late 1980s. These reforms have not only helped to curb inflation but have also encouraged Western corporations to view Vietnam as an attractive new market. During the Vietnam War in the 1960s and early 1970s and for nearly two decades after that conflict, economic relations between Vietnam and the United States were nonexistent. However, since open-trade policies have been instituted between the two countries, the demand for English instruction has grown tremendously. As Luu Ngoc Lan, producer of English-language instructional programs, states, "In the past some people learned English but it wasn't important. Now it's essential." As you read this article, think about what you already know about Vietnam. Then ask yourself how this prior knowledge might affect your understanding of the article.

■

1   Muzzy, a green extraterrestrial with British accent, recently landed in Vietnam. The BBC video character is designed to help children around the world learn English, and he is now watched every week by thousands of children on Vietnamese Television.

2   Demand in Vietnam for English-language teaching materials like the Muzzy video series is enormous. Why? The short answer is money.

3   The country's extensive market reforms, introduced in the late 1980s, have curbed inflation, boosted growth and encouraged Western companies to view Vietnam as an area of untapped opportunity—

and the new Western presence has set off a stampede to learn English, the worldwide language of business.

4   "The Vietnamese see English as a major tool in the fast-moving economic development of their country," said Muriel Kirton, director of the British Council in Hanoi. "All joint-venture companies here operate in English, even the Japanese, and English has become the lingua franca for all nationalities."

5   And not only in business: The government recently issued a decree that all state employees under the age of 45 must be conversant in English. The British Council, which has only been in Vietnam since the end of 1993, is offering a variety of English courses to meet the sudden demand.

6   According to Ms. Kirton, 180,000 people are studying English on any given evening in Hanoi, and language schools are springing up all over the country. The Hanoi Foreign Language College estimates that there are 200 centers for English-language instruction in Vietnam—which, at 71 million people, is one of the largest countries in Southeast Asia.

7   Berlitz International, which has language schools in Thailand and Hong Kong, has been studying setting up joint ventures in Vietnam, China and South Korea and plans to move into at least one of those countries this year.

8   "China is the huge big plum that everyone is looking at, and the sooner we get in there the better," said Michael Strumpen-Darrie, vice president for curriculum and training at Berlitz International's headquarters in Philadelphia. "Our most ambitious plans are for the Far East, and it will definitely happen in 1995."

9   Quoc Hung, vice rector of the Foreign Language College and a leading expert in his field, said: "The Vietnamese are thirsty for learning. Everyone, even the workers, are learning English. Some spend half their salaries doing so."

10   He added: "In the past French was the major language, and Russian was also important, but due to the recent open trade policy we are now exposed to more of the world, and in most other countries English is the language."

11   Sue Brooks, an American television producer living in Hanoi, agrees. With sponsorship from Telstra, an Australian corporation, she is about to start broadcasting a two-minute English-language program five nights a week on Vietnamese Television that will aim to teach one English expression each night in quick, colorful segments.

12   "The Vietnamese love MTV-style television," she said.

18

13   Television and radio are being used extensively as teaching vehicles, usually with support from Western multinationals. British Petroleum Co. is sponsoring a television program, "Starting Business English," adapted from a video course produced by the BBC.

14   David Nicholas, a spokesman for BP in London, said, "We need to recruit local staff, and it helps us if they can communicate with the larger BP world."

15   British Petroleum is the market leader in lubricants in Vietnam, and the company claims to have drilled more offshore wells there than any other oil company.

16   "The country is obviously an important market for us, and we want to facilitate Vietnam's entry into the business world," Mr. Nicholas said.

17   Luu Ngoc Lan adapted the "Starting Business English" videos for Vietnamese Television and produces a number of other English-language instructional programs.

18   "We bump into so many foreigners nowadays, and all modern Vietnamese know some English," he said. "Around 70 percent can talk English adequately. In the past, some people learned English but it wasn't important. Now it's essential."

19   Sue Brooks agrees. "A year ago, most taxi drivers couldn't understand where you wanted to go. Now they can. It's all about money at the end of the day, and if learning English means making money, they'll do it."

20   In contrast to Vietnam, there are relatively few native English-speakers living in China, and the availability of imported study materials there is limited. Berlitz, however, has developed a series of programs to teach English to Mandarin and Cantonese speakers.

21   John Okazaki, president of Berlitz Japan, recently returned from Beijing, where he said he saw a growing need for English courses. In fact, he said, the three most important skills for middle managers in China now are to be able to drive, to use a personal computer and to be proficient in English.

DISCUSSION QUESTIONS

1. In small groups, brainstorm with classmates about what you know about the Vietnam War. Consider how this information affects your understanding of the article.

2. What have your personal experiences been with learning a new language? Was it difficult or easy? What do you think is the best way to

learn a language? Do you see a need in the future for learning and using a foreign language?

3.   Do you think Americans spend as much time as people from other countries learning foreign languages? Why or why not?

4.   The writer of this article states that the demand for English proficiency is found not only in business but also in other areas such as government. Why do you think the need for English is spreading into other areas of Vietnamese life? Why might English proficiency be seen as an advantage in other areas?

5.   The director of the British Council in Hanoi claims that "The Vietnamese see English as a major tool in the fast-moving economic development of their country." How does language act as an economic tool? What are a language's specific functions in an economy, and how can knowledge of one particular language make a difference?

WRITING ASSIGNMENTS

1.   Write an informative report that details the changes in the Vietnamese's attitudes toward the English language since the end of the Vietnam War.

2.   Write a personal narrative that explores your experiences with learning a foreign language. Have these experiences had a significant impact on your life? Before beginning your essay, brainstorm on this topic using an invention tool such as the journalist's 5W questions (who, what, when, where, why).

3.   Interview someone who is bilingual. Ask questions that will help you determine what the experience of being or becoming bilingual has been like for the person you are interviewing.

4.   Write an argumentative essay that either defends or opposes the position that all students in the United States should be able to demonstrate proficiency in a language other than English by the time they graduate from high school.

Broader Horizons in MBA Programs

Lawrence Malkin

International Herald Tribune

■

In this selection, Lawrence Malkin explores the effort to attract more foreign students to MBA (Master of Business Administration) programs at American universities. Because these programs now stress globalization and international business, school administrators believe that multiple perspectives from around the world are needed. Prestigious business schools such as Pennsylvania's Wharton and New York University's Stern School have shown a dramatic increase in the number of foreign students applying and being admitted to MBA programs. While reading this article, think about the specific ways a more international focus in MBA programs will help both students and the businesses where they will eventually be employed.

■

1   NEW YORK—No department in America's universities is changing more quickly than its famed graduate schools of business. They are adapting to globalization of commerce in the real world by seeking out teachers and, above all, students from other countries to internationalize their courses.

2   Of the 450,000 foreign students at American universities in the last academic year, 87,000 were specializing in business, more than any other field. Of those, 16,719 were enrolled in programs leading to a Master of Business Administration, according to the Institute of International Education. They represented 14 percent of all foreign graduate students, second only to the 22 percent in engineering.

3   The typical MBA candidate is 28 years old and has several years of work experience. Admissions officers say foreign as well as domestic applicants closely monitor Business Week magazine's annual ranking of the top 20 schools before deciding whether to shell out $70,000 in tuition and living expenses for the two-year MBA course.

4   Most seek an advanced degree to enhance promotion prospects in their late 30s, when companies seek more breadth and strategic ability. Admissions officers look beyond an applicant's academic record to find young high-fliers who know what they want to do in business.

5   At the top five schools—Pennsylvania's Wharton, Northwestern's Kellogg, Chicago, Stanford, and Harvard, in that order—the percentage of international students ranges from 20 to 30 and in general has doubled in the past decade. With applications from Americans running well ahead of last year as the economy revives, the schools do not really need foreign students, but they definitely want them.

6   Widely criticized during the 1980s for producing managers who watched only the bottom line no matter what the human cost, the business schools are increasing their stress on management skills and transnational business problems because the students themselves demand it.

7   "We teach business, and business now is definitely global," said Steve Christakos, director of admissions for Kellogg, who formerly held the same post at Wharton. "How can we discuss it without having people right in the class who can remind us of the different ways of the world?"

8   Mr. Christakos views himself as recruiting an international "symphony orchestra" of students. At New York University's Stern School, which exploits its ties with Wall Street to specialize in finance, there was a high mark several years back of 40 percent foreign students, and half of them were Japanese. Stern's administration was relieved when the recession forced Japanese companies to cut back on sponsoring students and enabled the school to redress the balance.

9   Some 60 percent of Wharton's graduates say their jobs now involve significant international responsibilities, ranging from actually managing a foreign subsidiary to dealing with foreign suppliers and finance. That proportion was 30 percent only five years ago.

10   Stephen Kobrin, director of a special Wharton program offering a joint degree in business and international studies, said the presence of foreign students puts pressure on the faculty to think through problems from an international perspective: "Not just in the obvious areas such as marketing; we all know that what sells in America doesn't necessarily sell abroad. But different countries also have different capital markets, different relationships between business and government, and different organizations within the firm, where people are less mobile and more hierarchical than in America."

11   Then why seek an American MBA? To begin with, said Robin Hogarth, an Englishman who is deputy dean at Chicago and formerly taught at the London Business School and France's INSEAD, the business school curriculum was first developed in America and now is adapted in European and Asian schools, "so why not go for the real thing?"

12   Another reason is building up contacts for future business relationships; Japanese businesses especially assist their employees so the company can profit from a returning student's personal network.

13   The noted Wall Street economist Henry Kaufman, chairman of the Trustees of the Stern School and of the Institute for International Education, points out that "American schools have developed minds like W. Edwards Deming, who taught Japan productivity, and the management scholar Peter Drucker. Our financial institutions are in the vanguard of innovation from corporate finance to derivatives."

14   Among the top 20, Chicago, the font and origin of market economics, stresses theoretical rigor and practical application. Duke's Fuqua school stresses working in small teams to duplicate a work environment but so far has only a 17-percent foreign enrollment and is actively seeking to raise it. The Simon School at the University of Rochester, which was dropped from the top 20 because its location makes it less accessible to corporate recruiters, has the highest ratio among leading schools at 42 percent and thus can guarantee an international input in its study groups stressing entrepreneurial skills.

15   Harvard is tops in international prestige, but according to Business Week its administration is the most unresponsive to its students. Admissions Director Jill Sadule said Harvard is trying to do better and is offering an eight-week summer course in English for MBAs as well as an orientation course on things like how to open an American bank account and shop wholesale.

16   "All countries have their own ways of developing their own elites, and there used to be only one way, through a nation's elite universities," said Richard Edelstein, director of international affairs for the American Assembly of Collegiate Schools of Business. "What is developing now is a different multinational route through the firm."

DISCUSSION QUESTIONS

1.   In this article, Steve Christakos, director of admissions for Northwestern University's Kellogg School of Business, states that he is in the business of recruiting an international "symphony orchestra" of

students. Why do you think he has chosen this "symphony orchestra" metaphor to describe the new student population? Do you think it is an appropriate metaphor?

2. Why do you think universities have moved to a more international MBA curriculum? In other words, what do you think are the factors contributing to the changes in the curriculum as well as the student population?

3. Given your knowledge of the business world today, what do you think an MBA program should stress above all? In small groups, brainstorm on this question. Be as specific as possible in your responses.

4. The writer of this article discusses the international trend in MBA programs. Do you see this trend in other university programs? If so, consider why this trend might be occurring. If not, speculate about what programs might or might not benefit from such a trend.

5. In small groups, discuss the specific sorts of international problems and concerns a business might have to deal with in today's economy. In order to focus your discussion, you might choose a well-known business (for example, McDonald's, The Gap, Nabisco) and speculate about the kinds of international concerns it might have. Then consider how an MBA would be best prepared to handle these problems. Be prepared to share your findings with the rest of the class.

6. Business schools have for the most part always had programs or majors in international business. Why do you think there is much more emphasis now on globalization in MBA programs?

WRITING ASSIGNMENTS

1. Design a questionnaire that asks questions about globalization in business schools and/or MBA programs. Then interview professors, administrators, graduates, and/or students from a business school or MBA program, and write a report that compares and contrasts the different responses you received from your interviews. Finally, come to some conclusions about the results of your research.

2. Write an essay that explores the reasons why business schools, especially MBA programs, are emphasizing globalization in their courses as well as in their student populations. Be sure to use specific details and examples to support your general ideas and claims.

3. Choose a few business schools and/or MBA programs to investigate (for example, Pennsylvania's Wharton, Northwestern's Kellogg, NYU's Stern). Then research the programs' histories, philosophies, and goals. Come to some conclusions about which schools are best suited to prepare students for international business. Be prepared to present your findings to the class in an oral presentation.

CHAPTER ONE WRITING ASSIGNMENTS

1. Both the United World Colleges and the Menéndez y Pelayo International University stress incorporating the ideas of international peace and cooperation into the curriculum. Write a report that describes in detail a curriculum plan that would incorporate these ideals. Your report should cover the humanities and the social sciences, as well as math and science. Be sure to include specific examples and details to illustrate your plan.

2. Write an essay that responds to the following question: "To what extent and in what ways can globalization efforts in education benefit the international community as a whole?" Use the sources from this chapter as well as any outside readings you find to help you support your assertions.

3. The articles "Equality Means Progress, Says Swedish Minister" and "Courses in English Flourish in Vietnam" address the relationship of language ability to business success. Write an essay in which you respond to the following question: "Other than business use, why might knowledge of several languages be an important asset?" Be sure to use specific reasons and evidence to support your assertions.

Understanding the Impact of the Media

Although we may not realize it, the media have a profound effect on our lives. We may think we are not affected by the various messages sent to us through radio, television, billboards, or newspapers, to name a few of the more obvious media. In both subtle and overt ways, however, the media have a major impact on our daily lives. We may choose to buy a certain product over another because of advertising; we may vote for a particular political candidate because of information we receive during televised debates; or we may simply choose a different route to work one morning because of a traffic report we heard on the radio. Big or small, these examples and others should be a reminder of the tremendous impact the media have on our lives.

The articles in this chapter are intended to make you more aware of the media's impact. The chapter opens with an article entitled "Americanizing the Airwaves" in which Richard Covington reports on the influence American radio style and format have had in Europe. The article specifically addresses American radio phenomena such as "shock jocks" and niche programming and asks us to consider the extent to which American radio can be transplanted into a European environment.

Looking at a specific example of American radio, John Tierney discusses the overwhelming success of a new talk radio station, KSFO of San Francisco, that caters to a conservative audience. In his article, Tierney explores why this talk show and others like it keep listeners' interest level high. Apparently, San Francisco, a city known for its liberal bias, has a contingency of conservatives who are happy to find an outlet for their views on radio talk shows.

The universal appeal of radio is also explored in an article by Chris Hedges entitled "Traditional Ramadan Radio Tales Give Egypt a Medium for Its Message." During the holy month of Ramadan, Muslims fast during the day, eating meals only between sunset and dawn. In Egypt during this month, it has become traditional for friends and family to gather around the radio in the evening to listen to special serialized melodramas. These serials carry on Egypt's ancient tradition of storytelling. However, according to Hedges, the stories also serve a political end since they characterize government officials as "honest and intelligent," while militants are portrayed as "depraved and misguided."

Moving from radio to television, Erik Ipsen looks at the proliferation of business news shows on European television. He specifically addresses the ability of the market to sustain so many business programs. He also examines the nature of these shows and suggests that people may want more than simple facts and statistics.

In "'New Age' Newspaper Hits the Headlines" by William Glaberson we move from electronic to print media. The focus of this article concerns the efforts of one newspaper, the *Minneapolis Star Tribune,* to cater to the needs of its readers with a user-friendly format and focus groups. Although these techniques have been criticized by traditional journalists, Joel Kramer, publisher of the *Minneapolis Star Tribune,* insists that these journalistic innovations are the only way big-city newspapers can survive. He firmly believes that print journalists must consider their market while also maintaining high standards.

The chapter concludes with an article by Joseph Fitchett entitled "TV Advertising Alters Its Image." In this selection, Fitchett presents an interesting look at a new technology called Epsis, which allows the same live broadcast to transmit different images to various locales. At present, this technology is being used only for advertising purposes. However, many have raised ethical and regulatory questions about its continued use since there is obvious potential for abuse.

As these articles will demonstrate, the media, whether in the form of radio, television, or print, should not be taken for granted. They have a tremendous ability to influence our daily lives. While reading these selections, you might think about how the media affect you personally. What specific changes in your life, minor or major, can you say may have been influenced by the media? Why do we need to be conscious of the media's impact on our lives?

AMERICANIZING THE AIRWAVES

Richard Covington

International Herald Tribune

◼

Country-western, classic rock, alternative rock, "lite" rock, jazz and blues, classical, talk radio, and all-day news—the list goes on and on. These are a few of the radio station formats that American listeners are able to tune into. In contrast, European radio listeners are just beginning to get a flavor of diverse programming. The introduction of diversity as well as other "Americanizing" gimmicks into European radio programming is the focus of the following article by Richard Covington. In his commentary, Covington examines the changes occurring in European radio formats as a result of American influence. As Europe's radio audience expands with American radio gimmicks such as niche programming and shock jocks, more investors, especially American radio networks, are paying attention to this growing market. However, there will be differences between American and European radio. As Covington reports, "European personalities are likely to be tamer than their American counterparts, however, because of stricter regulation." Since European governments exercise more control over the airwaves than does the U.S. government, shock jocks such as Howard Stern are less likely to have free rein. Nevertheless, change is in the air for European radio. While reading this article, think about what you enjoy and what you don't appreciate when listening to the radio. What elements do you think European radio stations should borrow from American radio, and what do you think should be left behind?

◼

1   CANNES—Set to launch on Feb. 14, Talk Radio UK is promising more thorns than Valentine's Day roses. Its crop of so-called shock jocks, the station says, should outrage listeners.

2   But strong personalities are only a part of the Americanization of European radio, a trend that was much in evidence here at MIDEM, an international record, music-publishing and video-music market held last week. The transformation, moreover, is bringing more U.S. investors such as ABC Radio Networks and MTV Networks, more promotional gimmicks, targeted niche programming, outlandish personalities—and of course, more advertising revenue—to Europe's rapidly-expanding radio airscape.

3   Even in France, where stations are required to reserve 20 percent of their airtime for music from French artists—the government is loosening restrictions to allow media conglomerates such as Matra-Hachette SA and Luxembourg-based CLT Multi-Media to acquire additional stations.

4   Radio advertising revenues across Europe are booming and will approach $4 billion this year, according to a report by Zenith Media Worldwide, a division of the British advertising firm Saatchi & Saatchi Co. In Britain, for example, radio has outstripped print and television as the fastest-growing medium for the past three years, a trend expected to continue for the next five years, according to David Mansfield, commercial director of Capital Radio PLC, one of Britain's largest radio networks. In Germany, ad revenues exceeded $1 billion last year, according to Hamburg-based media company Gruner & Jahr GmbH.

5   This pitch of activity has caught the attention of American radio networks anxious to expand into this lucrative field. "The Americans are looking beyond their own saturated market toward Europe and Asia," said Simon Cole, chief executive of Unique Broadcasting Co., a European radio syndicating agency with offices in London and Paris. Among its panoply of services, Unique syndicates the audio portion of MTV Europe in 16 countries.

6   Moreover, in contrast to the American market, Europe is steadily adding new radio stations. While Los Angeles is bulging at the seams with some 60 commercial stations, London has a mere 16, with four additional ones slated to go on the air this year.

7   ABC Radio Networks, based in Dallas, Texas, has been in the forefront of the American invasion, distributing "top 40" formats by Los Angeles disk jockey Rick Dees to a number of European countries. "There's a trend in Europe for the countries that have been ignoring radio to start picking up on the pace of licensing new stations," said David Kantor, executive vice president for ABC Radio Networks. "This is bound to create greater diversity in programming and more advertising interest."

8   Global advertisers like Nestlé SA, Coca-Cola Co. and McDonald's Corp. will soon be expanding their European radio buys, he predicted.

9   Meanwhile, syndication—the practice of distributing a show or format to many stations—is another staple of American radio that is just starting to spread within European markets, one that Mr. Kantor said he expected to grow considerably as audiences become more sophisticated.

10   Another import from the United States is niche programming, or tailoring a station's format for a particular category of listener. This began revolutionizing radio eight years ago in France and Germany, but only two years ago in Britain. "In the old days, we used to program a single station to appeal to all listeners equally," said Marc Garcia, music director for the public network France Inter. "Old ladies leaving church, kids leaving school—everyone tuned in to the same station."

11   Still, Europe has a long way to go before radio audiences are as fragmented as they are in the United States, where some cities have five Country & Western stations and as many as 28 different formats overall. But with the proliferation of formats—Munich's latest station, SP4's Multi-Kulti, is devoted exclusively to world music, for example—Europe is catching up fast.

12   "It's a grave mistake to pick up American formats, lock, stock and barrel," warned David Campbell, chief executive of Britain's Virgin Radio PLC. "What bothers me is the practice of stations abandoning their formats and trying on another just because it's the hottest thing going."

13   So far, European radio has been fairly immune to radio personalities being elevated to cult status. "By and large, radio is more music-based than in the U.S.," Mr. Kantor said. "There has been very little interaction with listeners. As radio here loosens up, European superstars are sure to develop."

14   Shock jocks—radio disk jockeys known for outspoken opinions, profanity, and off-color jokes usually of a racist or sexist nature—began raising eyebrows in the United States in the 1970s. Two of the best known, Dom Imus and Howard Stern, are pioneers who are still on the air there.

15   Personalities, particularly for morning shows, generate an excitement about a station and have a bonding effect on listeners, said Arno Müller, a breakfast show host for the RTL radio network affiliate in Berlin. "The competition may copy your music, but it's much harder to copy your personality."

16   Virgin Radio's foray into shock jock talk shows cost the station two fines for profanity—the first for £5,000 ($7,750), the second escalating to £20,000. "The listeners didn't find it phenomenally successful anyway," Mr. Campbell admitted.

17   European personalities are likely to be tamer than their American counterparts, however, because of stricter regulation. "You won't be able to have a Howard Stern running amok, because governments exercise more control," said Mr. Kantor. Mr. Stern is currently facing $1 million in obscenity fines from the U.S. Federal Communications Commission.

18   As the veteran British talk show host Simon Bates, formerly of BBC's Radio 1 and now with Capital Radio's London News, said: "Many radio personalities are certifiably insane, seriously malformed mentally. I should know, I am one."

DISCUSSION QUESTIONS

1. According to Covington, "In Britain . . . radio has outstripped print and television as the fastest-growing medium for the past three years, a trend expected to continue for the next five years." Why do you think radio has become so popular? What are some of the characteristics of radio that would make it so popular? Why do you think that, according to Covington's sources, it has become even more popular than television?

2. Covington writes that "syndication—the practice of distributing a show or format to many stations—is another staple of American radio that is just starting to spread within European markets" and is "expected to grow considerably as audiences become more sophisticated." What do you think is meant by a sophisticated radio audience? Why would syndication develop as audiences become more sophisticated?

3. What do you think are the advantages and disadvantages of niche programming? Why do you think it has become so popular in the United States? What effect do you think niche programming has had on advertising?

4. At the close of the article, Covington quotes a British radio personality as saying, "Many radio personalities are certifiably insane, seriously malformed mentally. I should know, I am one." Do you agree with this statement? Why or why not? What do you think is the appeal of shock jocks?

WRITING ASSIGNMENTS

1. Write a proposal for a new radio show. Your proposal should include a description of the show's format, a rationale for the show, a description of the audience, a marketing strategy, and a list of potential advertisers and sponsors.

2. Covington writes that "Shock jocks—radio disk jockeys known for outspoken opinions, profanity, and off-color jokes usually of a racist or sexist nature—began raising eyebrows in the United States in the 1970s. Two of the best known, Don Imus and Howard Stern, are pioneers who are still on the air there." There are some people who think obscene or offensive language should be censored. Howard Stern, for example, has been slapped with $1 million in obscenity fines from the U.S. Federal Communications Commission. Others argue that these shock jocks are protected by freedom of speech. In an argumentative essay, respond to the following question: "To what extent should shock jocks be allowed to say whatever they want over the airwaves?" Use specific details and examples to support your argument.

3. For a few days, listen to one particular radio station that is geared to a specific audience. Keep a log of the sponsors for that station. What is being advertised? How often is it being advertised? What are the advertisements like? Then write an analytical essay that explores why the sponsors and ads you listened to were chosen for that particular radio station. What marketing decisions do you think were made when the sponsors and ads were approved? Use specific details and examples to develop your analysis.

SAN FRANCISCO'S LOUD VOICE
FOR THE RIGHT SOUNDS OFF

John Tierney

New York Times Service

■

In the following selection, John Tierney explores the recent growth of conservative talk radio programs in San Francisco. Although San Francisco has become one of the most liberal cities in the United States, it is now home to one of the country's most conservative talk radio stations, KSFO-AM. The 24-hour talk show has replaced a liberal program with a show called Hot Talk that caters to an extreme right-wing agenda. Many speculate that such programs are beginning to sprout in the San Francisco area as a reaction to the liberal environment for which the city is known. Since, as Tierney points out, conservatives are much more likely than liberals to listen to and participate in talk radio programs, the format has become an outlet for this political faction. As you read this article, consider why this medium might be so appealing to conservatives. What are the qualities of the talk radio format that attract conservatives? What do you think about these shows?

■

1   SAN FRANCISCO—Do people with AIDS need to quarantined? Should American citizens be paid a bounty to shoot illegal immigrants? Is President Bill Clinton controlled by a coven of communist lesbian members of the Trilateral Commission?

2   These are some of the questions up for discussion on Hot Talk KSFO-AM, a station taking rightist radio to new levels here. For the past week, while San Francisco's appalled politicians and homosexual-rights leaders have been rallying opposition, the station's callers and hosts have been casting themselves as beleaguered revolutionaries.

3   "These gay and lesbian Nazis, I don't know what else to call them, they're trying to steal our freedom," said Michael Savage, the afternoon host who bills himself as The Compassionate Conservative.

4   The host of a morning show, J. Paul Emerson, shouted, "Political correctness is over!" to the homosexual-rights groups that demonstrated outside the station earlier this month. "Take your signs and go to hell! That's the only place that you're going to get any attention, because that's where all your stinking butthead friends are!"

5   It may seem odd that San Francisco, often considered America's most leftist metropolis, now has one of the country's most rightist talk-radio station. But KSFO's extremism may be a logical reaction to the local culture.

6   The sudden transformation since Jan. 1—when the 24-hour talk station replaced its young, liberal hosts with conservatives—might shed some light on a much-debated question: Why does the right dominate talk radio?

7   The medium is biased toward conservatives in several ways, according to a survey by the Times Mirror Center for the People and the Press. Compared with liberals, conservatives are more likely to listen to talk radio, more likely to call in when they listen, and more likely to get on the air when they call. Exit polls taken after the last presidential election showed that frequent listeners to talk shows voted Republican, 3 to 1.

8   Some media experts attribute the bias to the force of a few hosts' personalities—notably, Rush Limbaugh, who claims an audience of 20 million—and a temporary dearth of entertaining liberals. Others see talk radio as particularly hospitable to conservatives.

9   "Talk radio is a venting mechanism for people who are angry and anti-institution," said Cliff Zukin of Rutgers University, who conducted the Times Mirror survey. "The theme is 'us against them,' which works for conservatives because government is always a good 'them.' Angry people can always find examples of government programs that don't work."

10   Besides government, the other great object of conservative callers' wrath is that entity known as the liberal media. This feeling of being ignored by the mainstream press is the main reason that conservatives cite for their embrace of an alternative medium.

11   "Talk radio is right-wing for the same reason that free weekly newspapers are left-wing," said Virginia Postrel, the editor of Reason, a libertarian magazine that is must reading for many talk-show hosts.

"They're both examples of how a newly abundant medium comes to be dominated by a group with intellectual vitality that is outside the political mainstream."

12 "The New Left was in that position in the 1960s when offset printing made weekly newspapers possible," Ms. Postrel said. "And the papers have retained their left-wing culture their readers and advertisers have come to expect."

13 "When the switch of music to FM radio opened up the AM band to talk radio in the 1980s, it was conservatives who had the vitality and the desire to flock to a new medium and create their own culture there," she added.

14 No other station seems to have a more extreme rightist culture than KSFO, perhaps because in no other city do conservatives feel so excluded. The station regularly promotes its new format by playing Peter Finch's line from the movie "Network": "I'm mad as hell, and I'm not going to take this anymore"—a cry echoed by the callers who rail at the local liberal orthodoxy.

15 "I came from the communist country," said a caller with an East European accent. "Now I am in Berkeley, a totally communist city. The homosexual community really is danger. Seems like in this area, we don't have the right for free speech. This is the only station like this in the Bay Area, and now liberals want to destroy it."

16 Jack Swanson, operations director at KSFO, said the audience's reaction reminded him of what he heard 15 years ago when he put a show called "Gay Talk" on the air in San Francisco.

17 "I think it was the first gay talk show on any commercial station in the country," Mr. Swanson recalled, "and we were flooded with gay callers saying, 'Thank God, you're there—I felt so alone until I heard your show.' That's the same kind of need we're meeting now. This is a community where essentially everything has been O.K. up until now except being a conservative. We're letting the last group out of the closet."

18 Mr. Swanson, who described himself as a liberal, said he chose the conservative format after seeing a station in Seattle—KVI-AM, the only other all-conservative talk station in the United States—crush its liberal competitors in the ratings.

DISCUSSION QUESTIONS

1. Tierney asks a much-debated question in his report: "Why does the right dominate talk radio?" How would you answer this question?

2. Tierney writes, "[The] feeling of being ignored by the mainstream press is the main reason that conservatives cite for their embrace of an alternative medium." Do you think the mainstream media are biased? Why or why not?

3. Tierney makes the point that right-wing radio talk shows are similar to left-wing free newspapers in that they are both alternatives to the mainstream press. Do you think this comparison is valid? Why or why not?

4. In "Americanizing the Airwaves" (page 29), Richard Covington discusses the impact of "shock jocks" on viewers. Do you think there are any similarities between shows such as KSFO's Hot Talk and the use of shock jocks in radio programming?

WRITING ASSIGNMENTS

1. Write an exploratory essay that responds to the following question: "Why do conservatives dominate talk radio?" Your essay should provide specific reasons and evidence to support your opinions and conclusions.

2. Write an analytical essay that responds to the following question: "What effect does talk radio programming have upon the general public?" In your essay, explore the advantages and disadvantages of this sort of radio format. Be sure to support your opinions with specific details and examples.

3. Tune in to a local talk radio program. Listen to the program for a set period of time of at least one hour. Then write a critique of the experience. Your essay should be more than a simple summary. Rather, you should comment on the format and style of the program. How did it affect you and why? You should also attempt to explain what you learned from the experience.

TRADITIONAL RAMADAN RADIO TALES GIVE EGYPT A MEDIUM FOR ITS MESSAGE

Chris Hedges

New York Times Service

■

Ramadan, the holy month in which Muslims fast during the day, eating only when the sun is set, is also a time for family and friends to come together in the evening to listen to favorite stories on the radio. As Chris Hedges reports in this article, the Egyptian radio serials continue the ancient Arabic art of storytelling that has been with the Arab community since before the "Thousand and One Nights." However, these programs are also used by the Egyptian government as a political tool to control militant Islamics. The stories often put the government in a good light and portray the Islamic militants as "depraved and misguided." While reading this article, you might think about the ways in which radio drama differs from other forms of entertainment such as television and the movies. What makes radio appealing to people?

■

1   CAIRO—There is an old Arabic superstition that warns that whoever tells stories during the day will grow horns and see his gold turn into iron. Night is the time for stories. And the best stories, as has been true for generations in the Muslim world, are saved for the languid evenings during the holy month of Ramadan.

2   At dusk during the holy month, which started Wednesday, Muslims break their daylong fast, performed as penance, with *iftar,* the evening meal. They feast on dates and figs, on *qatayif,* small pancakes filled with raisins and nuts, and on *bamia,* a beef stew with okra and onions.

3   And, while families gather around the table, many turn on the radio to follow the special serials that start on the first day of Ramadan and culminate on the last. These stories of love, intrigue and adventure help

envelop this country of nearly 60 million in a unity of purpose that briefly shuts out the widespread poverty, political unrest and misery.

4   And the serials carry on the ancient art of storytelling that Arabs have nurtured since before the "Thousand and One Nights."

5   But in the politically charged climate of Egypt, the serials are also an important part of the government's drive against Islamic militants, who are waging a violent campaign to create an Islamic state.

6   As portrayed in these melodramas, the police tend to be intelligent and honest. Islamic militants, when they appear, are usually depraved and misguided. And Egypt is shown as a land of hope and opportunity for those who work.

7   The militants, who denounce the serials, have threatened many of the writers, actors and directors involved, and some of them now have bodyguards.

8   "In the last couple of years, the government has increased its use of the radio serials to transmit its propaganda," said Fahmi Howadi, a writer on Islamic affairs. "The serials are now a powerful weapon in the government's war against the Islamic trend, although I find the government's message naive and unconvincing."

9   The serials, nevertheless, are extremely popular.

10   "The lower classes listened faithfully to these programs," said Samya Saaty, head of the sociology department at Ein Shams University. "The programs portray the problems many people face, from marital difficulties and poverty to drug addiction. People look to the dramas for solutions."

11   There are four main radio stations and each mounts serials for the month. The stations broadcast their programs at different times so listeners can switch from one to the next until *suhour*, the meal eaten just before dawn.

12   Egypt's television and cinema stars spent most of January in recording studios in Cairo's radio and television building producing the 15-minute episodes.

13   "When I was a young girl my friends and I would sit up nights and listen to the dramas during Ramadan," said Salwa Mohammed Ali, an actress who is playing in a radio serial. "I could barely wait until the next episode."

14   The writers, actors and the actresses often save their best scripts and performances for Ramadan. Many have also developed a fondness for radio drama, an art form that has died out in many other parts of the world.

15   "Radio invites people to imagine, to participate in the production," said Mrs. Mohammed. "It gives almost as much pleasure as reading."

16   The hottest serial this year is called "Rice With the Angels." The show, taken from an Arabian proverb about dreamers that says "they are eating rice with the angels," features some of the biggest names in Egyptian show business.

17   The serial tells the story of a beautiful girl, Shams, and a poor boy who loves her, Menadi, whose schemes to make money are thwarted by his lack of education and poverty.

18   "The message of this story is that people who dream must dream realistically," said the serial's script writer, Osama Anwar Okasha. "If our dreams are unrealistic they can be destructive. People must dream within their limitations and capabilities."

19   There are numerous scenes that hammer home this point.

20   "Shams doesn't want just love," the character Menadi tells his friend Essam. "She wants someone who will snatch her away from this life, someone who will take her higher and higher. This is her dream. It is my dream, too."

21   "But you cannot hold down your jobs," Essam points out. "You have no weight. You do not take responsibility."

22   "This is not a time for people to crawl up a ladder rung by rung," Menadi replies. "It is a time for people to jump."

23   In the story Menadi is falsely accused and arrested in the killing of a German, who first appears as a kindly old man who lives in Menadi's alleyway.

24   The German, it turns out later, was a former Nazi who persecuted Jews. In the end, the police will discover that the assassination was carried out by the Israeli secret service, the Mossad, and Shams and Menadi will get married when he is freed from prison, chastened and realistic about his life.

25   "This is just entertainment," said Naglaa Fathi, a movie star who appears in the serial.

26   "The whole country fasts at the same time, eats at the same time. We all come together for Ramadan. The only problem, for us, comes from all the people who keep asking us how the story will end."

DISCUSSION QUESTIONS

1.   Hedges writes that "Many have also developed a fondness for radio drama, an art form that has died out in many other parts of the world." Why do you think this art form may have died out in certain parts of the world? Why do you think it might be popular in other parts of the world?

2. The article states that "The programs portray the problems many people face, from marital difficulties and poverty to drug addiction. People look to the dramas for solutions." Why do you think people might look to these dramas for solutions? How can dramatic entertainment help people find solutions for problems?

3. Hedges quotes a radio serial actress as saying, "Radio invites people to imagine, to participate in the production. It gives almost as much pleasure as reading." What are the qualities of radio that might prompt this actress to make this statement? Do you agree with her statement? Why or why not?

4. To what extent do you think radio dramas can bring people of the same culture together? Can you think of other forms of entertainment in other cultures that have an effect similar to these radio dramas?

WRITING ASSIGNMENTS

1. In small groups, write a radio drama similar to the ones described in this article. Assign different acting roles to the people in your group. Be prepared to perform the drama in front of your class. You might want to begin by looking at some old radio drama scripts in order to learn about this style of writing. You can get these scripts from the library.

2. In its prime, American radio drama of the 1930s and 1940s was as popular as television is today. Based on library research, write an informative report about American radio drama of the 1930s and 1940s. What were some of the favorite shows? Who were the most popular stars? Who were the audience and sponsors? Be sure to use specific details and examples to develop your report.

3. The article explains that radio dramas are a special event during Ramadan. After doing some library research, write an informative report that explores the Muslim holy month of Ramadan. What is the significance of this holy month? What traditions are associated with it? Be sure to develop your report with specific details and examples.

THERE'S NO BUSINESS
LIKE BUSINESS SHOWS

Erik Ipsen

International Herald Tribune

■

The following article by Erik Ipsen looks at the recent boom in the number of televised business news shows in Europe. While some people in the television industry have been questioning the increase in the number of business news programs and wondering how many of these shows the market can support, others feel that the European audience is wide enough to support the growth of this industry. As you read this article, you might think about the growth of this market in the United States. Have cable news shows started to emphasize more business coverage? What do you think might be some effects of an increase in business news shows both in Europe and North America?

■

1   LONDON—The question of just how much televised business news Europe can take was posed on Wednesday with the inauguration of a new channel that promises 24-hour business coverage.

2   The latest entrant is Bloomberg Information Television Europe, a division of Bloomberg LP, a business news service. The new service follows the launch of European Business News by Dow Jones & Co. early this year.

3   It also competes with market heavyweights such as Cable News Network Inc. and NBC Super Channel, which have in recent months upgraded and expanded their business coverage.

4   CNN now boasts five hours a day of business coverage and has plans to expand that. In the United States, CNN plans to launch a business channel early next year.

5   "We follow the money," said Albert Bozzo, managing director for CNN Business News Europe. "And right now business is booming."

6   Others insist that Europe can sustain more than the one or possibly two business channels, which are widely assumed to mark the saturation point. "I think there is room in this market for more players than most people think," said Michael Connor, managing director of European Business News.

7   But analysts predict that the news channels face an uphill fight not just for advertisers but for distribution. They say that in such vital markets as Germany, many cable systems are already full.

8   CNN and Super Channel already enjoy a huge lead. Market leader CNN, for instance, says it reaches 70 million homes in Europe. European Business News, meanwhile, scored a coup on Wednesday by broadcasting on Rupert Murdoch's Sky Channel in Britain, which reaches 3.2 million homes.

9   Bloomberg, meanwhile, bills its service as "24 hours a day, seven days a week," but it has yet to sign up with a single distributor to carry more than 18 hours of its programming a day.

10   In fact, on its first day of operation, Bloomberg's business service was carried on just two cable systems in Britain, with a total audience reach of just 500,000 homes. It was also being carried for one hour a day on a channel called LIVE-TV, which reaches 900,000 viewers.

11   Bloomberg executives have said they are in negotiations with six cable operators on the Continent and hope to have distribution to 1.5 to 2 million homes by year end.

12   Bloomberg's service splits the TV screen into five sections of rolling text and data on everything from sports scores, weather reports and horoscopes to currency and stock prices. In the top left corner of the screen, a news reader presents facts that comprise the sole audio aspect.

13   In the end, analysts say the channel with the most staying power will win, but Bloomberg says it has an advantage in terms of cost. To set up and run the European television venture, it hired 10 new staff members, compared with the hundred journalists hired by European Business News. "We are spreading our resources in a more productive way," said Stuart Bell, European managing director for Bloomberg.

14   Despite Bloomberg's lead in terms of volume of information, critics say it fails to put the data into context.

15   Mr. Bozzo of CNN said, "Information is only part of the news. Our value added is trying to bring meaning to the numbers."

16   EBN similarly eschews a facts-only approach. EBN's approach is to balance currency, bond and stock coverage with what Mr. Connor calls a "business dimension" to topics such as technology and culture.

17   The question the channels face is whether there are enough advertisers to go around. Mr. Connor said that advertising revenues on EBN were "coming along" but were "never as good as you like them to be."

DISCUSSION QUESTIONS

1.   Why do you think promoters of a 24-hour business news show feel that there is a market for their program? What do you think might be the appeal of a 24-hour business news show? Why business news?

2.   Ipsen quotes a representative of CNN as stating, "Information is only part of the news. Our value added is trying to bring meaning to the numbers." What do you think might be meant by this statement? How can meaning be brought to numbers, and why might it be important to do so?

3.   The article states that "The question the channels face is whether there are enough advertisers to go around." Think about the types of people who might listen to these shows. What sorts of advertisers do you think business shows might attract?

WRITING ASSIGNMENTS

1.   Write a news brief suitable for a business news show. Before writing the news brief, watch several television news programs so that you become familiar with the format and style of these shows. Be prepared to present your news brief to the class.

2.   Ipsen writes that "EBN's [European Business News] approach is to balance currency, bond and stock coverage with what Mr. Connor calls a 'business dimension' to topics such as technology and culture." Choose a local, national, or international current events topic. Then write an essay that explains the business and financial ramifications of this topic. For example, you might look at the economic effect of a flood or hurricane. Or you might look at the impact of a new housing development on the business community of your city.

3. Write an informative report about the growth of televised business news shows. How and when did the shows originate? What companies are the leading contenders? How successful do you think this form of news will be in the future? You will need to do some outside research to develop your essay.

"NEW AGE" NEWSPAPER HITS THE HEADLINES

William Glaberson

New York Times Service

■

In the following selection, William Glaberson provides an interesting look at the changes one newspaper, the *Minneapolis Star Tribune,* is undergoing in an attempt to boost productivity and improve service. According to Glaberson, however, the *Star Tribune* has been accused of replacing journalistic tradition with gimmicky "new age techniques" and political correctness. As you read this article, think about what you like to see in a newspaper. What needs of its readers should a newspaper fulfill? What do you like about the newspapers you read? What would you like to see changed in these newspapers?

■

1   MINNEAPOLIS—Joel R. Kramer, the publisher of the Minneapolis Star Tribune, would like to answer his critics. He says he is shaking up journalistic traditions to save big-city newspapers from extinction.

2   Mr. Kramer has plenty of critics to answer. The paper, where he was once editor, has a long tradition of solid journalism. But with Mr. Kramer as publisher since 1992, it has also become perhaps the most ridiculed newspaper in the country, described by critics inside the paper and out as a headquarters of political correctness and New Age journalism jargon.

3   The Star Tribune has dived into just about every experiment being tried by any newspaper anywhere. The paper is dividing its reporters into teams; trying "employee empowerment" techniques to get journalists involved in decision making; using focus groups to measure what readers want; experimenting with "interactivity," and redesigning the paper to be more reader-friendly.

4   "I'm not sure there's a current journalism fad that our managers have not embraced," said Robert Franklin, a longtime reporter and a former city and state editor.

5   The Star Tribune, which is owned by Cowles Media Co., is financially healthy and has a steady circulation. Nonetheless, the paper is in the process of reorganizing just about everything in sight, from its corporate and newsroom structures to the look of its pages.

6   Mr. Kramer has said he is searching for new solutions to the problems that are threatening dailies across the country. In the process he has, in effect, opened a debate inside the Star Tribune over how America's midsize newspapers are to cope with such challenges as declining readership and shrinking advertising.

7   "My number one goal is to keep the institution of metropolitan journalism healthy and financially viable so it can continue to be done," he said.

8   Mr. Kramer's moves to improve service to what he calls the paper's "reader-customers" have brought skewerings from national writers, local critics and many of the paper's own staff members. The Wall Street Journal and the Washington Post have poked fun at the changes, especially the cultish new titles given to nearly everyone in authority. (Yes, the managing editor is now the news leader and there really is a newsroom director of player personnel and a leader of strategic integration.)

9   Mr. Kramer has also broken down the traditional wall in journalism between newspapers' business and news staffs, giving his top editor bottom-line responsibility for the paper's revenue from readers, including circulation. "The people responsible for news should also be responsible for success with readers," he said.

10   In a savage critique, the alternative paper here, the Twin Cities Reader, recently parodied the Star Tribune's message. "We're so terrified of losing subscribers, we're willing to try anything," said one invented memo The Reader asserted could have been written by Tim J. McGuire, the Tribune's editor, who now has the added title of general manager of the reader-customer unit.

11   "We hope to offer the visceral dialogue found on talk radio with the formless beauty of focus-group journalism," said another of the ostensible memos.

12   Among the management's other changes has been a ban on the use of what it says are offensive Indian nicknames like Redskins in sports articles; working to increase cooperation between the news and business staffs; inventing new publications like one aimed at real estate brokers, and giving reporters new assignments to meet what

are said to be the interests of readers. There is a new columnist who tests products like panty-hose and mosquito repellent, and there are plans for a "relationships" beat.

13   At a time of closings, layoffs and consolidations in the newspaper industry, Mr. Kramer and his supporters at the paper say print journalists need to keep doing the best of their traditional work, like investigative reporting. But they say journalists also need to be flexible enough to try new ways of doing their jobs.

14   Being the butt of jokes and the object of derision, they say, may be the price of confronting the threats to the entire newspaper industry. "There's trouble out here in River City," Mr. McGuire said, "and we as an industry are trying to forge a future. We here are trying to take hold of that future, rather than having it take hold of us."

15   Some of the criticism, Mr. McGuire said, comes from people who simply resent change. "A lot of the political-correctness criticism," he said, for example, "comes from people who don't want to stop using racism and sexism in their language."

16   And many journalists, Mr. McGuire said, naively insist that they do not want to worry about whether readers want their journalism. "The only way we're going to be independent and strong is if we understand we've got to make some money," Mr. McGuire said. "That's how this works. That ideological purity is not going to work anymore."

17   But some critics at the paper say the frenzy for change and the focus on internal organizational issues have made the Star Tribune wander too far from simply gathering the news and printing it. "Just as politicians are being led by polls, we're being led by focus groups and market research," said Mike Meyers, an economics writer at the paper.

18   Joe Rigert, who has been with the paper for 30 years, said repeated meetings about collaboration and the team approach had distracted reporters. "I don't get it," he said. "I don't understand how this is going to serve readers. You serve readers when you've got reporters out in the field talking to people."

DISCUSSION QUESTIONS

1. Why do you think the writer of this article uses the term *New Age* in the title? What does *New Age* mean to you, and how might the term relate to this article?

2. Glaberson writes that the publisher of the *Minneapolis Star Tribune,* Joel Kramer, "is searching for new solutions to the problems that are threatening dailies across the country." In small groups, discuss what you think might be the problems that newspapers are having today. How do you think these problems might be solved? Be prepared to share your ideas with the rest of the class.

3. The article states that the *Minneapolis Star Tribune* has given new titles to people in authority. For example, the managing editor is now the news leader. Why do you think the decision was made to change the titles of key personnel? Do you think changing someone's title will have much effect on anything? If so, what? If not, why not?

4. According to Glaberson, the publisher of the *Minneapolis Star Tribune* has tried to break down traditional lines between business and news staffs. He states that "The people responsible for news should also be responsible for success with readers." Do you think this is a good philosophy? What do you see as the advantages and disadvantages of such a strategy?

5. Glaberson quotes an economics reporter from the *Minneapolis Star Tribune* as saying, "Just as politicians are being led by polls, we're being led by focus groups and market research." What do you see as the potential results of newspapers being controlled by market research and focus groups? What might the advantages and/or disadvantages be of such an approach to journalism?

WRITING ASSIGNMENTS

1. Choose a local newspaper to review. Then write a critique of the newspaper. What aspects of the newspaper appeal to you? What needs to be improved? Be sure to support your opinions with specific reasons, details, and examples.

2. Interview a newspaper professional from your community. Before interviewing this person, decide on a focus for your interview. For example, you might choose to focus on the future of journalism in the United States or the person's professional development as a journalist. Whatever you decide, be sure to create an interview guide before you talk with your interviewee so that your interview will have direction.

3. Write a letter to the editor about something you read in your community's newspaper. You should probably choose a news item that in some way bothered you or made you think more about the topic. Your letter should refer specifically to what you read. Be sure to use details and examples to back up your opinions. Then send the letter to the newspaper.

4. As a term-long class project, create an alternative newspaper for your school. Although your school probably already has a newspaper, this one could present alternative perspectives or contain different features. You might also consider creating a newspaper or newsletter specifically designed for your class. You will need to work cooperatively in groups and figure out how the various tasks involved in newspaper production will be handled.

TV ADVERTISING ALTERS ITS IMAGE

Joseph Fitchett

International Herald Tribune

■

At the finish of the Tour d'Espagne, the Spanish bike race, history was made not just by the cyclists but also by the advertising industry. As the cyclists sped past the finish line, viewers in Spain saw a banner advertising the Spanish beer Aguila. Viewers in all other parts of Europe watching the same race saw the cyclists speed by an Amstel advertising banner, not an Aguila banner, at the finish line. In the following selection, Joseph Fitchett explores both the practical and ethical considerations of a new technology that allows advertisers to alter an advertising image during a live broadcast. As you read this article, think about the positive as well as the negative implications of this new technology. Is it possible that such technology could be abused? How might the abuse be prevented? What are some potential positive outcomes of this new technology?

■

1 PARIS—The first time it happened, almost nobody noticed because only a few million viewers watch the Tour d'Espagne, the Spanish bike race. And only now has the company talked about it for the first time.

2 The results were conclusive. Watching the live broadcast of the finish, viewers everywhere saw the riders pump the final yards as the TV cameras zoomed into close-ups on the strained features of the riders.

3 It looked like routine sports coverage. It was, except for one detail: Viewers in Spain saw the winner speed past a sponsor's banner advertising the Spanish beer, Aguila, while screens everywhere else in Europe showed the same rider pass the same banner advertising Amstel. Both brands belong to the Dutch beverage giant Heineken, which was delighted for Aguila, the local beer that sponsored the

race, to appear for Spanish consumers while in other countries the prime exposure went to Amstel, Heineken's international brew.

4   This success of this experiment has changed forever what viewers are likely to see when they watch live broadcasts of international sports events. The French Open tennis tournament, a World Cup final, a Formula One race—where athletes compete in an arena studded with advertisements—the event will be real, but some of the decor is likely to be virtual reality.

5   From now on, sponsors and advertisers can differentiate the on-site billboards in a live broadcast so that they target specific markets around the world—beer ads for Germans (who like beer with their sports), billboards at Wimbledon in Japanese for Japan, with American brands for the United States.

6   The ability of this French technology to modify images in real time—in live broadcasts, which have become part of our sense of visual reality—has revolutionary potential. It will raise ethical and regulatory problems, but it is also set to corner a $100 million-a-year European market.

7   And it provides an object lesson in the conversion of military technologies to civilian applications with commercial potential.

8   "Nothing is as simple as it seems anymore," says Philippe Isambert, a fast-talking scientist who can spare only a nanosecond grin to acknowledge a visitor's problems sorting out the implications. Mr. Isambert manages the research team that spent five years developing this technology—baptized Epsis—in labs just outside Paris for Matra Defense & Space, part of the Lagardère Groupe, a privately-owned French conglomerate.

9   For Epsis, a commercial product, Matra harnessed two of its most powerful military technologies: the guidance systems enabling smart missiles to seek out targets they have been programmed to destroy and the massive computing power used in France's nuclear submarines.

10   The $1 million machine is owned and operated by Symah Vision, a Lagardère Groupe subsidiary, which sells the service to the sponsors of sports events to enhance the advertising value of the broadcast rights they sell.

11   Epsis fits into a panel truck so that it can drive right up to the stadium and plug into the broadcast system—taking the pictures as they emerge from the director's mix, changing them (at a rate up to 50 images a second) and sending each new version to a different satellite for broadcast.

12   Ahead of time, explains Pierre Pleven, Symah Vision's director-general, the truck records the camera angles that will be used to cover the event, then stores these images in the Epsis computer with reference points enabling the system to "see" when a billboard is about to come on screen.

13   Like a missile seeking a target to match the image in its memory, Epsis detects the billboard, locks on and tracks it as the cameras swing and the screen image sways. Like a missile, Epsis gets help in predicting movement thanks to an algorhythm that is still classified.

14   "What makes Epsis more sophisticated than a missile in terms of computer vision is its ability to keep remodeling the billboard incredibly fast so that it always looks natural in the three-dimensional landscape," Mr. Pleven explains.

15   This enables Epsis to replace the billboard, in the digitalized TV picture, with its own image chosen from the library of brand names or slogans in its memory. An art director, skilled in computer-assisted graphics, has to bring the right touch to the job in order to make the billboard perfectly realistic.

16   In the last few weeks, the Epsis team has extended the machine's capabilities so that it can keep this virtual billboard in place even when racers or tennis players pass in front of the real one.

17   The possibilities, of course, include some interesting perspectives: If environmentalists complain that billboards pollute sports, the actual signs can be removed since what advertisers want is the television advertising.

18   There are also some grimmer possibilities: Couldn't the technology be used to broadcast a doctored image of a scoreboard? Theoretically, yes, the Symah Vision team acknowledge.

19   But they have given a public undertaking to disclose any changes they make with Epsis and they do not plan to sell the machines, even though they are protected with patents. Instead, Symah Vision will sell the service, to be paid as a percentage of the extra revenues generated by its ability to multiply and target the broadcast ads.

20   The bottom line about the project's significance comes from Claude Gomy, the executive vice-president of Matra Space & Defense. He runs a task force under owner Jean-Luc Lagardère that aims to find synergies between defense technology and the commercial markets served by Hachette, the group's publishing company, especially its cutting-edge multimedia department, which is headed by Arnaud Lagardère, son of the founder.

21   "We're fortunate because we have the matrix for bringing together the scientists who know what the technology can do and the marketeers who know what the consumers need," Mr. Gomy said. He sees the Matra Hachette Multimedia division leading other commercial applications derived from defense electronics.

22   The real breakthroughs, Mr. Gomy added, are achieved not by simply retooling weapons into toys but by combining basic technologies, such as the computing architecture and the space observation systems elegantly reused in Epsis.

23   But the spinoffs may not stop there. The Matra technologies have matured in the last decade by criss-crossing between civilian and military projects. "The next phase may see the Epsis technology spin into a satellite or some other defense program," Mr. Gomy said.

DISCUSSION QUESTIONS

1.   The article describes a new technology called Epsis that allows an advertisement to be altered during a live broadcast so that viewers in one location might see a different advertising image than viewers in another location, even though the same event is being broadcast. Using the information in the article, discuss in small groups how this innovation is technologically possible.

2.   Fitchett writes that the "success of this experiment has changed forever what viewers are likely to see when they watch live broadcasts of international sports events." To what extent do you think this change is for the better? Support your opinion with specific reasons.

3.   The article states that this new technology "provides an object lesson in the conversion of military technologies to civilian applications with commercial potential." Can you think of any other technological innovations in the commercial market that have begun with the military?

4.   Fitchett states that "The ability of this French technology to modify images in real time—in live broadcasts, which have become part of our sense of visual reality—has revolutionary potential. It will raise ethical and regulatory problems, but it is also set to corner a $100 million-a-year European market." What do you think Fitchett means by the term *visual reality*? What sorts of ethical and regulatory problems might this technology raise?

5. In what other ways do you think this new technology might be used? What specific markets do you think might benefit from this technology?

WRITING ASSIGNMENTS

1. Fitchett writes that the ability to alter advertising images during a live broadcast "will raise ethical and regulatory problems." Write an exploratory essay that examines the nature of these problems. What specific sorts of ethical questions might be raised with this new technology? In what ways might the technology be abused? Is it possible to control and regulate the use of this technology? Be sure to support your opinions with specific examples and details.

2. Fitchett uses the term *visual reality*. Write a definition paper in which you attempt to define this phrase. What could or might be meant by this term? Use specific examples and details to support your ideas.

3. Write a proposal for a new use of the Epsis technology. Other than altering advertisements during live broadcasts of sporting events, how else might this technology be used? Your proposal should include a description of your idea as well as a rationale for it. Be as specific as possible in your presentation of the proposal.

CHAPTER TWO WRITING ASSIGNMENTS

1. Interview someone who is professionally involved with the media. Drawing on what you have learned from the articles in this chapter, prepare a set of questions to use with your interviewee. Be sure your interview has a specific focus. Try to ask questions that elicit more than simple yes and no responses.

2. Several of the articles in this chapter concern radio. Drawing on information from these articles as well as outside research and your own experience, write an essay in response to the following question: "To what extent does radio influence our daily lives?" You should begin your writing process by using a prewriting technique such as clustering or brainstorming to help give your essay direction.

3. Drawing on the readings from this chapter as well as other sources, write a paper that compares and contrasts the impact of print and electronic media on their respective audiences. How are they different? How are they similar? Do you think these media are best suited for different purposes? Use specific examples and details to support the ideas presented in your analysis.

4. Drawing on at least two sources from this chapter, write an essay in response to the following question: "To what extent can the media help to create better understanding among nations?" You may also choose to include information from other sources in your essay. Be sure to support your claims with specific details and examples.

Contending with Violence around the World

A young woman is attacked and robbed. A gunman opens fire in a crowded restaurant. A federal building is bombed by terrorists. Indeed, it is rare that we can listen to or watch a news broadcast that does not contain a report about some act of violence inflicted upon an individual, an innocent group of people, or even an entire community. We do not need to consult statistical studies to recognize that the incidence of violence in our society is increasing. What factors are contributing to this increase in violence? Are there ways to prevent violence? What can we learn from societies where violence is relatively low? These and other questions are explored in this chapter.

The chapter opens with an article by T. R. Reid entitled "Japanese Are Shaken by Shooting of Official." In this selection, Reid reports on the shooting of Takaji Kunimatsu, Japan's director general of the National Police Agency. Kunimatsu, who was leading the investigation of a 1995 poison gas attack of the Tokyo subway, was shot outside his apartment building just ten days after the subway attack. Many suspect that there is a connection between the shooting and the nerve gas attack and that the terrorist group Aum Shinrikyo is responsible. What is most disturbing, however, is that these two incidents represent a growing concern on the part of Japanese citizens that they are no longer safe. Although rates of violent crimes are lower in Japan than in any other free country, according to Reid's article, the people of Japan are afraid. As a headline of Japan's leading newspaper, the *Yomiuri Shimbun,* asked, "What Happened to Our Safe Society?"

Similarly, Parisians were stunned by the subway bombing of a busy Métro station in the Saint-Michel district of Paris during the summer of

1995. Police suspected either a fundamentalist Islamic group or a Serbian group. According to Marlise Simons in "Paris Terror Attack Gives Up Few Leads," many Parisians remembered that the Paris Metro was a target of Algerian terrorists during the Algerian war in the 1960s, when Algeria wanted independence from France. Police have asked businesses, cinemas, and large stores to increase security measures, and Prime Minister Alain Juppé stated, "We will systematically continue actions of precaution and prevention."

The concept of prevention is also examined in "Agony of Killer's 'Only Living Victim'" by Debra West. In this article, West reports on how a fifty-five-year-old woman named Jeremy Brown is working to reform parole laws. Brown was attacked in 1994 by Reginald McFadden, who had been sentenced to life in prison in 1969 for murder but was paroled in 1994. Less than three months after his release, McFadden went on a rampage of violent crime, including his attack on Brown. Brown lived to tell her story and warns that similar tragedies will occur unless the parole laws are reformed.

The selection entitled "Juveniles Fuel Soaring Violent Crime in America" also issues a warning. The article explains that the incidence of violent crimes committed by juveniles has increased dramatically in the United States. In the past, juvenile delinquents were primarily involved in nonviolent property crimes. Between 1984 and 1992, however, homicides involving handguns increased fivefold among juveniles. In a statement to the press, United States Attorney General Janet Reno warned, "Unless we act now to stop young people from choosing a life of violence and crime, the beginning of the 21st century could bring levels of violent crime to our community that far exceed what we have experienced."

In "After Shooting, Los Angeles Man Becomes an Instant Hero" by Seth Mydans, we see how a need to feel free from harm has prompted some people to take the law into their own hands, making them heroes in the eyes of many. Mydans reports that William Masters of Sun Valley, California, a Los Angeles suburb, was hailed as a hero for shooting two youths who were spraying graffiti underneath a freeway overpass. One youth was fatally shot; the other was wounded. Although some people called the shooting racially motivated because Masters is Caucasian and the youths were Hispanic, others think Masters was simply protecting himself and the community.

In contrast to the sentiments surrounding the Los Angeles shooting, "London's Longtime Loathing for Guns Begins at Last to Fade" by William E. Schmidt explores the belief of the British that limiting gun ownership will help prevent crime. In addition, the long-standing tradition that British police officers, or "bobbies," should carry only wooden nightsticks rather than guns echoes this conviction. However, as Schmidt points out, rising crime in Britain is forcing law enforcement officials to reconsider the policy. Although police officers are not pleased with the prospect of being required to carry firearms, the day may come when they will have to. As one British bobby states, ". . . if you carry a gun, you have to be ready to use it, and I don't think I can do that."

The chapter concludes with an article by Patrick E. Tyler called "In Rural China, 'Gold Lords' Challenge the State." In this selection, Tyler gives an account of the gold rush occurring in the remote and rural countryside of mainland China. According to Tyler, the gold rush is creating a state of lawlessness and violence in the countryside. This gold fever pandemonium is the result of gold lords and entrepreneurial miners protecting their interests and territory. Although the violence in the countryside has been an embarrassment to Communist Party leaders, they have not been able to curb the lawlessness. As one "gold boss" stated, "Even if the government wanted to control us, we are stronger than they are right now, and our guns are normally much better than the ones carried by the Public Security Bureau."

While reading the selections presented in this chapter, think about the nature of violence. Where does it come from? What does it feed on? Why do certain types of situations seem to breed violence? And, finally, how can we as individuals and as members of our communities help to lessen violence?

JAPANESE ARE SHAKEN BY SHOOTING OF OFFICIAL

T. R. Reid

Washington Post Service

■

A week after a nerve gas attack in Japan's subway, the person heading the investigation of the attack, the director general of Japan's National Police Agency, Takaji Kunimatsu, was shot outside his apartment building by a masked bicyclist. In this article, T. R. Reid examines the fear that hit the Japanese people after both the gas attack and the shooting occurred within ten days of each other. Some suspected that the nerve gas attack and the shooting were related since Kunimatsu was the chief investigator of the gas attack. According to this article, however, police were reluctant to make a connection between the two incidents. Many think that a secretive cult named Aum Shinrikyo was responsible for both the subway attack and the shooting. What remains clear is that the people of Japan are not accustomed to this violence, and they are afraid. As you read this selection, consider the question posed at the start of the article: "What happened to our safe society?" What happened to the sense of security in Japan? In the United States? Around the world?

■

1 Tokyo—As the head of the national police force lay in a hospital with four bullet wounds, and the terrorists responsible for last week's subway gas attack remained at large Thursday, the people of Japan face a frightening question: "What happened to our safe society?"

2 So asked the headline in the evening's edition of the Yomiuri Shimbun, Japan's biggest newspaper, as a nation that is accustomed to safety, civility, and peace in every neighborhood at any hour suddenly experiences its second shocking crime in 10 days.

3   Following their standard practice, the police said almost nothing about possible clues or suspects in the shooting Thursday of Takaji Kunimatsu, director general of the National Police Agency. Mr. Kunimatsu, was shot outside his apartment building about 8:30 A.M. by a masked man who rode up on bicycle, fired at least four times, and raced away in a misty morning rain.

4   Mr. Kunimatsu, 57, was reported in stable condition Thursday night. As the head of National Police Agency, he had been in charge of the nationwide investigation into the terrorist poison gas attack on the Tokyo subways on March 20 that killed 10 people and injured about 5,000.

5   Mr. Kunimatsu's investigators have focused on a secretive cult named Aum Shinrikyo, led by a bearded Buddhist guru named Shoko Asahara, whose meandering and often wildly illogical writings overflow with fear and hatred of the National Police Agency.

6   The police would not discuss any connection between the two crimes. The Aum sect denied any responsibility for either one.

7   But other analysts were less reluctant. "At the very moment the police are carving open the deepest secrets of the poisoning case, the top officer of the police was shot," said a crime expert, Yukio Akatsuka. "Naturally you can see a connection there."

8   The ownership of guns is essentially banned in Japan. Members of the organized crime network, the *yakuza*, are known to traffic in smuggled guns, and normally any shooting here prompts suspicion of these gangsters.

9   But attacking the national police chief is not their style, and analysts said it was unlikely that the yakuza was responsible for the shooting.

10   According to news reports, the police investigation has turned up an enormous amount of evidence linking the Aum cult to the nerve gas that was used in the subway killings.

11   Former cult members say they were taught that any necessary measure was acceptable to protect the cult and its leader, Mr. Asahara, who styled himself the "Venerated Master." The guru, an admirer of Hitler, has repeatedly criticized the National Police Agency, which employs every police officer in Japan. He has asserted that the police are trying to kill him and his followers.

12   Indeed, one suggested motive for the subway attack is an attempt to kill officials of the police agency. The poison gas was released on five trains that were scheduled to stop at the station nearest the police agency headquarters close to 8:30 A.M., when the offices open for business.

13   Mr. Asahara also asserts that the Central Intelligence Agency and the U.S. military have attacked him. Evidently for that reason, the U.S. Embassy here issued a warning to all Americans in Japan to be on guard until the subway case is solved.

14   There has been some criticism of the police as moving too slowly on the subway case, as well as a case nine months earlier in the city of Matsumoto in central Japan, where a fog of nerve gas wafted through a residential neighborhood and killed seven people. In both cases, the weapon was the same rare nerve gas, sarin.

15   But despite evidence that may link the 8,000-member Aum cult to sarin gas, no arrests have been made in either case.

16   The attack on the national police director Thursday presumably will not enhance the reputation of the force.

17   The police said two officers had been detailed to guard Mr. Kunimatsu around the clock in case of an attack. But the guards said they did not see the bicyclist approach their chief as he walked to a waiting limousine just outside his apartment door.

18   The attacker was described as a man roughly 40 years old wearing a black coat and a white surgical mask. The latter would not be particularly unusual here, because Japanese people who have a cold or cough routinely wear masks to keep from spreading germs.

19   That kind of concern for others is one of the reasons for Japan's record for public safety. In a highly egalitarian country where nearly everyone who wants a job has one and most people are roughly as well off as everybody else, rates of violent crime are lower than in any other free country.

20   Last year this nation of 125 million people had 38 shooting deaths.

21   But however low the rate of crime, dry statistics cannot compete with raw fear that is fueled by sensational cases. Today, the people of Japan are afraid.

DISCUSSION QUESTIONS

I. In small groups, discuss the question being asked by the Japanese people: "What happened to our safe society?" You may want to discuss the question in terms of different communities. Your town or city? Your school? Your state? Your nation? The world? Make a cluster or brainstorming chart of your discussion. Be prepared to share your thoughts with the rest of the class.

2. Reid writes, "In a highly egalitarian country where nearly everyone who wants a job has one and most people are roughly as well off as

everybody else, rates of violent crime are lower than in any other free country." What do you think is the connection between being a "highly egalitarian country" and having a low crime rate?

3. The article mentions that owning a gun in Japan is illegal. To what extent do you think the banning of private ownership of guns lowers the crime rate? Do you think such a ban would work in the United States? Why or why not?

WRITING ASSIGNMENTS

1. Write an exploratory essay in which you respond to the following question: "What happened to our safe society?" Be sure to use specific details and examples to support your thesis. You should use a prewriting strategy such as clustering or brainstorming to help you explore your ideas.

2. Research the subway nerve gas attack that occurred on March 20, 1995. Write an informative report on your findings. Your report should include details of the actual attack as well as information about the investigation. Be prepared to present your findings to the whole class.

3. Reid has described Japan as "a highly egalitarian country." Research what you think this term might mean. Then write an essay that focuses on the relationship between egalitarianism and a low crime rate. Your essay should respond to the following question: "To what extent does egalitarianism help prevent crime?"

PARIS TERROR ATTACK
GIVES UP FEW LEADS

Marlise Simons

New York Times Service

■

Acts of terrorism have been increasing worldwide, as has the destruction they cause. The bombings of the World Trade Center and the Oklahoma City federal building are two examples of terrorism in the United States that will remain etched in our memories. The following selection by Marlise Simons details the events of a terrorist bombing in the Paris subway in the summer of 1995. The attack occurred during the evening rush hour at the busy Saint-Michel Métro station. The bomb had been placed under a seat and exploded just as the doors of the express train opened. Four people were killed instantly, and three others died later from severe burns. Nearly eighty people were treated for injuries or shock. Police speculate that the open door helped save lives. According to this article, police suspect that either Algerian Islamic fundamentalists or a Bosnian Serb group may be responsible for the blast. As you read this article, consider the effect that living in fear of terrorism has on people's lives. How should governments respond to terrorism? How can we protect ourselves from terrorist acts?

■

1   PARIS—With the death toll from the bombing in the Paris subway rising to seven, French police Wednesday hunted for leads that would enable them to determine who was behind the worst terrorist action here in almost a decade.

2   The government ordered police reinforcements in Paris and other cities, with random security checks during the night on the roads and at the borders. Security was visibly tightened to calm public fear at

airports, railroad stations and at the Channel Tunnel linking France and England.

3   French television reported a spate of bomb hoaxes Wednesday, including one that forced the evacuation of about 8,000 people from the Louvre and another that closed the shopping complex at Les Halles for an hour.

4   The police said they had received a number of calls overnight from people claiming responsibility but they had not enough reasons to believe any of them.

5   The nearest attribution of blame so far has come from Interior Minister Jean-Louis Debré, who said: "The Islamic link is possible, the Serbian link is not impossible." However, other links should not be ruled out.

6   But while Algeria's Islamic fundamentalists have threatened attacks against France because of its support for the Algerian military government and the Bosnian Serbs have been fiercely criticized by Paris, there is still apparently no firm lead to suggest that either of these groups decided to strike at France in the heart of its capital.

7   The explosion was evidently set for maximum impact during the evening rush hour at the busy Métro station of Saint-Michel. The bomb aboard the southbound train of the RER-B suburban express set off a fire and sent glass and metal flying at passengers. The blast occurred just as the doors opened onto the platform, which police said had probably saved lives.

8   Four people were killed immediately and three others have died during the night from severe burns. The police have not released the names of the victims. Another 11 are listed in serious condition and close to 80 people have been treated for injuries or shock.

9   The intersection at the Place Saint-Michel, with its cafés and fountain, appeared as busy as usual on Wednesday. The station reopened and the damaged train has been towed to a police laboratory, where investigators sifted through the wreckage for clues. One investigator said the bomb, which had been placed under a seat, was a "rustic" rather than a sophisticated device triggered by a timer. Laboratory results that might reveal meaningful information about the bomb and its makers are expected in the next few days.

10   France, which is normally secretive about its police actions, Wednesday announced its anti-terrorist actions with much publicity. A government spokesman said that many police had been called back from vacation and that the government was deploying 1,000 extra

police in Paris and another 800 in other cities, including Marseille, Lyon and Nice, and it was keeping several thousand special forces of riot police on standby. Security checks and ostentatious police patrols were visible at places where crowds gather, such as soccer stadiums, department stores and train stations.

11   "We will systematically continue actions of precaution and prevention," Prime Minister Alain Juppé told reporters after Wednesday morning's cabinet meeting.

12   The police prefect of Paris and other authorities have called on representatives of businesses, cinemas, museums and large stores to increase their surveillance. The French remember that during the terrorist attacks of the 1980s, launched by pro-Iranian Lebanese groups, explosions came in series just a few days apart in places like stations, stores and post offices.

13   Older Parisians also recalled that the Paris Métro was a special target during the Algerian war in the early 1960s, before France granted Algeria its independence.

14   The newspaper Le Monde was one of several that speculated whether Tuesday's attack was also linked to Algeria. It said that on July 17, the Algerian newspaper La Tribune reported that the fundamentalist Armed Islamic Group had threatened that it would carry out "bomb attacks in Paris to punish the French government." It said that two terrorist squads had left for Belgium and Germany, one of which, it alleged, was responsible for assassinating an influential imam at a Paris mosque on July 11.

15   Over the past year, French police have several times rounded up suspected Islamic fundamentalists, expelled some and jailed others.

DISCUSSION QUESTIONS

1. In small groups, discuss what you know about terrorism. How would you define it? What specific acts of terrorism do you remember? Why do you think it occurs?

2. How do you think both governments and individuals can help to prevent terrorism? Do you think it is possible to prevent terrorism?

3. The article states that several people called the police after the Paris bombing claiming to be responsible for the blast. Why do you think people and/or organizations make these claims? What do they have to gain by pretending to be responsible for an act of terrorism?

4. Simons states that "France, which is normally secretive about its police actions, Wednesday announced its anti-terrorist actions with much publicity." What do you think can be gained from making anti-terrorist tactics public? What can be gained from keeping police work secretive?

WRITING ASSIGNMENTS

1. Write an informative report about a specific terrorist act. You might want to choose a fairly recent incident, such as the Oklahoma bombing, or one from the past, such as a hijacking. Be sure to include enough detail so that someone who knows nothing about the event will learn something after reading your report. Be prepared to share your findings with the class in an oral presentation.

2. Write an essay that responds to the following question: "To what extent can terrorism be prevented around the world?" Be sure to include specific reasons and evidence to support your claims. You may also want to consult other sources to help you develop your ideas.

3. Many films have dealt with the subject of terrorism, including *In the Name of the Father* and *Black Sunday*. Watch a video of one of these films and then write a critique of the film. Your critique should be more than a summary of the film. Rather, it should assess the film's production values, such as the quality of the acting and the script. In addition, you should address the question of terrorism itself by questioning how the film represented terrorism. Was it realistic or contrived?

AGONY OF KILLER'S
"ONLY LIVING VICTIM"

Debra West

New York Times Service

■

In the following selection, Debra West reports on how Jeremy Brown, the fifty-five-year-old rape victim of a paroled murderer and suspected serial killer, is using her position as the "only living victim" of a serial killer to help reform New York State's parole laws. Reginald McFadden, Brown's attacker, was pardoned by the governor of Pennsylvania in 1994 for the 1969 killing of an elderly Philadelphia woman. Less than three months after his pardon, McFadden went on a crime spree. After testifying at McFadden's trial, Brown stated, "I am the only living victim of Reginald McFadden, a psychopath who was sentenced to life in prison for murder in 1969. A psychopath who was also set free to murder again in 1994." As you read this article, you might think about our current penal system and parole laws. To what extent are criminals rehabilitated in prison? Do you think it is ever appropriate to pardon a person who has been given a life sentence? Do you think our justice system needs reform?

■

1   NEW CITY, New York—Reginald McFadden, a pardoned murderer and suspected serial killer, has been found guilty of rape, but the moment belongs to his rape victim, who went before the cameras at the courthouse here and declared herself a victim no longer.

2   Immediately after the guilty verdict was announced, the woman, Jeremy Brown, a 55-year-old social worker, stood at a news conference and described the agony of being cross-examined by Mr. McFadden, who served as his own lawyer in the three-week trial.

3   "I think it is perfectly ludicrous that I was tortured by this man for five hours and then to have to sit there and answer his ridiculous questions," Ms. Brown said. "I think it's crazy."

68

4   "I am the only living victim of Reginald McFadden," she added, "a psychopath who was sentenced to life in prison for murder in 1969. A psychopath who was also set free to murder again in 1994."

5   Unlike most rape victims, who seek to remain anonymous, Ms. Brown said she was speaking openly to call attention to a system that had permitted Mr. McFadden's release.

6   "We spent all this money and all this time when it was so obvious that he was guilty," she said. "My fantasy was that we would just march him down Main Street and burn him and throw rocks at him."

7   Acknowledging that her words reflected rage rather than a rational view of law and order, she said, "It's true. I'm a social worker—but I had a lot more compassion before this happened."

8   The authorities say Mr. McFadden went on a crime spree last summer, less than three months after being pardoned by the governor of Pennsylvania for having killed an elderly Philadelphia woman in 1969. He has been charged in the murders of two Long Island residents and is a suspect in a third killing.

9   The circumstances of his 1994 release have since been found to be marked by bureaucratic mixups. The resulting controversy has had political repercussions in Pennsylvania and has generated a debate over the rights of criminals to start life over and the rights of citizens to feel free in their homes.

10   Thursday, after less than two hours of deliberation, a jury concluded that Mr. McFadden was guilty of having attacked Ms. Brown at her South Nyack home on the evening of Sept. 21, 1994. Over the next five hours, the jurors concluded, he raped her three times, beat her several times and robbed her of her cash and jewelry.

11   Mr. McFadden faces up to 50 years in prison if given the maximum penalty on each count. Sentencing was set for Sept. 7.

12   Mr. McFadden, 42, had no reaction when the verdict was read Thursday. As he left the courtroom in shackles, however, he placed his hands together at chin level, stared at the victim, gave three small claps and smiled.

13   Ms. Brown said Thursday that she felt most abused by the people who had helped secure Mr. McFadden's freedom, members of an Islamic group known as Irfan. He converted to Islam in prison, and Irfan members petitioned the parole board for his release. Afterward, Ms. Brown asserted, they abandoned him.

14   "When somebody is sent away for life," she said, in a flash of anger, "I don't see why Americans are hell-bent to get him out. I've had no word of support from those people. They spent a lot of years getting him out of prison and then they dropped him like a hot potato."

15   The Pennsylvania Board of Pardons, convinced that he had repented his crimes and reformed his ways in prison, voted, 4 to 1, in 1992 to commute Mr. McFadden's sentence.

16   The board insisted that he spend two years in a halfway house. But by the time Governor Robert P. Casey signed the release papers, 18 months had passed and parole officials mistakenly believed they were obligated to release Mr. McFadden unconditionally.

17   Ms. Brown has not returned to her job as a social worker. Nor has she returned to the house where she was brutalized. But she said Thursday that she had begun healing.

18   She plans to use her position as "the only living victim" of a serial killer to seek reform of New York state's parole laws.

19   She has already had success in Pennsylvania. On June 1, the governor signed a bill requiring that parolees with violent criminal pasts spend at least one year in a prerelease center and be supervised weekly for six months if they move out of state.

DISCUSSION QUESTIONS

1.   In small groups, discuss the following question: "To what extent does our justice system help to prevent further crimes?" Be prepared to share some of your views with other members of the class.

2.   West writes, "On June 1, the governor signed a bill requiring that parolees with violent criminal pasts spend at least one year in a prerelease center and be supervised weekly for six months if they move out of state." Speculate about the term *prerelease center*. What do you think a prerelease center might be? What should it do? How would it work? Do you think it could work?

3.   Why do you think criminals who have been sentenced to life imprisonment or who have committed violent acts are sometimes paroled or pardoned? What are the issues parole boards and/or other authority figures might consider when making this determination?

4.   West writes that this controversial trial has resulted in much debate over "the rights of criminals to start life over and the rights of citizens to feel free in their homes." What is your opinion of this debate? Whose rights should be considered more important? Do you think it is possible to reach a compromise on this issue?

WRITING ASSIGNMENTS

1. Jeremy Brown states that she is "the only living victim of Reginald McFadden, a psychopath who was sentenced to life in prison for murder in 1969. A psychopath who was also set free to murder again in 1994." Write an essay that responds to the following question: "Under what circumstances, if any, should criminals be paroled?" Be sure to support your opinions and ideas with specific evidence and reasons.

2. Write an essay that responds to the following question: "To what extent do you think the United States correctional system rehabilitates criminals convicted of violent crimes?" Be sure to support your opinions and ideas with specific evidence and reasons.

3. Write a problem-solution paper in which you explore one specific problem of our correctional system and offer potential solutions for the problem. Your essay will require some outside research.

4. West writes that the governor of Pennsylvania signed a bill "requiring that parolees with violent criminal pasts spend at least one year in a prerelease center and be supervised weekly for six months if they move out of state." Write a paper in which you explore the function of this prerelease center. What are its goals and objectives, and how will it accomplish these goals? Your essay should be developed with specific details and suggestions.

JUVENILES FUEL SOARING VIOLENT CRIME IN AMERICA

International Herald Tribune

■

The following selection examines the increase in violent crimes committed by juveniles. According to a recent Justice Department study, arrests of juveniles for major violent crimes have grown from 83,400 in 1983 to 129,600 in 1992, and homicides committed by juveniles have nearly doubled in this same time period. The study questions the usefulness of several juvenile crime-prevention initiatives, such as midnight basketball leagues, since most juvenile crime is committed between 3:00 p.m. and 6:00 p.m. Many people are worried about this increase in juvenile crime because for decades, according to sociology professor Dean Rojek, juvenile criminal activity was generally limited to property crimes. As Attorney General Janet Reno asserts, "Unless we act now to stop young people from choosing a life of violence and crime, the beginning of the 21st century could bring levels of violent crime to our community that far exceed what we have experienced." As you read this article, think about Reno's comment. What do you think we need to do to help prevent juvenile crime? What do you think Reno meant when she said that we must "act now"?

■

1 WASHINGTON—Juveniles have become the driving force behind the alarming increases in violent crime in the United States, with arrests for murder, rape, robbery and aggravated assault growing sharply over the last decade as guns and drugs become more available, a new Justice Department study shows.

2 The study, presented as the most comprehensive of its kind, shows that juvenile arrests for major violent crimes grew from 83,400 in 1983 to 129,600 in 1992. The number for homicide alone more than doubled to 2,202 in 1991, from 969 in 1984.

3   If that rate continues, the report projects a staggering 261,000 arrests of violent youth offenders by the year 2010—a doubling of the current figure.

4   The report also calls into question some of the most popular crime prevention programs adopted by cities, states and the federal government in the last few years, including curfews and midnight basketball leagues.

5   The report found, for example, that the peak time during which youths age 6 to 17 commit violent crimes was from 3 P.M. to 6 P.M., between the end of the school day and dinner.

6   "What you see here is a road map to the next generation of crime," said Attorney General Janet Reno at her weekly news briefing. "Unless we act now to stop young people from choosing a life of violence and crime, the beginning of the 21st century could bring levels of violent crime to our community that far exceed what we have experienced."

7   "For decades violent crime was driven mostly by adults, with kids involved mostly in property crime," said Dean Rojek, professor of sociology at the University of Georgia. "What's been changing is that you have juveniles becoming much more involved in violent offenses, with the use of weapons. If we add to this more babies, you could have a multiplier effect."

8   The report by the department's Office of Juvenile Justice and Delinquency Prevention chronicles a number of disturbing trends that have developed over the last decade including:

• Between 1984 and 1993, the number of homicides among juveniles involving handguns increased fivefold. Eighty percent of juvenile homicides now are committed with a gun. A spokesman for the White House, Rahm Emanuel, said that President Bill Clinton found the projection of a doubling in arrests for juveniles by 2010 "very disturbing."

• From 1980 to 1992, reports of children abused and neglected almost tripled, to 2.9 million from 1 million. The report cited several studies that showed a clear link between child abuse and neglect, and future juvenile delinquency and adult criminality. But Howard Snyder, one of the authors of the report and director of systems research for the National Center for Juvenile Justice, said it was unclear how much of the increase in cases might be attributed to better reporting of child abuse.

9   Melissa Sickmund, one of the report's two authors, said that current crime statistics and projections portend a worsening crisis.

10   "The rates are high enough now that this is a scary proposition," she said. "Juvenile detention facilities are already crowded. Public safety demands that you take care of bad kids. These kids grow up. I don't think we can afford to have a nation of criminals."

11   Large urban centers where crack-cocaine and firearms were more available showed the most pronounced problems with juvenile violence. New York had the highest violent juvenile offender rate, followed by Florida, New Jersey, Maryland and California.

12   "Violence is tied to poverty and drug use," said Mr. Snyder, the report's other author.

DISCUSSION QUESTIONS

1. In small groups, think of some reasons why juveniles are committing more violent crimes than they did in past years. What are some of the factors contributing to this increase in violent crimes committed by juveniles? Make a brainstorming list or cluster and be prepared to share it with other members of the class.

2. Drug use and poverty, according to this article, have been cited as factors leading to violent criminal activity by juveniles. Why do you think these two factors might produce an increase in juvenile crime? Try to explain the connection.

3. West writes, "The report also calls into question some of the most popular crime prevention programs adopted by cities, states and the federal government in the last few years, including curfews and midnight basketball leagues." These programs have been both supported and criticized by politicians and others. What is your opinion of these crime-prevention tactics? Do you think they work? Do some work while others don't? Support your ideas with specific reasons and evidence.

4. West quotes sociology professor Dean Rojek as stating, "What's been changing is that you have juveniles becoming much more involved in violent offenses, with the use of weapons. If we add to this more babies, you could have a multiplier effect." What do you think Rojek means by the term *multiplier effect*? How important do you think this effect might be for the future safety of communities?

WRITING ASSIGNMENTS

1. The use of crime-prevention programs such as midnight basketball leagues has been a much-debated issue. While some people feel these programs help keep juveniles out of trouble, others think that money is being inappropriately spent on such programs. Research this topic and then write an essay that responds to the following question: "Should the government support and fund crime-prevention programs such as midnight basketball leagues for youth?" Be sure to support your opinions with specific reasons and evidence.

2. Write a causal analysis essay that explores the connection between poverty and violent crimes committed by juveniles. What are the characteristics of poverty that may contribute to juvenile violent crime? Support your main points with specific details and examples.

3. Write an informative report that details the crimes committed by juveniles in your community. What trends do you see? Has this sort of crime increased in recent years? What has been done to prevent it? Your report will require some research. Be prepared to present your findings to the class.

After Shooting, Los Angeles Man Becomes an Instant Hero

Seth Mydans

New York Times Service

■

William Masters, a Los Angeles area resident, has been hailed by some as a hero for shooting two young men who were spraying graffiti underneath an overpass of the Hollywood Freeway. At 1:00 a.m., Masters came across the two youths while they were spraying graffiti under the overpass; he wrote down their license plate number. In the ensuing confrontation, Masters fatally shot Cesar Arce and wounded David Hillo. In the following selection, Seth Mydans examines the reaction of the general public to this event. For many Los Angeles area citizens, Masters was a welcome hero. However, others viewed Masters' actions as racially motivated, considering them anything but heroic. As Cesar Arce's sister said, "He's not a hero. He's a killer." As you read this selection, think about both sides of the debate. Why do you think so many people consider Masters a hero? Why might some others think just the opposite? What is your opinion?

■

1   Los Angeles—William Masters had often rehearsed the moment in his head when, on one of his late-night walks, he would pull out his 9-millimeter pistol, level it at a criminal and shout, "Freeze!"

2   It was his duty as a citizen, he said in an interview last week, to be armed, trained and ready to defend the victims of crimes.

3   It happened a little differently the week before last. Beneath an overpass of the Hollywood Freeway at 1 A.M., Mr. Masters confronted two young men who were spraying graffiti, argued with them and shot them, killing one, 18-year-old Cesar Arce.

4   The police accepted his assertion that the men had threatened him with a screwdriver and tried to rob him, and he was released from custody without being charged. Instantly, Mr. Masters became the latest celebrity in Los Angeles, a vigilante hero to many people, the toast of talk shows and letters to the editor.

5   "William, you're not a hero to me, you're a saint," said Guy in Palmdale, a caller to a KFI-AM radio show.

6   Another caller, Diane in the Van Nuys district, said, "I don't care if he's Looney Toons or what, but we need more guys like him around."

7   Since the shooting on Jan. 31 in the Sun Valley neighborhood in the San Fernando Valley, Mr. Masters, 35, who works as a movie extra, has fed these sentiments with pointed comments that express the kinds of fears and resentments that appear to animate people like Guy and Diane.

8   "People were relieved that here was a murder victim who was not murdered," Mr. Masters said. "Instead, one of the murderers died."

9   Asked if he was afraid of facing charges, he said, "Where are you going to find 12 citizens to convict me?" Describing his assailants with a racial slur, he said, "This situation is what everybody lives in fear of."

10   His actions and his words have become a focal point in a city where graffiti on walls and freeway signs symbolize to many people a spread of crime and deteriorating neighborhoods and an inability of government to maintain order.

11   Graffiti-busting is one of the few ways citizens have found to take the law into their own hands, forming neighborhood groups to hunt down young vandals and report them to the police.

12   Mr. Masters went one step further, and people are now comparing him with Bernard Goetz, a white man who shot four black youths on a New York subway train when they threatened him with a sharpened screwdriver, and with the main character in the recent movie "Falling Down," in which a frustrated man rampages through Los Angeles exacting vigilante justice.   .

13   "Kudos to William Masters for his vigilant anti-graffiti efforts and for his foresight in carrying a gun for self-protection," writes Sandi Webb, a member of the Simi Valley City Council, in a letter to The Daily News.

14   "If Sun Valley refuses to honor Masters as a crime-fighting hero, then I invite him to relocate to our town. I think he will find Simi Valley to be a much more compatible place to live."

15   It was in Simi Valley that an all-white jury found four police officers not guilty of assault in 1992 in the beating of a black motorist, Rodney G. King.

16   As with so many disputed issues here, race and ethnicity are moving again to center stage. Mr. Masters is white, and those he shot were Hispanic.

17   Last Wednesday, a group of Hispanic lawyers demanded a reopening of the investigation of the shootings. When District Attorney Gil Garcetti denied the request, they said they would call for a U.S. civil-rights investigation. They noted that Mr. Arce was shot in the back and that Mr. Masters had described the men he shot in racial terms.

18   Mr. Arce's sister, Lilia, has been her brother's chief defender.

19   "He's not a hero," she said of Mr. Masters. "He's a killer."

20   The crucial moments before the shootings are in dispute between Mr. Masters and the man he wounded, David Hillo, 20, who was treated and released from a hospital for a gunshot wound in his buttock.

21   It was past midnight and Mr. Masters, who owns five guns and subscribes to law-enforcement publications, said he was taking his usual armed, late-night walk through a barren neighborhood near the Hollywood Freeway. His critics suggest he was looking for trouble, but he insists that it is his right to walk on any street, any time.

22   When he came upon Mr. Arce and Mr. Hillo spray-painting a freeway pylon, Mr. Masters and Mr. Hillo agree, he wrote the license number of their car on a scrap of paper. The men saw him and demanded the paper from him.

23   At that point, the stories diverge. Mr. Masters said Mr. Hillo brandished a screwdriver and tried to rob him, and Mr. Arce lunged at him, leading him to shoot in self-defense. Mr. Hillo denied this, saying that Mr. Masters fired without provocation or warning.

24   The police said that Mr. Masters's version was more compelling and that he had acted justifiably in self-defense. They set him free after holding him for what he said was six hours.

25   "In this case—and I don't want this to sound callous—this was not a difficult decision, unfortunately," said Robert L. Cohen, the deputy district attorney who handled the case. "It's clear that what he did came under the law. Would a reasonable person in a like or similar case have reacted in the same way? And I think the answer is yes."

26   He added: "We don't think Masters is a hero. It's just a tragedy."

DISCUSSION QUESTIONS

1. In small groups, explore the meaning of the word *hero*. What are its various connotations? Then discuss whether or not you think Masters fits your definition of what a hero should be.

2. Mydans mentions that a member of the Simi Valley City Council stated that "If Sun Valley refuses to honor Masters as a crime-fighting hero, then I invite him to relocate to our town. I think he will find Simi Valley a much more compatible place to live." Mydans then notes, "It was in Simi Valley that an all-white jury found four police officers not guilty of assault in 1992 in the beating of a black motorist, Rodney G. King." Why do you think Mydans makes this point? What does it have to do with the rest of the article?

3. Masters is described in this article as a vigilante hero. How would you describe him? Why?

4. Mydans closes this article with a quote from Robert L. Cohen, the deputy district attorney who handled the case. Cohen states, "We don't think Masters is a hero. It's just a tragedy." Comment on Cohen's statement. Why do you think Cohen made this statement? What do you think he means? Do you agree or disagree with the statement?

WRITING ASSIGNMENTS

1. Mydans writes that "people are now comparing him [Masters] with Bernard Goetz, a white man who shot four black youths on a New York subway train when they threatened him with a sharpened screwdriver, and with the main character in the recent movie 'Falling Down,' in which a frustrated man rampages through Los Angeles exacting vigilante justice." The Bernard Goetz case occurred in the 1980s. Research this case and then write an essay that compares and contrasts the Masters and Goetz cases. Be sure that you focus your essay with a thesis that expresses your opinion of how the two cases compare.

2. The article mentions the film *Falling Down*. Rent the film and then write a paper that examines the connection between the film and the Masters case. Be sure to develop your essay with specific details and examples from the film.

3. Write an essay that responds to the following question: "To what extent do factors of race and ethnicity enter into criminal investigations?" Be sure to support your opinions with specific examples and evidence. You may need to do some outside research to develop your essay.

4. Robert L. Cohen, the district attorney who handled the Masters case, asserts, "It's clear that what he did came under the law. Would a reasonable person in a like or similar case have reacted in the same way? And I think the answer is yes." Write an essay in which you discuss the validity of Cohen's statement. To what extent do you agree or disagree with Cohen's statement?

London's Longtime Loathing for Guns Begins at Last to Fade

William E. Schmidt

New York Times Service

■

In this selection, William E. Schmidt reports on the changing attitudes toward the use of firearms by British police. Ever since the founding of Scotland Yard in 1829, British police officers, known as bobbies, have not carried firearms. Rather, they have carried concealed wooden nightsticks. Recently, some British police officers have replaced the nightsticks with more powerful truncheons, but the use of firearms is still extremely rare and limited to special antiterrorist and royalty security squads. According to Peter Waddington, the director of criminal justice at Reading University, the bobbies' authority comes from respect, not fear. Bobbies themselves prefer not to wear sidearms. As one officer has stated, "Besides, if you carry a gun, you have to be ready to use it, and I don't think I can do that." However, changes in society are forcing Scotland Yard to reconsider this long-standing tradition, and many are concerned about the eventual outcome. As Inspector David Davenport asserts, "The day will eventually come, I suppose, when most officers will be carrying arms. But when it does, I don't think any of us will be very happy about it." Throughout this article, Schmidt contrasts the British tradition of not issuing bobbies sidearms with the United States' practice of having police officers carry firearms. As you read this article, think about the different attitudes British and American citizens have about police carrying firearms. How are tradition and culture connected to these attitudes?

■

1   LONDON—Constable Damien Finbow says he does not want to carry a gun. After all, in the nine years he has patrolled London's sometimes mean streets, he can recall only four times when he has had to draw his nightstick to defend himself.

2   "If I wore a gun, I know I'd be worried about losing it in a fight," said Mr. Finbow, one of 24,000 uniformed patrol officers and detectives who, armed with nothing more lethal than a truncheon, keep the peace in this metropolis of 7 million people. "Besides, if you carry a gun, you have to be ready to use it, and I don't think I can do that."

3   But as he and a lot of other police officers here reluctantly acknowledge, the growing violence and a changing criminal culture are pushing the police to rethink their 166-year-old policy of policing without guns.

4   Last summer, for the first time ever, a handful of London patrol officers began wearing sidearms, and the number of armed response vehicles on the streets was more than doubled, from 5 to 12.

5   "The day will eventually come, I suppose, when most officers will be carrying arms," said Inspector David Davenport, who supervises patrols in the West End. "But when it does, I don't think any of us will be very happy about it."

6   The trouble with drugs, guns and violence in Britain is nowhere near the scale it is in the United States. In London, for example, firearms were involved in fewer than 2 percent of all assault cases last year.

7   Still, assaults on police officers in London jumped 15 percent last year, to nearly 4,000.

8   Whereas the police in the United States and on the Continent routinely carry sidearms, only about 2,500 officers among Scotland Yard's 27,000 are authorized to use firearms, and most of those are members of special squads involved in antiterrorist work or diplomatic and royal protection duties.

9   To ensure better protection for patrol officers, the Home Office last summer authorized police agencies to begin issuing, as standard equipment, truncheons 22 to 26 inches long (55 to 65 centimeters), worn openly on belts. These batons replaced the smaller, 10-inch wooden nightsticks that for decades were the only weapon most police officers were permitted to carry, concealed in their uniform.

10   In a bid to find other alternatives to sidearms, the Home Office also is testing the feasibility of arming officers with mace or pepper sprays. Most departments have made available body armor, designed principally to protect against knife attacks, which remain a far greater hazard than firearms.

11   "I think we all value the traditional image of the British bobby," said Paul Condon, superintendent of the Metropolitan Police Department. "But we have to police the real world, and the equipment and training must have some link to the real work."

12 The Home Office predicts, however, that most officers will remain unarmed for a long time, in keeping with the force's tradition of restraint and the government's long-standing policy of limiting gun possession nationwide.

13 The image of the unarmed bobby dates back to the founding of Scotland Yard in 1829, and it has been sustained over the years by a web of interlocking cultural and criminal realities.

14 Because the government had adopted tough laws over the years limiting gun ownership, the number of legal and illegal guns in circulation, though growing, remains relatively small.

15 And since few police officers have been armed, there has been little reason, until recently, for either the police or wrongdoers to expect violent confrontation.

16 "In the old days, your garden-variety English criminal might have carried a gun when he needed it for a job, but otherwise left it at home," said John Jones, a retired detective superintendent who ran a squad dealing with gun crime in south London. "The thinking was, the police don't carry guns, so why should I?"

17 It is a measure of the sensibility here, in contrast to the United States or the rest of Europe, that even now the police in London are required to file an incident report whenever they draw their nightsticks, since that is the most aggressive measure most police officers here may take.

18 Even now, London constables say they are careful not to draw their nightsticks unless they feel they are in physical danger.

19 As a result, many are able to recall exactly the times they have drawn their truncheons, the way many U.S. officers know how often they have drawn or fired their service revolver.

20 "It is a bit perplexing why people comply with the police, when the power that the policeman is able to utilize is limited," said Peter Waddington, director of criminal justice at Reading University. "But the contract between the people and the citizenry has always been rooted in the notion that people comply with an officer not out of fear, but out of respect. Over the years, each time someone has surrendered without resistance it has given the culture another self-sustaining twist."

21 But now, Mr. Waddington says, the balance is shifting, due to cultural changes within Britain brought about by immigration, as well as television and films. People are not as bound by the rules and rituals of the past, he said, and are less reluctant to use force to challenge the authority of the police.

DISCUSSION QUESTIONS

1. Schmidt writes, "Because the government has adopted tough laws over the years limiting gun ownership, the number of legal and illegal guns in circulation, though growing, remains relatively small." Do you think that if similar laws were established in the United States the number of guns in the United States would also remain small? As you consider this question, think about societal and cultural factors that might affect the outcome.

2. Schmidt quotes Peter Waddington, director of criminal justice at Reading University, as stating, "It is a bit perplexing why people comply with the police, when the power that the policeman is able to utilize is limited." Why do you think British citizens respect the authority of bobbies who do not carry firearms? Do you think this type of situation could ever exist in the United States?

3. Schmidt writes, "The image of the unarmed bobby . . . has been sustained over the years by a web of interlocking cultural and criminal realities." Speculate about what this "web of interlocking cultural and criminal realities" might be. What factors contribute to this "web"?

4. Schmidt mentions that immigration and the media have played a role in the shifting cultural climate that surrounds the issue of bobbies carrying firearms. In what ways do you think the media and immigration might affect this issue?

WRITING ASSIGNMENTS

1. Write an informative report that investigates the traditions of British bobbies. What were the circumstances surrounding the beginning of this police force? What code does the bobby follow? Where did the name *bobby* come from? These are just a few questions you might want to explore. You will need to do research to develop your report. Be prepared to present your findings to the class.

2. Write an essay that compares and contrasts the role of the British bobby with that of a patrol officer in the United States. You may need to do some outside research to help you develop your thoughts. Be sure to support your ideas with specific details and examples.

3. Schmidt writes, "Because the [British] government has adopted tough laws over the years limiting gun ownership, the number of legal and illegal guns in circulation, though growing, remains relatively small." Write an exploratory essay that responds to the following question: "To what extent do you think government controls on firearms in the United States would help decrease crime?" Be sure to support your claims with specific evidence and reasons.

In Rural China, "Gold Lords" Challenge the State

Patrick E. Tyler

New York Times Service

■

In the following report, Patrick E. Tyler explores the violence that has erupted in China's vast countryside over a gold rush. The "gold fever" that has been spreading throughout rural China has also led to lawlessness and violence. In a scramble to get rich, gold diggers seeking their fortunes and protecting their territory have sometimes resorted to violence. According to Tyler, "gold lords" in the Hunan Province have been "blamed for a crime wave so serious that a local newspaper complained that with all the robbery, murder and brawling, 'not even the chickens and the dogs feel secure.'" Since there are not enough local police to combat this problem, and the gold diggers often have more powerful arms than the police, lawlessness has taken over the countryside. As you read this selection, think about the connection between the desire for wealth and the proliferation of violence. How are the two related? Can you point to other situations in which the temptations of wealth have led to violent lawlessness?

■

1   XINING, China—A frenzied and chaotic gold rush is under way across vast expanses of rural China, where newly wealthy "gold lords" and the peasants who toil and fight for them are challenging the authority of the state.

2   Here in the far western province of Qinghai and in other parts of China, modest gold deposits, long under the exclusive control of the Communist Party and state mining combines, are being overrun by a wave of entrepreneurial and well-armed private miners.

3   "I've heard the bullets whizzing by my ears and seen people beside me dying," said a woman in her 40s, who got rich and went bust during four years as a "gold boss" in a remote mountain region 400 miles west of here. "Even if the government wanted to control us, we are stronger than they are right now," she said, "and our guns are normally much better than the ones carried by the Public Security Bureau."

4   Lawlessness and violence, much of it induced by gold fever, has spread to every province rich in minerals and continues to embarrass the Communist Party leadership, no longer sure of its control over the 900 million rural Chinese.

5   The chaos here is part of a broader breakdown of government authority in large parts of the country as Beijing has relaxed its rigid economic controls and millions of people have joined the scramble to get rich.

6   The new stress on making money over the last decade has made getting rich by digging gold respectable, if not altogether legal, and has also stripped away the priggish revulsion of the Mao Zedong era for all that glitters—whether jewelry, religious adornments or just hoarded bars of gold.

7   Gold industry researchers say China, Hong Kong and Taiwan are leading the world in wholesale and retail gold purchases, a surging demand that drives the gold rush here.

8   For millions of poor Chinese, the seemingly meager payoff for leaving farm or factory to dig gold is enticing. Here, a couple of hundred dollars made over the course of a summer from backbreaking work on mining teams is the local definition of "getting rich." (In rural areas, the average annual income is only about $120 a person.)

9   And so the gold seekers come, lugging their tents and mess kits and mud-crusted sheepskins for warmth and leaving behind farms or low-paying factory jobs. With an estimated 130 million Chinese designated as "surplus labor" in the countryside, the pool of potential miners tempted by tales of riches in the mountains is huge.

10   Across Qinghai Province, known for its high plateau grasslands, its sweeping mountain ranges and barren deserts, tens of thousands of Chinese peasants, often supervised by "gold lords," are shredding mountainsides with explosives, poisoning rivers with their runoff and weakening government control of vast, remote tracts in western China.

11   The environmental damage is bedeviling central authorities concerned that the country's already degraded base of natural resources is being depleted.

12   The Qinghai Daily newspaper recently complained that widespread and unregulated gold mining had seriously damaged state-owned mining areas, added to soil erosion along major rivers and pushed some rare animal species, like the snow leopard and white-lipped deer, toward extinction.

13   The prospectors are oblivious, however. One mining camp was dumping tons of sediment into a tributary of the Yellow River within sight of police patrols and near a large highway sign that proclaimed the river a "land and river erosion protected area."

14   But the local police, undermanned and sometimes outgunned, seem uninterested in extending their reach much beyond the city.

15   Last year, 2,000 miners from rival towns near here faced off on a mountainside. In dispute was the prime gold digging turf. Armed with handguns, machine guns and homemade cannon, they fought a marathon battle, leaving several dead and forcing the provincial authorities to dispatch 50 members of the People's Armed Police to separate the fighters.

16   Even Mao's birthplace in Hunan Province has not been spared an invasion by "gold lords." Seven were executed late in 1993 for setting up illicit operations outside Mao's hometown, Shaoshan. They were blamed for a crime wave so serious that a local newspaper complained that with all the robbery, murder and brawling, "not even the chickens and the dogs feel secure."

17   China's top judicial authorities have warned that security problems in rural China "are escalating enormously."

18   For tens of thousands of Chinese peasants dreaming of wealth, the reality of the gold rush means only the chance to work for $1.25 a day in biting cold and at high altitude, conditions so harsh that many try to flee only to be captured and returned to work in leg irons for the duration of their contracts.

19   "I was sure I was going to die," said Yan Demin, 32, part of the first wave of prospectors who, in the mid-1980s, headed for Qinghai's central mountains. Many struck it rich, but Mr. Yan and his friends "lost our trucks when they sank six feet into the mud" in the mountains.

20   "We had to walk out for three and a half days with no food," he said. "All you think of is home, of your wife, of your children, your mother, your father. Even if I knew where some gold was, I wouldn't go back."

21   They are peasants, or surplus farm laborers, the urban unemployed or just workers taking a few months off from their government or factory jobs to strike out for the mountains.

22   For six months of work, many go home with a few hundred dollars, and the lucky ones go home with a few thousand.

23   "If you make a thousand yuan"—$120— "you get rich," said Zhou Zhongfu, 31, who came down from the mountains this year after only 25 days because there was not enough water in the streams to wash the sand through the sieves. "If you make 500 yuan, it's O.K., but this year we lost money."

24   Many of the "gold lords" here come from syndicates organized by an underworld society dominated by China's Muslin minority, which has built a black market to service the soaring demand for decorative gold and jewelry among prospering Chinese.

25   Officially, all private mining is illegal in China, but as one longtime employee of the local Communist Party Committee asked, "What is really legal or illegal out here?"

26   Twenty miles east of here, a farmer named Li Chunxi organized 50 peasants to run an open-pit gold mine on a tributary of the Yellow River. The police come by each day, he said, but after he paid a "fee" of $300 to mine the riverbed, they don't bother him anymore.

27   On a good day the group can gross $400 by working in three shifts around the clock. Hardly pay dirt for backbreaking work.

28   Others are getting richer.

29   "I was a gold boss for four years," said the woman who made and lost her fortune. She has lived through countless gun battles and made more than $30,000 her first year as a gold boss.

30   She is just over 40, with a hard, piercing stare and speaks like a gangster in the Chinese dialect of Qinghai.

31   "This is all illegal," she said, referring to her mining exploits. "I hope you can protect my identity because if they find out, they will come and get me."

32   She did not say who "they" were.

33   "The first thing we would do when we struck gold," she said, "was set up a pillbox on the mountaintop and train more of our workers how to use guns; then we would use our blankets to make a flag, which meant: this mountain belongs to us. That's the way we marked our territory."

34   Then the digging began.

35   A small army of workers used dynamite to gouge rock and sand from the mountainsides and then "wash" it through cascades of sieves where the gold appeared.

36   If another gold boss cast "the red eye" of envy toward her claim, work might be interrupted for a gun battle. If some workers died in rock slides or gunfights, "it's the same as one or two chickens dying," she said.

37   Now bankrupt because, she said, her partner cheated her, she works in a factory office here in the provincial capital, but she cannot wait to get back in the game.

38   Another gold boss named Mi Zhanglu is said to have paid someone in the provincial government $70,000 for a mountain named Ha Shen Zhang near the western city of Golmud and has since been mining $5 million in gold a year from its ores.

39   "No one knew the mountain had so much gold in it," said one miner, an admirer of Mr. Mi. According to local lore, Mr. Mi was once so poor he and his wife had only one pair of pants between them.

40   "Now he drives a Land Cruiser and communicates with a cellular phone and his whole mountain is guarded by men with guns and cellular phones," the miner said.

41   Instead of going to the mountain, some villages buy tons of rock from Mr. Mi's syndicate and crush it in a huge homemade milling machine. The crushed rock contains traces of gold, which will bond with liquid mercury dumped into the vat by villagers. In the end, a puddle of mercury bonded with gold is heated and the gold is separated.

42   In Shangwuzhuang, 30 miles north of here, the Muslim villagers are making $50 to $100 a day milling the rocks. Most have renovated their houses, bought motorcycles for the young men, and with their surplus riches, they are making plans.

43   "Perhaps we will use the money to make a pilgrimage to Mecca," said Ma Jun, taking his turn at the mill.

DISCUSSION QUESTIONS

1. In small groups, discuss what you know about the American gold rush of 1849 that took so many people to the West Coast. Do you see any similarities between the gold rush of 1849 and the one now occurring in rural China? Make a brainstorming list or cluster that attempts to compare and contrast the two events. What do you think might be learned from comparing and contrasting both gold rushes?

2. Tyler writes that "Lawlessness and violence, much of it induced by gold fever, has spread to every province rich in minerals and continues to embarrass the Communist Party leadership, no longer sure of its control over the 900 million rural Chinese." Do you think the only way to stop this sort of lawlessness is through government control? What are some ways this lawlessness could be controlled?

3. Tyler states that private mining is officially illegal in all of China, but he also quotes a longtime member of the Communist Party Committee as asking, "What is really legal or illegal out here?" What do you think this person means by this question?

4. The article mentions that the gold rush in China has led to environmental problems. In what way might the gold rush be seen as an act of violence against the environment?

WRITING ASSIGNMENTS

1. Write a short research essay that compares and contrasts the gold rush of 1849 in the United States with the current gold rush in rural China. You will need to consult outside sources for this paper. Be sure to support your main ideas with specific details and examples.

2. Imagine that you are working on a committee investigating the problem of lawlessness in the gold rush areas of rural China. Write a problem-solution paper that offers suggestions for combating the violence associated with this gold rush. Try to make your proposal for reform as specific as possible with details and examples.

3. Imagine that you are a young Chinese person who wishes to leave the city to find a fortune of gold in the hills of rural China. However, your parents object to your going on this adventure. Alternatively, imagine that you are the parent of a young person who wishes to join the gold rush, and you do not want him or her to go. Write a letter which will persuade your parent or child of your position. Be sure to support your arguments with specific evidence and reasons.

CHAPTER THREE WRITING ASSIGNMENTS

1. Imagine that an international conference on terrorism is being held. The central theme of the conference is "How Can We Combat Terrorism?" Representatives from nations around the world are attending this conference. Write a roundtable dialogue in which the participants discuss this central theme. Your roundtable should include representatives from at least six different nations. The discussion should refer to specific acts of terrorism and suggest ways to prevent future terrorist acts.

2. Write a paper that explores the nature of violence. Your paper should examine the origins and roots of violence. What feeds violence? Why are some societies more prone to violence than others? Be sure to use specific examples, details, and evidence to support your opinions and main points.

3. Write a paper that explores the relationship between terrorism and extremist groups. What acts of terrorism have been connected to extremist groups? Why do these groups commit acts of terrorism? Has extremist terrorism increased or decreased in recent years? Be sure your essay has a focused thesis that is developed with specific details.

4. In an exploratory essay, respond to the following question: "To what extent can individuals help to prevent crimes?" Your essay should include specific details and examples that support your main ideas and opinions.

CHAPTER FOUR

Living in a World at War

This chapter has been named "Living in a World at War" because it is sometimes hard to imagine how we, as human beings, manage to continue our day-to-day lives while wars around the world destroy life. Unfortunately, war seems to be a common thread from one nation to another; it is a constant across time as well as geographical locale. Few parts of the world have not been affected by the devastation of war at one time or another in history. War is therefore a global concern, one that people study in an attempt to prevent future conflict. Throughout history, people have asked why wars start and how they might be prevented. The aim of this chapter, then, is to explore the difficult questions raised by war.

The chapter opens with an article by Alan Cowell entitled "Dresden: 'It Was How You Would Imagine Hell.'" February 1995 marked the fiftieth anniversary of the Allied firebombing of Dresden, Germany, in which more than 35,000 civilians were killed and irreplaceable buildings and artwork were destroyed. Cowell reports on the services held in commemoration of the air raid. In his report, he gives details of the firebombing but more specifically addresses the emotional impact this raid has had on the people involved. His article also confronts questions of guilt and blame for an attack that targeted so many civilians.

Similarly, "War-Torn Nation Faces a Hidden Foe for Years to Come" by Paul Taylor examines the devastating effect that instruments of war can have on civilians. Taylor describes the effects land mines have had on the civilians of Angola, especially the children, in a civil war that has lasted more than twenty years. As Taylor reports, both sides of this civil war have specifically targeted civilians in an attempt to demoralize the general population. He also notes that during the Cold War these land mines were manufactured in both the former Soviet Union and the United States. Humanitarian groups are currently trying to rid the nation of these mines and to heal both the physical and emotional wounds inflicted by them.

Humanitarian groups such as Human Rights Watch are also extremely concerned about the civil war in Rwanda. In "Hutu Chiefs Gearing for War," William Branigin reports on the attempts of such groups as well as the United Nations to curtail the sale of arms to Rwandan Hutus. However, as Branigin points out, the extent to which these groups have been able to prevent arms sales to aggressive forces in Rwanda has been limited.

While the sale and use of conventional arms proliferate, the development of even more deadly weapons has been with us for many years. The article "When Both Sides Stood Ready for Bacterial Warfare" by Denis Warner exposes the little-known dangers of bacteriological warfare that both the Axis and Allies were ready to implement during the final days of World War II. However, as Warner points out, both sides ultimately recognized the devastation that such weapons would bring and decided not to use them.

Yet the potential danger of germ weaponry and other forms of war remains. The policing of these dangers is addressed in the final selection of this chapter, "A New Nuremberg Could Just 'Break the Frozen Sea'" by Anthony Lewis. In this article, Lewis asks whether or not the Nuremberg trials that followed World War II were able to effect any lasting principles that might stop aggressive war. Although the Nuremberg trials defined the waging of aggressive war over fifty years ago as a crime against humanity, the incidence of such wars continues.

As you read through the selections in this chapter, think about why wars continue to develop. What are the root causes of war? Are the origins of various wars similar? Can we learn something from any perceived similarities? How might exploring the causes of war help stop them? How else might war be prevented?

Dresden: "It Was How You Would Imagine Hell"

Alan Cowell

New York Times Service

■

Over fifty years ago, during the final months of World War II, Dresden, Germany, was the site of an Allied air raid that killed more than 35,000 civilians and destroyed much of the extraordinary architecture for which Dresden was known. In the following article, Alan Cowell reports on ceremonies that were held in Dresden in commemoration of the air raid. While the article gives details of the firebombing, its real focus is the emotional impact the air raid still has today on the lives of those who were involved. As you read the article, consider the concepts of guilt and blame in relation to this historic event. To what extent are questions of guilt and blame still relevant concerns?

■

1   DRESDEN—From his position as navigator of a Lancaster bomber, Colin Campbell said, the city seemed like a "carpet of fire" glimpsed between the clouds.

2   Eighteen thousand feet below, in what Germans called "Florence on the Elbe," Helga Siewers, a young German Red Cross nurse, knew that part of the fiery carpet was woven from the 1,000 straw mattresses she and others had spread in a school as beds for 750 refugees fleeing the advancing Soviet Army.

3   She knew, she said, because the mattresses were burning directly above them, threatening to roast them in the basement where she and the refugees had taken shelter. They eventually made their way out of the inferno.

4   Elsewhere, Matthias Griebel, then a boy of 8, ran from a cellar where he had been sheltering when fire swept through it.

5   "The bombs had thrown people into the trees," he said. "The streets had broken up. The water mains had broken. The gas pipes were on fire. It was how you would imagine hell."

6   John Greenwood, now a stock broker in St. Louis, remembers that the next day, when his B-17 was one of the 311 American Flying Fortresses unloading a third wave of bombs onto Dresden, "the fires were still burning."

7   The city's destruction, he said, had been "just a normal type of raid."

8   The recollections are old and varnished with time. Yet, in their retelling, they paint a troubled and painful backdrop for the commemorations here on Monday of the 50th anniversary of the British and American raids that wiped out Dresden on Feb. 13–14, 1945.

9   The attack killed more than 35,000 civilians and destroyed architectural treasures. It stands as one of the most ambiguous anniversaries in a year that marks a half-century since the end of World War II.

10   The raid itself came in three stages, starting on the night of Feb. 13, 1945.

11   The first sirens sounded at around 9:45 P.M., and soon afterward night turned into day as warplanes escorting 243 British four-engined Lancaster bombers droned over the city, dropping flares to light the way for the bombardiers.

12   A second wave of 529 Lancasters—Mr. Campbell's among them—came three hours later. And the 311 American B-17s came the afternoon of the 14th. Altogether, they dropped more than 3,300 tons of bombs, many of them incendiaries.

13   The questions raised by the firebombing of Dresden are manifold. But they all revolve around what Mr. Griebel, now curator of Dresden's City Museum, called "the question of guilt."

14   There is a lingering sense among many Dresdeners that the raid was brutally unfair.

15   "The war was almost over, and we had one of Europe's most beautiful cities," said one resident, advancing two of the points made by those who consider the Allied raid to have been vindictive and even criminal.

16   These people argue that because the target of the British bombing was a civilian residential area, and because the Germans were in retreat, there was little strategic reason for the raids.

17   But the accusations seem more than offset by the sense that the ultimate blame lay not with the Allied pilots, or with the British strategy of bombing civilians to break German morale, but with Hitler.

18   "It was both cause and effect," said Mr. Griebel. "A fire went out from Germany and went around the world in a great arc and came back to Germany."

19   Less poetically, Douglas Radcliffe, head of a British veterans's association, said: "This was one air raid on a nation that wasn't sitting around singing hymns and sipping tea, but had the whole of Europe by the throat."

DISCUSSION QUESTIONS

1.   What effect do the quotations from survivors of the raid, both civilians and military personnel, have on you as a reader? What do you think the article might be like without these quotations?

2.   What do you think the author means when he writes, "The recollections are old and varnished with time. Yet, in their retelling, they paint a troubled and painful backdrop for the commemorations"? Why do you think he chooses to use figurative words such as *varnished, paint,* and *backdrop*?

3.   The author states that the questions raised by the Dresden firebombing all concern the question of *guilt*. Speculate about the meaning of the word *guilt*. What does it mean to feel guilty? What does it mean to be guilty? What does it mean to assign blame? Why do you think so much attention has been placed on this issue of guilt? What are the potential benefits of this focus? What is the potential downside?

4.   Many Dresdeners argue that the firebombing was brutally unfair because the war was almost over and the attack was directed at civilians and one of Europe's most beautiful cities. However, others argue that the ultimate blame should be placed upon Hitler and those who supported his aggression on Europe, not upon the Allied strategy of breaking German morale. What is your opinion? Is all fair in war? Support your response with specific reasons.

5.   The fiftieth anniversary of the Dresden firebombing has been commemorated with memorial services and dedications. What can we learn from this commemoration that might benefit future generations?

6. The author writes, "The questions raised by the firebombing of Dresden are manifold. But they all revolve around . . . 'the question of guilt.'" Can you think of any other issues besides guilt that should be addressed?

WRITING ASSIGNMENTS

1. Research the Dresden firebombing that occurred on February 13–14, 1945. Then write an informative report that details the events of those days as well as the lasting ramifications of this historical event.

2. Write an exploratory essay that investigates the question of guilt as it relates to the Dresden firebombing. The aim of this assignment is not to argue that one side or another is guilty but rather to explore the motivations of the people behind these emotions. Why is there such an emphasis on the question of guilt? Why is there a need to assign blame? What drives these human emotions? You might begin this writing assignment by freewriting on the question, "How important is the question of guilt in the Dresden firebombing?" Try switching points of view as you write. In other words, freewrite for ten minutes as yourself, then for another ten minutes as if you were one of the pilots, and then a final ten minutes as if you were a civilian survivor of the raid. Take breaks in between each freewrite. Use the information from your freewriting sessions to help you develop your thoughts.

3. Find a person who either is a veteran of World War II or remembers the war. Interview that person about his or her memories of the Dresden firebombing or another significant battle of the war. Write out your interview questions before you begin. After the interview, write up your findings in the format of a magazine interview.

WAR-TORN NATION FACES A HIDDEN FOE FOR YEARS TO COME

Paul Taylor

Washington Post Service

■

The following selection is a disturbing story about the effects of land mines on the people of Angola, a country devastated by civil war. The author of the article, Paul Taylor, reports statistical information about the numbers of unexploded mines and mine casualties, but he also offers a glimpse into the lasting terror these weapons continue to inflict upon innocent people— especially the children of Angola. According to Taylor, the psychological and emotional reactions of children who are victims of land-mine explosions are markedly different from the responses of children exposed to other effects of war. While the more common reaction of children with war injuries is to want to become a nurse or doctor, children wounded by land mines are completely numb. As one psychologist reported to Taylor, "In some ways these children are the living dead." While reading this article, think about this psychologist's statement and its potential meanings.

■

1   Kuito, Angola—Evangelisto, 10, was walking to a river with his mother. Domingo, 12, was fetching firewood. Rosetta, 13, was looking for food in the fields. Juan, 11, was playing in front of his house.

2   This much, they all can remember.

3   But at the edge of the terror beyond, faces go blank, aching eyes cast downward and tongues fall still. How does a child talk about losing a limb?

4   "I don't think I have ever worked with a group as sad as this," said Magne Raundalen, a Norwegian psychologist and Unicef consultant who has interviewed more than a thousand child victims of war

around the world. He had just finished a group therapy session here with a dozen children who had stepped on land mines.

5   Somebody once called land mines the devil's seed. If so, he planted one big crop in Angola. The country is home to an estimated 70,000 land-mine amputees—nearly 1 percent of its population. And there are more to come.

6   Angola still has an estimated 10 million unexploded land mines underfoot—one for every inhabitant. They were laid with minimal record-keeping during 20 years of a civil war in which both sides have made civilians their primary targets.

7   Even though a fragile cease-fire has been in effect for three months, the rate of mine injuries will probably increase in the future, as peasants return to fields that are newly accessible because of the break in fighting but remain infested by some of the most fiendish weapons man has created.

8   An anti-personnel land mine is an instrument of terror. Its intention is not to kill but to maim. "You kill a guy with a land mine, he's dead. End of story," explained Nick Bateman, a former British army officer who is co-directing a mine-removal project here for the Halo Trust, a London-based relief organization. "But you blow his leg off, you tie up a medic for a day, and you demoralize his friends and family for years."

9   And if your victim happens to be a child, you might destroy more than a body.

10   "In some ways these children are the living dead," Mr. Raundalen said of his emotionless therapy group. "Some lost their legs two or three years ago. Some, 10 years ago. But the shock and the trauma are still there, still blocking the grief."

11   Mr. Raundalen, who has written two books about the children of war, came here to advise Unicef on setting up a counseling program to address the psychic wounds of Kuito's young amputees. Ten of the children in his group were missing one leg. One had lost both legs. One has lost the sight in an eye. About half have lost one or both parents.

12   For an excruciating hour, the visiting psychologist tried to strike some emotional chord with them. At first he offered soothing questions. Later he tried jarring questions. It did not seem to matter. He could not connect. ·

13   "When you sit with a group of war-affected children, they often can become very animated describing their experiences," Mr. Raundalen said later. "But land-mine victims tend to be different. The injury comes with no warning. It is so sudden. There is no time to prepare.

And the consequences are so devastating. You are reminded of it every day. So you remain emotionally numb."

14 A sampler of the exchanges:

15 "Did your leg actually fall off when the mine blew up?"

16 "I don't remember."

17 "What did the doctor do with the leg after he cut it off?"

18 Shrug.

19 "Do you sometimes dream about your leg?"

20 "No."

21 "Do you feel angry?"

22 "No."

23 "Are you angry at the doctor for cutting it off?"

24 Shrug.

25 "What do you feel like when you talk about it?"

26 "Nothing."

27 "What do you want to be when you grow up?"

28 Shrug.

29 "Are you sad?"

30 "Yes."

31 Mr. Raundalen said later: "Often children with war injuries will say they want to grow up to be nurses or doctors. These children have no feelings in that direction. They have no sense of the future. They do not even know how to connect with each other. Here were 12 kids who had a natural bond, and they were sitting together in a room, all alone."

32 After coaxing, some of the children did say they would like to have artificial limbs. But that seems a distant dream. Fewer than 10 percent of Angola's amputees have them, and at the current rate of production of a few thousand a year nationwide, the number of new mine victims is likely to exceed the number of new prostheses.

33 Mine victims in Angola are lucky just to have proper crutches. A high percentage hobble around with the help of a single stick, fashioned from a tree branch, sometimes with a rag tied around the top. Occasionally, one sees a double amputee shuffling down the street on his or her hands. The double amputee in Mr. Raundalen's group was carried into the room on her brother's back.

34 Small wonder that amputees in Angola are bitter. Some have organized demonstrations to demand more services. Other resign themselves to a lifetime of begging. "The Ministry of Health simply doesn't have the money to do anything for them," said Jean-Luc Tonglet, director of Handicapped International, a French aid organization that is setting up workshops to make prostheses.

35   When it comes to government priorities, the problem actually is less one of wallet than of will. With more than $3 billion a year in oil-export revenues, Angola is one of sub-Saharan Africa's wealthiest countries. But the vast bulk of its earnings since independence from Portugal in 1975 has gone to weapons purchases and war profiteers.

36   That leaves a gap that the international community has partly filled. In addition to making plans last week to send 7,000 peace-keeping troops here—at an estimated cost of $1 million a day—the United Nations and various private relief organizations have spent $1 million a day for the past two years feeding and medicating Angolans.

37   One humanitarian program just gearing up with the latest out-break of peace is the painstakingly slow task of mine removal.

38   The Halo Trust project in Kuito offers a sense of the scale of the problem. This is the most war-ravaged city in the country. In 1993–94, it was reduced to rubble during 16 months of siege, shelling and door-to-door fighting. At different stages of the battle, government and rebel forces occupied shifting sections of the city. Sometimes they faced off across a single street, lighting each other's cigarettes, bartering for food and playing cards during lulls in fighting.

39   As they have done all over Angola for the past two decades, each side planted thousands of land mines here. It is the way a poor-man's army keeps a population penned in, a key installation defended or a retreat unencumbered.

40   In early 1993, just as the civil war was resuming after a brief break for peace, the human rights group Africa Watch, in New York, published a study that said 37 types of land mines had been used in the country. Most were produced in the Soviet Union, which backed the formerly Marxist government during the Cold War phase of the conflict. At least seven types were manufactured in the United States, which until 1990 supported the anti-Communist rebel movement, UNITA.

41   One of the U.S.-manufactured land mines here, the M16 A1, is a diabolical creation. It is a "bounding" anti-personnel mine. When activated by a trip wire or the pressure of a foot, it jumps about four feet off the ground, where its explosion "has the power to rip the heart out of anyone standing within 100 feet," the Africa Watch report said.

42   Two weeks ago, the Halo Trust team began work here at a bombed-out elementary school. Two former British army officers direct 24 Angolans as they comb the school's one and a half acres of grounds. At a site like this—littered with shells, shrapnel and unexploded ordnance—each two-man team might cover only a square yard an hour. Halo's Mr. Bateman estimates the unit will spend a month on the site.

43   "And we may not remove a single land mine," he said. (After two weeks, they had not.) "But we will remove a question mark. When we're done, the community will have its school back." Or it will eventually, once the war debris is carted off and the walls and roof are rebuilt.

44   Removing mines is nerve-racking work, but the Angolans on the crew do not seem to mind. They earn $50 a month, 10 times the salary of a teacher in this country. Plus, "we are seen as heroes in the community," said Jose Antonio, 30, a former soldier. "The people know we are doing dangerous work."

45   If the peace holds, joint teams of government and rebel soldiers will start to work on mine removal. South Africans, who supplied UNITA with many of its mines, may return to remove them. But even in the best of scenarios, Angola's land mines are going to be around a long time. So are its broken spirits.

46   At one point, Mr. Raundalen tried to soothe Arao Jose, 16, by telling him, "I know how you must feel."

47   The boy glanced at his own lower body, then at the doctor's. His response came not in words, but in a look. It was sad and angry and sly. It said: No you don't.

DISCUSSION QUESTIONS

1.   Taylor states that if a victim of a land mine "happens to be a child, you might destroy more than a body." What do you think he means by this statement? What else might be destroyed and why?

2.   Taylor writes that both sides of this civil war have made civilians the primary targets of these land mines. Speculate about the reasons enemies might choose such a strategy. What is your opinion of military weapons that are targeted at civilians?

3.   Reread the first paragraph of this article. Why do you think the author chooses to begin with these examples? What purpose do these examples serve? How do they affect you as a reader?

4.   The author states that a land mine is intended "not to kill but to maim." Speculate about the potential reasons for using such a strategy. What are the short-term as well as long-term consequences of this type of warfare?

5.   Taylor writes that these land mines were produced in both the former Soviet Union and the United States. What other wars or military conflicts can you think of in which more powerful countries have supplied

weapons to the warring factions? In small groups, speculate about the reasons for and the consequences of this common practice.

6.   Much of this article deals with the impact of land-mine wounds on the emotional health of children. In small groups, discuss what you think the future holds for these children and what sorts of therapy you think might help them the most.

WRITING ASSIGNMENTS

1.   Write an informative report that details the history of the Angolan civil war. Be sure to include information that explains the origins as well as the consequences of this war. Your report should include a status report on the present situation in Angola. Use a variety of sources (such as newspapers, books, interviews) to develop this report.

2.   The author concluded this article with an account of an exchange between a victim and a therapist. Reread this conclusion. Then write a dialogue that you might have with one of these children. What might you want to say? What do you think one of these children might say?

3.   Although Angola is one of the wealthiest countries in Africa's sub-Sahara, its wealth goes not to helping victims of this war but to buying more weapons. According to this article, the international community helps to fill this gap with aid from humanitarian organizations and the United Nations. Write a persuasive letter to a humanitarian organization of your choice to request aid for the victims of this war.

4.   Read the article in this chapter entitled "Dresden: 'It Was How You Would Imagine Hell.'" The articles on the firebombing of Dresden and the land mines in Angola both focus on the impact of war on civilians. Think about other wars, both present and past, and their effects on civilians. Then write an essay that responds to the following question: "Can military attacks on civilians ever be justified in wartime?"

HUTU CHIEFS GEARING FOR WAR

William Branigin

Washington Post Service

■

In the spring of 1994, the African nation of Rwanda became embroiled in a bloody civil war. In the following months, the government forces and militias of the majority Hutus killed minority Tutsis and moderate Hutus in what the United Nations has called a "campaign of genocide." The Tutsi-led Rwandan Patriotic Front countered this slaughter with a force composed of 50,000 fighters living in exile camps near the Zaire border. The war has resulted in an estimated half-million deaths and an unprecedented exodus of refugees. In this article, William Branigin reports on the involvement of the United Nations, human rights groups, and other countries in attempts to resolve this conflict. While reading the article, think about the similarities you perceive between this civil war and others (such as the one in Bosnia), as well as the nature and extent of outside involvement in these conflicts. To what extent should outside forces become involved in civil conflicts?

■

1 WASHINGTON—Secret arms deliveries to the exiled perpetrators of last year's massacres in Rwanda are raising fears among human rights groups, U.S. officials and the United Nations of renewed warfare in the turbulent central African region.

2 Reports of the arms shipments and an upsurge of military activity by the forces of the former Hutu-led Rwandan government, quartered in refugee camps primarily in eastern Zaire, prompted the UN Security Council last month to call for UN observers to be stationed in the area to monitor an international arms embargo.

3 However, central African countries have rebuffed the UN bid, fueling concerns about an increase in fighting between rival tribes in both Rwanda and neighboring Burundi.

4   The rebuffs from Rwanda's neighbors, particularly Zaire and Tanzania, represent another setback for the United Nations and concerned governments trying to maintain peace in a troubled part of the world.

5   The bloodshed in Rwanda in three months last year claimed an estimated half-million lives—far more than the death toll of the war in Bosnia to date—and resulted in a refugee exodus unprecedented in its combination of speed and scale.

6   According to the United Nations, a measure of stability has returned to Rwanda since the spring of 1994, when government forces and militias of the majority Hutus slaughtered minority Tutsis and moderate Hutus in what UN reports called a "campaign of genocide."

7   But human rights groups, U.S. intelligence sources and UN officials say that Hutu leaders, who fled with an estimated 2 million Hutu civilians in the face of defeat by the Tutsi-led Rwandan Patriotic Front insurgency, have formed a force of up to 50,000 fighters in their exile camps, acquired new weapons and ammunition and stepped up cross-border raids in preparation for a violent return to Rwanda. Most of the camps are in eastern Zaire, near the Rwandan border.

8   U.S. officials also express concern about the prospect of fighting in Burundi, where Hutu-Tutsi discord is similar to Rwanda's.

9   "The Hutus are rearming, and Hutu extremists from both countries are starting to work together," a senior Clinton administration official said.

10   "Incursions across the border are on the increase, becoming more frequent and more organized," said a UN official who monitors Rwanda. The Hutus, he said, are obviously armed. "What is less clear is where these arms come from."

11   Alarmed by reports of secret arms deliveries to the Rwandan Hutus, the Security Council last month expanded an arms embargo on Rwanda to include Hutu camps in neighboring countries and called for UN military observers to be stationed in the area, notably at airfields in eastern Zaire.

12   In meetings last month with leaders of Burundi, Rwanda, Uganda, Tanzania and Zaire, a UN envoy, Aldo Ajello, "emphasized the Security Council's great concern over increasing reports of military activities that threatened to destabilize Rwanda," a UN report said.

13   The report said the "uncontrolled circulation of arms" in the area was "a major cause of destabilization, especially in Rwanda and Burundi." However, it said, Mr. Ajello encountered "strong opposition

to the deployment of United Nations observers as proposed in the Security Council resolution."

14 Tanzania refused the deployment outright, Uganda argued that the Security Council's concerns were misplaced, and Zaire rejected the premise for the observers: that Zaire was giving the former Rwandan government forces arms and training.

15 The U.S.-based group Human Rights Watch recently charged that the UN arms embargo, imposed in May 1994, has not been properly enforced and that weapons have reached the former Rwandan government forces, mostly through the airport at Goma, Zaire.

16 A report by the Human Rights Watch Arms Project said four months of field investigation in central Africa had turned up evidence that several countries, including France, Zaire, South Africa, the Seychelles and China, have assisted the Hutu effort.

17 France and Zaire strongly supported the government of President Juvénal Habyarimana of Rwanda, whose death in an unexplained airplane crash on April 6, 1994, sparked the slayings in Rwanda.

18 "Zairian forces close to President Mobutu Sese Seko have played a pivotal role" in the rearming by giving "shelter and protection" to the former armed forces and militias and allowing the use of Zairian territory and facilities "as a conduit," the report said.

19 It said Zairian officials have profited from the arms shipments through kickbacks from private arms dealers and cargo companies.

20 Zaire has denied any involvement in rearming the Hutus.

21 The Human Rights Watch report said France sent at least five arms shipments that arrived at the Goma airport after the embargo took effect. It said the weapons, including artillery, machine guns, assault rifles and ammunition, were taken into Rwanda by members of the Zairian military and delivered to the fleeing Rwandan Army in Gisenyi.

22 According to the report, the French consul in Goma said the arms were supplied under prior contracts with the Rwandan government.

23 Now the French government denies that any arms were delivered after the embargo.

DISCUSSION QUESTIONS

1. In small groups, discuss what you know about the war in Rwanda. What have you heard on the news? What have you heard other people say? What have been some of your responses to this conflict? Share this information with the rest of the class.

2. Branigin writes that a United Nations report has called the Hutu massacre of Tutsis "a campaign of genocide." What connotations does the term *genocide* have for you? What are some possible meanings of this term? What sort of effect do you think this term might have on other audiences (world leaders, the general public)? Why do you think this term was used in the report?

3. Branigin reports that intelligence efforts by the Human Rights Watch Arms Project have determined that several countries, including France and Zaire, have supplied arms to the Hutus. Speculate about some of the reasons nations might choose to supply arms to other countries. What are some of the economic as well as moral implications of such involvement?

4. According to this article, Human Rights Watch has charged that the United Nations arms embargo has not been properly enforced. What is your opinion of the United Nations? To what extent can it police conflicts all around the world? Can it do it alone? Should it do it alone? Can you make any suggestions?

5. What similarities and/or differences do you see between the Rwandan conflict and the war in Bosnia or other civil conflicts? How might knowledge of these differences and similarities be helpful to those trying to resolve the conflicts?

6. According to this article, there seems to be two types of outside involvement at present in the Rwandan War—those who wish to decrease the supply of arms to the warring factions and those who continue to provide aid in the forms of arms and other necessary goods. Speculate about the motivations of the two types of interested groups. What concerns and issues propel one group to respond by supplying arms and the other to respond in the opposite manner?

WRITING ASSIGNMENTS

1. Spend some time reading about the country of Rwanda as well as the history between the Hutus and Tutsis. Then write an informative report that explores the origins of this conflict. Be prepared to present your findings to the class.

2. Arms trading is not only a problem in the Rwandan conflict but has also been the focus of many controversial news events. Do some research on arms-trading controversies. Then write an essay that explores the ethical and moral implications of such an activity.

3. Write a letter to a human rights group such as Human Rights Watch in which you express an interest in finding out what the group is doing and give your opinion about what you think should happen to resolve this conflict. In order to write a more informed letter, you will need to do some research.

WHEN BOTH SIDES STOOD READY FOR BACTERIAL WARFARE

Denis Warner

International Herald Tribune

■

In this selection, Denis Warner reports on the development of deadly bacterial weapons during World War II. By the end of the war, both the Allies and the Axis were prepared for bacterial warfare, but bacterial weapons were never used. As you read Warner's account, think about the differences between bacterial warfare and other types of weapons. Are there any differences? Have we used weapons in the past or do we presently use weapons that have the potential to do as much damage as bacterial weapons? What might the consequences of bacterial warfare be for humanity?

■

1   MELBOURNE—Memories of bloody beachheads and of ships blasted by kamikaze planes in the closing months of the Pacific war remain vivid after a half-century. Yet it is material from previously secret archives that tells us how dangerous those days really were, not just for the combatants but for much of mankind.

2   In December 1944, on the initiative of Vice Admiral Jisaburo Ozawa, vice chief of the navy general staff, the Japanese Navy devised a secret plan code-named "PX Operation." Its aim was to use a particular type of submarine, which carried two seaplanes, to release rats and mosquitoes carrying deadly diseases onto the U.S. mainland and Pacific islands held by the Americans.

3   The Japanese Navy had made little progress in its bacteriological research. It was obliged to call on the services of Lieutenant General Shiro Ishii, who set up the notorious bacteriological warfare facility

known as Unit 731 in the suburbs of Harbin, in northern Manchuria. As a result, the plan became a joint army-navy venture.

4   The navy blessed the scheme. But at the last moment, on March 26, 1945, when all was ready to go, General Yoshijiro Umezu, chief of the army general staff, vetoed the plan. "Germ warfare against the United States would escalate the war against all humanity," he said.

5   He thus spared the world from what could have been a disaster of unparalleled proportions. Documents in the National Archives in Washington leave little doubt that the United States would have responded in kind.

6   Months before the Japanese attack on Pearl Harbor, Henry Stimson, the U.S. secretary of war, had learned that the Axis powers led by Nazi Germany might be planning to use bacteriological weapons. This led to the formation of the War Research Service, which signed contracts with scientists at Harvard, Cornell and other universities to work on deadly botulinum toxin and anthrax spores.

7   By the end of 1943, a large area in Camp Detrick, Maryland, had been set aside as the main center for U.S. bacteriological research. Horn Island, Mississippi, became a field testing station.

8   In January 1944, a directive from Mr. Stimson to General George C. Marshall, the army chief of staff, instructed the War Department to undertake a program of research, experimentation and preliminary production of biological weapons. At the same time, General Marshall charged the Army Service Forces with responsibility for preparing the United States to wage biological warfare.

9   Major General William Porter, head of the Chemical Warfare Service, reported in February 1944 that eight months would be needed to construct a plant to produce biological agents. He recommended immediate construction of a facility to produce botulinum toxin, anthrax spores and other agents.

10   In March, Lieutenant General Brehon B. Somervell, head of the Army Service Forces, estimated that eight months after the date of approval, the plan would have a monthly output of 1,000 anthrax spore bombs, or 275,000 botulinum toxin bombs. He said that production on this scale would place the United States in a position to supply biological agents just when "the current timetable for operations in the Pacific would indicate our approach to the Japanese homeland."

11   However, General Somervell noted that the United States was committed to refrain from using poisonous gases or other inhumane

devices of war, except in retaliation. He noted that General Marshall had supported a recommendation that biological warfare not be used against Germany or its satellites except in response to a similar attack.

12   Japan fell into a different category. General Marshall wanted plans made to use biological weapons against Japan following Germany's defeat, as General Somervell recalled, but had urged that no final decision be made prematurely.

13   General Somervell sought permission from the Joint Chiefs of Staff to produce offensive materials and develop measures by Jan. 1, 1946, for possible use against the Japanese home islands.

14   The British were engaged in a similar project; they had kept the Americans fully informed. In April 1944, Lord Ismay, chief of staff to Britain's defense minister, wrote to Field Marshall Sir John Dill, the British representative on the Combined Chiefs of Staff in Washington, that the United States hoped to inaugurate a plant soon that would produce bacteriological bombs at a rate of 25,000 to 50,000 a month. A much larger plant was also planned, he said, adding that Churchill had approved a proposal for Britain to place a preliminary order for 500,000 of these bombs.

15   Lord Ismay said that there could "of course, be *no* [underlined by him] question of either country using this form of warfare except by way of retaliation for its adoption by the enemy, and then only after consultation with one another."

16   The question of formulating a combined U.S.-British policy on the issue was considered but discarded. Nonetheless, General Marshall informed General Eisenhower by a top-secret signal that the U.S. Joint Chiefs of Staff had advised their British counterparts of their agreement that general information on bacteriological measures should be issued to medical and intelligence staff in the military forces of both nations. This was to prevent them being taken by surprise should the enemy launch a germ warfare attack.

17   Like General Umezu and Sir John Dill, many on the Allied side viewed bacteriological weapons with great distaste. By the time the war ended, however, the weapons were available. They almost certainly would have been used but for General Umezu's veto of the Japanese plan.

18   After the surrender of Japan, the International Military Tribunal for the Far East, set up by the Allies, sentenced General Umezu to life imprisonment.

DISCUSSION QUESTIONS

1. Warner opens the article with descriptive images of World War II and then states that we were unaware of just how dangerous that time was for all of humanity. What is the effect of this opening on you as a reader?

2. In small groups, discuss the possible long-term and short-term consequences of bacterial warfare. Be prepared to discuss your findings with the whole class.

3. Speculate about the differences and similarities between more conventional weapons and bacterial weapons. Why do you think there was so much concern over the use of bacterial weapons during the World War II? Do you think weapons that have been used in recent years might be put in the same category as bacterial weapons?

4. According to Warner, both United States and British military leaders said that bacterial weapons would only be used in response to the use of bacterial weapons by the enemy. Why do you think these military leaders made this decision?

5. Warner relates that General Yoshijiro Umezu, Japan's chief of the army general staff, vetoed the use of germ warfare and cites Umezu as stating, "Germ warfare against the United States would escalate the war against all humanity." What do you think Umezu might have meant by this statement? In what way might the war have been altered if germ warfare had been employed?

6. Warner ends this article with the following detail: "After the surrender of Japan, the International Military Tribunal for the Far East, set up by the Allies, sentenced General Umezu to life imprisonment." Why do you think Warner chose to end the article in this manner? What is your reaction to this information?

WRITING ASSIGNMENTS

1. Write an essay that attempts to define the phrase *war against all humanity*. What is a *war against humanity*? Use specific examples from history to help develop your thoughts.

2. Research the development of bacteriological warfare during World War II. Write an informative report that investigates the origins and consequences of this form of warfare.

3. Write an essay that describes what the world might look like today if the Allies and the Axis had engaged in bacterial warfare over fifty years ago. The tone of your essay should be persuasive. In other words, your description should serve as a warning.

A NEW NUREMBERG COULD JUST "BREAK THE FROZEN SEA"

Anthony Lewis

The New York Times

■

After World War II, an international court was established in Nuremberg to try Nazis suspected of committing "crimes against humanity." One outcome of the Nuremberg trials was that the waging of aggressive war was deemed a crime under international law and those judged responsible for such crimes were to be prosecuted and punished. Today, over fifty years after the Nuremberg trials, many people are asking whether these trials established any lasting principles that can be applied to other crimes against humanity. In this article, Anthony Lewis reports that an international tribunal has been established to try people charged with war crimes in the former Yugoslavia. However, Lewis contends that the world's response to atrocities seems to go only as far as political self-interest. As you read this article, ask yourself whether you think it is possible to preserve and enforce the principles set forth at the Nuremberg trials over fifty years ago.

■

1 BOSTON—On April 6, 1992, Serbian forces besieged the capital of Bosnia, Sarajevo. It seemed grotesque, then, that a city known for its relaxed charm, its easy mix of Muslims and Serbs, Croats and Jews, should be under attack by virulent nationalism. Surely such anachronistic savagery could not go on for long. The world would not allow it.

2 Three years later the siege of Sarajevo continues. Serbian guns have destroyed the city's most prominent buildings. The Serbs hold 70 percent of Bosnia, and have "cleansed" that territory of many of its non-Serbian inhabitants. And the world has done nothing—nothing effective—to stop them.

3   The world's political leaders and diplomats still talk, but they hardly seem to care. Even the informed Western public's attention has drifted away. But the reality remains. An aggressive war has been waged, and essentially won.

4   The waging of aggressive war was defined 50 years ago as a crime under international law. That was a principal achievement of the Nuremberg trials. Nazi leaders were convicted of the offense. The question is whether Nuremberg did something more lasting than judge the monstrous acts of the Nazi regime. Did it establish principles that the world will apply to other acts of aggression and genocide?

5   That question was explored this past weekend at a conference put on by Boston College Law School. It was entitled "Judgments on Nuremberg: The Past Half-Century and Beyond." And even those who thought they knew about the Nuremberg trials found it a gripping event.

6   A session I attended brought together six men who were on the Nuremberg prosecution staff. Thomas Lambert, now a professor at Suffolk University Law School in Boston, said a key accomplishment of the trials was to lay down the rule of individual accountability: "Those who plotted the war—the captains and the kings—bore responsibility."

7   Mr. Lambert quoted an extraordinary remark by the first chief prosecutor at Nuremberg, Supreme Court Justice Robert Jackson. He told his staff that they had to produce "an ice pick to break up the frozen sea within us."

8   What Justice Jackson meant was that human beings may be unmoved by horror in the large, even by mass murder. It is individual suffering and death—the story of an Anne Frank—that makes us understand. One of the great accomplishments of the prosecution at Nuremberg was to detail the Nazi inhumanities in evidence that fills 15 large volumes.

9   "Nuremberg was a moment when the life of reason leapt forward," Mr. Lambert said. It showed that "even if we cannot abolish aggressive war, we can condemn it."

10   How lasting the principles of Nuremberg will prove to be is now very much in the balance. For the first time since then, an international tribunal has been established to try charges of war crimes: in the former Yugoslavia. The United Nations has also authorized prosecutions for the genocidal events in Rwanda.

11   The Yugoslav tribunal should soon hold its first trial, of a Serbian concentration camp guard charged with atrocities. The prosecutors hope to build from that beginning to cases against the leaders—"the captains and the kings," in Mr. Lambert's phrase—who plotted the aggression and by propaganda roused ordinary people to atrocities.

116

12 Unlike the defendants at Nuremberg, most of those suspected of crimes in the former Yugoslavia are not in custody—and of course will not voluntarily bring themselves within the jurisdiction of the court. But the court's rules allow for the bringing of indictments against absent individuals and publication of the evidence on which the indictments are based.

13 Beyond Bosnia, the nations of the world remain highly selective—cynical—in their condemnation of military aggression.

14 When Turkey invaded northern Iraq to kill Kurds, the U.S. government winked. President Bill Clinton is going to visit Boris Yeltsin in Moscow despite Mr. Yeltsin's butchery in Chechnya.

15 Perceived self-interest can so easily mute political responses to inhumanity. We need a reaffirmation of Nuremberg to make us understand aggression's price.

DISCUSSION QUESTIONS

1. What is the tone of the introductory paragraph of this article? How does the tone prepare you as a reader for what follows?

2. Why do you think Lewis refers to the Serbian attack on Sarajevo as "anachronistic savagery" (paragraph 1)? What is the effect of this phrase on you as a reader?

3. Lewis writes that three years after the Serbian attack on Sarajevo, "The Serbs hold 70 percent of Bosnia, and have 'cleansed' that territory of many of its non-Serbian inhabitants." How is the word *cleansed* being used here? What are some connotations of this word?

4. Lewis argues that, although the Nuremberg trials deemed the waging of an aggressive war an international crime, an aggressive war has in fact been waged by Serbia, yet the world has done very little to stop the Serbs. To what extent do you think the world can enforce the principles set forth by the Nuremberg trials? To what extent can individual nations or the United Nations police the aggression of other nations?

5. Lewis quotes a remark made by the first chief prosecutor at the Nuremberg trials, Supreme Court Justice Robert Jackson. Jackson stated to his staff that they would need "an ice pick to break up the frozen sea within us." What do you think Jackson meant by this remark? How might this comment relate to the situation in the former Yugoslavia as well as similar arenas of aggressive war?

6. Lewis asserts that "Perceived self-interest can so easily mute political responses to inhumanity." What do you think Lewis meant by this

statement? What specific examples can you think of that might help you to illustrate what Lewis may have intended with this comment?

7. Lewis points out that "a key accomplishment of the [Nuremberg] trials was to lay down the rule of individual accountability: 'Those who plotted the war—the captains and the kings—bore responsibility.'" To what extent can someone who claims that he or she was simply following orders be held accountable?

8. Lewis quotes Thomas Lambert, a member of the Nuremberg prosecution staff, as saying, "Nuremberg was a moment when the life of reason leapt forward. . . . even if we cannot abolish aggressive war, we can condemn it." What do you think Lambert meant when he made this statement? To what extent can international condemnation help prevent aggressive war?

WRITING ASSIGNMENTS

1. Write an exploratory paper than responds to the following question: "To what extent does self-interest (individual and/or national) determine responses to inhumanity?" Use specific examples from history and current events to support your thesis.

2. Research the history of both the Yugoslavian and Rwandan conflicts. What are the root causes of these conflicts? Then write an essay that compares and contrasts the origins of these two conflicts in an attempt to determine why aggressive wars start and how they might be prevented.

3. Write an exploratory essay that responds to the following question: "To what extent should the international community police the aggressive actions of individual nations?"

4. The title of this article is "A New Nuremberg Could Just 'Break the Frozen Sea.'" Write a descriptive definition of the phrase *break the frozen sea*. What is the "frozen sea"? How and why should it be broken? You might begin by using prewriting strategies such as clustering or freewriting to help focus your understanding of this phrase.

CHAPTER FOUR WRITING ASSIGNMENTS

1. Both the articles "Dresden: 'It Was How You Would Imagine Hell'" and "War-Torn Nation Faces a Hidden Foe for Years to Come" explore the specific targeting of civilians in military attacks. What is your opinion of such attacks? While some argue that targeting civilians is inhumane, others might argue that, in certain situations, it is strategically necessary. Reread these articles and consider other military attacks in which citizens were involved. Then write an essay in which you respond to the following question: "Is the targeting of civilians in a military attack ever justified?" Support your opinions with specific examples, evidence, and reasons.

2. Write an exploratory essay that attempts to define the root causes of war. What are some of the common underlying causes that fuel wars? Be sure to use specific details when addressing this question.

3. The United Nations is mentioned in several of the articles in this chapter. Write a research paper that details the birth of the United Nations, its mission, and its influence on the world to date. Your essay should draw some conclusions about the effectiveness of this organization.

4. Many of the articles in this chapter concern civil wars (Rwanda, Angola, the former Yugoslavia). Research the origins and causes of one conflict and write an essay outlining your findings.

5. Several articles in this chapter address the responsibility of the international community to stop aggressive war. Write an essay that responds to the following question: "To what extent can the international community prevent aggressive warfare?" Be sure to support your opinion with specific evidence and details.

CHAPTER FIVE

Staying Healthy around the World

Health-related stories have wide appeal and are frequently covered in the news. We read or hear reports about a miracle drug for weight loss discovered in France, a new surgical procedure for heart patients performed in Germany, the uses of acupuncture in Asia, or the pros and cons of socialized medicine in various countries. Health issues often become the focus of heated debate, because maintaining good health is so vital to our survival. The articles in this chapter, therefore, look at a few of the many health-care issues currently concerning people around the world.

The chapter opens with an article entitled "So Doctors Without Borders Is Leaving the Rwanda Refugee Camps" by Alain Destexhe, secretary-general of the international relief group known as Doctors Without Borders. In his article, Destexhe relates the dilemma Doctors Without Borders faced in its attempt to help Rwandan refugees who were fleeing from civil war. Although international relief from this organization and others saved tens of thousands of lives, the aid also inadvertently gave the Hutu aggressors the ability to restart the civil war. Although relief organizations asked international forces from the United Nations to police the refugee camps, Western countries would not send troops. Consequently, Doctors Without Borders had to make the difficult decision either to abandon their work with Rwandan refugees or to see their aid being diverted into war efforts.

The next selection, "Smoking Is under Fire in China," examines the increased attention smoking has been receiving in China. Pressure from international health organizations has prompted Chinese officials to enforce an old law prohibiting smoking in public places and to enact a new regulation that bans nearly all tobacco advertising. Some worry, however, that the motives behind the enforcement of these laws have more to do with commercial interests than with concern for the health of China's people since a ban on tobacco advertising will give China the opportunity to develop its own tobacco industry.

In Daniel Goleman's article, "If You Can't Lose Weight, You Can at Least Learn to Like Yourself," a new approach to dealing with weight problems is examined. Psychotherapists have recently developed a treatment to help overweight people ease the emotional distress that so often accompanies weight difficulties. Although the new therapy is not designed to facilitate weight loss, it does not discourage weight loss either. Rather, it is intended to help people who are unable to lose weight learn to accept themselves for who they are. Although obesity does present physical health problems, it is hoped that this new psychotherapy will help an overweight person's emotional health.

Another innovative health treatment is explored in Jane E. Brody's article "Can Hormones Turn Back Clock?" In this report, Brody looks at the use of hormones to treat symptoms of aging. While the hormone estrogen has been used for some time to ease the effects of menopause, the growth hormone, a product of the pituitary gland, is now being employed. This latest hormone therapy is said to enhance the quality of life in aging people by helping them remain stronger and leaner. Although the findings are not conclusive, early results suggest that the therapy has had a positive impact on antiaging efforts.

The chapter concludes with an editorial about the current state of health-care reform in the United States. Entitled "Health Care Once Again," the editorial comments on the efforts being made by the United States government to ensure access to health care for all citizens. However, the need to maintain quality while cutting costs continues to stall the process.

While reading these articles, you might think about the relative importance of health-related issues around the world. Do health priorities differ from region to region? Are there universal concerns related to health care?

So Doctors Without Borders Is Leaving the Rwanda Refugee Camps

Alain Destexhe

The New York Times

■

Alain Destexhe is secretary-general of the international relief group Doctors Without Borders. In this commentary, Destexhe discusses the ethical dilemma Doctors Without Borders faced when treating refugees from the Rwandan civil war. In this conflict, the ethnic Hutu waged a campaign of genocide against Tutsi civilians. As a result of the civil war, thousands of Hutu ended up in disease-ridden refugee camps in Zaire. Although the physicians of Doctors Without Borders saved tens of thousands of lives during a cholera epidemic in the camps, they eventually decided that they could no longer provide the Hutu refugees with medical assistance because their efforts were being taken advantage of by the militant Hutu, who were diverting food, supplies, and funds to rebuild their military strength. Consequently, the organization made the difficult decision to withdraw from all refugee camps controlled by the Hutu-led government. While reading this article, you might think about the process of making an ethical decision. What factors need to be weighed when confronted with a dilemma such as the one Doctors Without Borders faced?

■

1 BRUSSELS—How can physicians continue to assist Rwandan refugees when by doing so they are also supporting killers? That is the ethical dilemma that has forced Doctors Without Borders (*Médicins sans frontières*) to decide to withdraw from all camps in Zaire and Tanzania, starting with our Feb. 8 retreat from the one at Kibumba, Zaire.

2 The Rwandan refugees, most of whom are ethnic Hutu, have not fled from persecution or famine. They were terrorized into the exodus by their Hutu-led government last summer after its military

defeat. Disease came only after they were in the camps. An international relief effort saved tens of thousands of lives during a cholera epidemic in Goma, Zaire.

3   The camps have turned into prisons. The Hutu who led the genocidal campaign against Tutsi civilians last spring are now holding hundreds of thousands of refugees hostage while they plot their counterattack against the new government in Rwanda.

4   They have created a miniature Rwanda in the camps—refugees are organized in groups according to the regions and villages they come from. Any dissident voices are quickly silenced. Our volunteers have stood by helplessly as refugees were kidnapped or even hacked to death.

5   International aid is the key to the Hutu leaders' efforts to restart the war. Food represents power, and the camp leaders, who control its distribution, divert considerable quantities toward war preparations. They also skim off a percentage of the wages earned by the thousands of refugees employed by relief agencies. Thus in the last seven months international aid has allowed the militias to reorganize, stockpile food and recruit and train new members.

6   Not until this month did the refugee leaders realize that they needed to improve their public image. They allowed the UN High Commissioner for Refugees to establish a registration program to make sure that food supplies match the real needs.

7   Some aid agencies claimed this as a major victory, but it does little good as long as the murderers remain in control.

8   The only hope of breaking their grip is an international force to police the camps, as many aid organizations have requested. But Butros Butros Ghali, the United Nations secretary-general, says Western countries have refused to provide troops.

9   More than 500,000 people, mostly Tutsi, were slaughtered in less than two months last year, and if Rwanda is ever to return to stability it will need a contemporary version of the Nuremberg trials. Yet the United Nations has offered only a slow-moving international tribunal. Legal proceedings against some of those who ordered the massacres have been initiated in France and Belgium, but all proceedings are being blocked or delayed.

10   The humanitarian crisis in the camps has been over for some time. Despite the diversion of food by the militias, Rwandan refugees are better fed in the camps than most Africans, although they are completely dependent on foreign aid.

11   Thus agencies such as ours are caught in a lose-lose situation. Either we continue being reluctant accomplices of genocidal warmongers, or we withdraw from the camps, leaving the refugee populations to the mercy of their jailers.

DISCUSSION QUESTIONS

1. In small groups, discuss what you know about the causes and consequences of the civil war in Rwanda. You may want to refer to the article in Chapter Four entitled "Hutu Chiefs Gearing for War." Be prepared to share your thoughts with the rest of the class.

2. Destexhe writes that "agencies such as ours are caught in a lose-lose situation. Either we continue being reluctant accomplices of genocidal warmongers, or we withdraw from the camps, leaving the refugee populations to the mercy of their jailers." What factors do you think these agencies took into consideration when making their decisions? How does one go about making a choice between two bad options? Do you think Doctors Without Borders made the right decision? Why or why not?

3. Can you think of any similar "lose-lose situations" in the world today? How are they being handled?

4. What do you think is the significance of the agency's name, "Doctors Without Borders"? What does the name mean to you? Why do you think this name may have been chosen?

5. Destexhe writes, "The only hope of breaking their [the Hutu's] grip is an international force to police the camps. as many aid organizations have requested. But Butros Butros Ghali, the United Nations secretary-general, says Western countries have refused to provide troops." Discuss why you think Western countries have refused to provide troops.

WRITING ASSIGNMENTS

1. Investigate the humanitarian work done by Doctors Without Borders. How big is the organization? Where is it based? Who supports it? How long has it been in existence? Then write an informative report based on your research. Be prepared to share your report with the class.

2. Imagine you are a physician working for Doctors Without Borders in a camp for Rwandan refugees. You have been told that you must withdraw from the camp because the political situation demands retreat. Write an entry in your journal that expresses your feelings about this "lose-lose situation." Alternatively, write about it in a letter to a friend or relative.

3. Write an argumentative paper that either defends or rejects the possibility of an international force being deployed to police refugee camps to allow relief agencies to do their work in safety. You may need to do some research to develop your thoughts. Be sure to support your opinions with specific reasons and evidence.

SMOKING IS UNDER FIRE IN CHINA

Bloomberg Business News

■

This selection reports the enforcement of both an old law in China that prohibits smoking in public places and a new law that bans nearly all tobacco advertising. Traditionally a sign of prosperity, smoking in China has recently been scrutinized by international health organizations and Chinese health officials. However, some people believe that the recent smoking regulations have not been motivated by concerns for the people's health; they suspect instead that monetary interests are behind the bans, since they allow for the development of an exclusively Chinese tobacco industry with its own advertising campaign. As you read this article, compare and contrast the controversies surrounding tobacco smoking in China with those now being debated in the United States. What are the similarities and differences?

■

1   SHANGHAI—Smoking, once a sign of prosperity and distinction in China, is increasingly under fire these days.

2   Shanghai officials are enforcing an old law that prohibits smoking in public places, and a nationwide advertising law that has just gone into effect seems to ban nearly all tobacco advertising.

3   But some say its motives may be as much commercial as health-related.

4   Andy Pan, who handles cigarette accounts in China for the advertising agency BBDO Worldwide, said, "China is trying to develop its own tobacco industry and grow its local advertising industry, and this gives them the chance without being too obvious about it." BBDO is part of Omnicon Group Inc.

5   "This does make life more difficult for us, yes," said Robert Fletcher, public affairs director of Rothman's Far East, which makes almost

2.5 billion cigarettes a year in its joint venture in northern China's Shandong Province.

6   With annual sales of 1.72 trillion cigarettes, China accounts for 30 percent of all cigarette sales worldwide. China's cigarette tax is a leading source of income for the government.

7   With Westerners increasingly quitting the habit, Philip Morris Cos., R. J. Reynolds Inc., BAT Industries PLC and Rothman's International PLC have all signed agreements to make cigarettes in China.

8   These companies currently have about 2 percent of the Chinese market.

9   "What we're seeing behind the scenes is the reorganization of the Chinese tobacco industry, and that's a lengthy process," Mr. Fletcher of Rothman's said. "They have only recently developed national brands," he said, and these laws "give them a little breathing room."

10   Another step that could buy local manufacturers more time is to make foreign cigarettes more expensive.

11   Du Shaoyong, deputy secretary of the Chinese Smoking and Health Association, said the association and the Ministry of Health were advocating a tax increase to finance anti-smoking campaigns.

12   Shanghai started enforcing its anti-smoking law largely in response to pressure from international health organizations, which "want China to discourage smoking instead of glorifying it," according to officials in the municipality's industry and commerce department, who asked not to be named.

13   Tobacco advertisements have been banned in newspapers and magazines and on television and radio as part of China's first advertising law. The move was made just as the country was required to expand foreign access to its cigarette market to live up to its end of a trade agreement with the United States.

14   The law also bans tobacco advertising in waiting rooms, theaters, meeting halls, stadiums and other public places. Theoretically, only point-of-sale advertising in stores is permitted, but there is some confusion over whether bars, for example, qualify as public places.

15   The advertising industry could lose as much as 1 billion yuan ($117 million) in contracts if Chinese authorities strictly enforced the new law.

16   Brenda Chow, director of public affairs for BAT, said: "We're waiting for details from the authorities. We're not sure what is allowed."

17   Ms. Chow said BAT had not pulled together a budget for advertising in China this year, because the situation has been "so volatile."

DISCUSSION QUESTIONS

1. Why do you think smoking in China was, as the reporter writes, "once a sign of prosperity and distinction"? Do you think smoking has ever been viewed in this manner by people in the United States or in other countries?

2. The reporter states that the new smoking laws may be motivated as much by commercial as by health-related interests. Explain.

3. In small groups, discuss the similarities and differences between anti-smoking campaigns in the United States and those of other countries. Do you think some countries are more relaxed about smoking regulations than others?

4. The article states that China started enforcing antismoking regulations "largely in response to pressure from international health organizations." To what extent do you think outside organizations should be able to dictate national policy in health-related issues?

WRITING ASSIGNMENTS

1. This article states, "Smoking, once a sign of prosperity and distinction in China, is increasingly under fire these days." Write an informative report that details the history behind the introduction of tobacco in China. When was it first imported? Has it ever been cultivated in China? How popular is it? What segment of the population smokes? Why was smoking associated with "prosperity and distinction"? What is the future of tobacco in China?

2. Using this article as a starting point for an analysis, write a paper that compares and contrasts attitudes toward smoking in China with those in the United States. To what degree is smoking in both countries accepted? When and why have smoking laws been enforced in these two countries? What societal values motivated smoking reform in these two countries? If you are more familiar with two other countries, you may compare and contrast the issues of smoking in those countries.

3. Interview someone who has been a smoker for a long time. In your interview, try to determine what effect various smoking regulations

(advertising bans, public-smoking bans, and so forth) have had on this person. Have they altered this person's smoking habits in any way? What does this person think of these regulations?

4. Write an essay in which you respond to the following question: "To what extent does a government have the right to regulate smoking?" Be sure to use specific examples and details to develop your points.

If You Can't Lose Weight, You Can at Least Learn to Like Yourself

Daniel Goleman

New York Times Service

■

In this selection, Daniel Goleman reports on a new treatment for people struggling with weight problems. The therapy is not a new diet, exercise regime, or medication. In fact, it will not help people lose weight. Rather, it is a therapy program designed to ease the emotional suffering that so often accompanies weight problems. Although the treatment is not intended to help people lose weight, it is not meant to discourage weight loss either. Since weight problems are so often lifelong battles, and the success rate of permanent weight loss is so low, this therapy is intended to help people who simply cannot lose weight to accept themselves for who they are. As you read this article, think about how our perceptions of people are too often determined by appearance. What do you think might be some consequences of this type of thinking?

■

1   NEW YORK—Given the difficulty of losing weight, psychotherapists have come up with a treatment aimed at easing the psychological suffering that comes with being overweight.

2   The therapy is not meant to discourage people from trying to lose weight, nor to deny the very real increased health risks that added pounds bring. Instead it seeks to ease emotional suffering.

3   But, the results show, once overweight people get over the acute self-consciousness that keeps them, say, from exercising in public, they are often better able to keep to their fitness regime.

4   "About 95 percent of people who lose weight in university-based clinical weight-loss programs have gained it back five years later," said Dr. Kelly Brownell, director of the Yale Center for Eating and Weight Disorders. "There's a collision between biology and culture. For some people there are biological barriers to losing weight at all, while others aspire to unrealistically lean ideals."

5   While other studies have come up with somewhat more optimistic estimates of the numbers of people who keep lost pounds off—as high as 25 percent—the odds against lasting weight loss are daunting. "The genetic research suggests that some people just have to live with being overweight," Dr. Brownell said. "Of course, this does not mean you should stop encouraging people to lose weight," Dr. Brownell added.

6   Pointing to the public health problems, like heart disease and diabetes, that plague overweight people, Dr. Brownell said, "having obese people simply accept their weight is like telling smokers to keep smoking. But what's needed are ways to tell more precisely who can and cannot lose weight, and help those who cannot to accept themselves as they are."

7   The approach has gained indirect support from a report this month in The New England Journal of Medicine that described the metabolic adjustments that make substantial and lasting weight loss a losing battle for so many people.

8   "Obese people are stigmatized and discriminated against," said Dr. Thomas Cash, a psychologist at Old Dominion University in Richmond, Virginia. "We help them with the emotional costs of these prejudices." His book describing the program, "What Do You See When You Look in the Mirror," was published in January by Bantam Books. "We say, do the healthy things—and one of those is to learn to accept your body in a world that does not," Dr. Cash said.

9   For the chronically overweight, the embarrassment, self-recrimination and obsession with their appearance "is an element of suffering in their lives that they can be freed from, whether or not they lose weight," said Dr. James C. Rosen, a psychologist at the University of Vermont, who reported results from the new therapy program in the journal Behavior Therapy.

10   People who are extremely overweight can experience such acute embarrassment that they avoid socializing, or spend hours preoccupied with arranging their clothes in the mirror or weighing themselves, Dr. Rosen said.

132

11   The 51 women in the treatment program were, on average, 52 percent over their ideal weight. The least overweight was about 25 pounds (11 kilograms) over her ideal weight, and one woman weighed more than 400 pounds.

12   The program had no effect on their weight, nor was the purpose of the therapy to help them shed pounds. Instead, it focused on freeing them from self-reproach, endless rumination about their appearance and their reluctance to appear in public.

DISCUSSION QUESTIONS

1. Goleman writes that the therapy program "focused on freeing them [overweight people] from self-reproach, endless rumination about their appearance and their reluctance to appear in public." Discuss what such therapy might entail. What might program participants be asked to do? What do you think should be included in such a program?

2. In small groups, explore why overweight people are stigmatized in today's society. What societal influences make being overweight so difficult to handle emotionally?

3. Goleman quotes the author of "What Do You See When You Look in the Mirror," Dr. Thomas Cash, as stating, "We say, do the healthy things—and one of those is to learn to accept your body in a world that does not." Do you agree that accepting one's body when others do not is a healthy practice?

4. Goleman writes that "once overweight people get over the acute self-consciousness that keeps them, say, from exercising in public, they are often better able to keep to their fitness regime." How else might a reduction in self-consciousness help people lose weight?

WRITING ASSIGNMENTS

1. As part of her dissertation, a graduate student of psychology pretended to be overweight by putting padding under her clothes. For several weeks, she recorded her experiences with daily life in a journal. She found that people did in fact treat her differently. Try a similar

experiment for a few hours, and, afterward, describe your experience in a personal narrative.

2. Write an informative report that investigates the relationship of emotional health and weight problems. Has much research been done in this area? What are some of the findings?

3. Write an exploratory essay that responds to the following question: "What societal influences affect how we accept our appearance?" Be sure to use specific details and examples to support your opinions.

CAN HORMONES TURN BACK CLOCK?

Jane E. Brody

New York Times Service

■

In the following selection, Jane E. Brody looks at the advances being made in hormone therapy for people over sixty years old. Although researchers believe that hormone treatments will not necessarily extend life, they hope that these treatments will improve the quality of life for people as they age. Estrogen therapy has been used for some time with menopausal women, but particular interest is now being directed at the growth hormone. Once thought to be of little use after the body had reached its final height, the growth hormone shows great promise in helping people stay stronger, leaner, and more mobile as they age. While reading the article, think about the positive outcomes that might result from hormone therapy in aging adults. Specifically, in what ways could hormone treatments improve an older person's quality of life that a younger person might take for granted?

■

1   NEW YORK—Why do some people in their 80s look, act and feel vigorous and energetic while others need help just to get through the chores of daily living? A good part of the answer may lie in their hormones. If studies now under way bear out their initial promise, hormone treatments for people over 60 may help to turn back the clock and, though without extending life, greatly enhance its quality.

2   Researchers are exploring the rejuvenating effects of several hormones that undergo rather striking declines with age. These include, but go beyond, replacing estrogen, which declines sharply in women after menopause. The safety of estrogen replacement, particularly with regard to the risk of breast cancer, is hotly debated and raises a cautionary note about the wisdom of replacing other hormones that fall with age.

3   A major focus of the new research is growth hormone, a product of the pituitary gland that gradually declines with age and until recently was not thought important to older people. Researchers are considering replacing testosterone loss in older men. There is also keen interest in a hormone of the adrenal cortex called DHEA or dihydroepiandrosterone, which is said to enhance immune function and life span in rats.

4   Whether or not nature has some hidden agenda for the ebbing of these hormones with age, for example in slowing people down as the life span wanes, it is now recognized that as people live to their 80s and beyond, the effect of declining hormones may contribute significantly to chronic, debilitating and costly illnesses.

5   "For every major hormone system that's been studied, we find age-related changes that suggest they could have meaning to the aging process," said Dr. Marc R. Blackman, chief of endocrinology at the Johns Hopkins Bayview Medical Center in Baltimore.

6   Among the well-known attributes of aging that hormone loss may bring about are the loss of muscle mass and strength, an increase of body fat, particularly fat around the abdomen, a weakening of the bones, a decline in immune responses and a general loss of energy.

7   While no one expects to turn a frail 80-year-old into an iron man, the hormonal effects under study could help to save old people from some of the burden of illness and to preserve their independence.

8   More than 7 million Americans now need long-term care costing tens of billions of dollars a year because they can no longer perform daily activities without help. Without an antidote for age-associated disabilities, by the year 2030 nearly 14 million people will need such care.

9   Several years ago, the National Institute on Aging in Bethesda, Maryland, made available some $2 million for exploring hormone replacement in people 60 and older. Nine research teams are now midway through their studies, which focus on growth hormone and other "trophic factors," substances that promote growth or maintenance of tissues.

10   "Trophic factors may not be the 'fountain of youth,' as some have suggested, but they may have promise for halting or reversing degenerative changes in bones, muscles, nerves and cartilage, which lead to frailty," said Dr. Stanley Slater, deputy associate director for geriatrics at the institute. Some form of growth hormone therapy, if its early promise is sustained, might help people "stay stronger, leaner and more mobile" as they age, he said.

11   But it would be wrong to make too much of these early findings, researchers caution. Dr. David Clemmons, an endocrinologist who

studies growth hormone at the University of North Carolina in Chapel Hill, said: "Just because you make a person's hormone profile more youthful does not mean you will arrest or reverse aging. You'll still have wrinkles and gray hair."

12 Growth hormone, along with the special factors that trigger its release or carry out its effects on the tissues, are the stars of current anti-aging studies. The hormone was once thought to be important in making the body reach its final stature, though of no great consequence afterward. But several important studies have shown this is not the whole picture.

13 The interest in growth hormone picked up significantly after advances in genetic engineering made it possible to synthesize the hormone in bacteria.

DISCUSSION QUESTIONS

1. The title of this article is phrased as a question. Why do you think Brody chose to use a question as the title? What rhetorical purpose does the question serve?

2. Brody indicates that estrogen replacement in women has been a questionable practice since some studies have revealed a connection between the use of estrogen and an increased risk of breast cancer. Do you think hormone replacement in general might have other disadvantages we should consider? Think about what you might want to ask a doctor if you were presented with the possibility of having these treatments.

3. What relationship might exist between emotional health and improved physical health as a result of hormone therapy? To what extent does a healthy body make for a happier person?

4. What are some of the financial impacts of hormone therapy? How might this therapy affect the financial situations of individuals, families, and health providers?

5. Are there any ethical issues surrounding hormone treatments that should be considered?

6. Brody writes, "Whether or not nature has some hidden agenda for the ebbing of these hormones with age . . . the effect of declining hormones may contribute significantly to chronic, debilitating and costly illnesses." Speculate about whether nature has "a hidden agenda." If so, what might it be?

WRITING ASSIGNMENTS

1. Keep a log for a few days in which you enter all activity that requires moderate to heavy physical exertion (such as carrying groceries, using the gas pump, or vacuuming). Then write a paper using the data from your log to explore what being elderly might feel like. Your paper can take the form of a creative narrative or a more formal analysis.

2. Research the uses of hormone therapy for the elderly. Then write an informative report that details the advances made in this area of scientific research. Be prepared to share your findings with the class.

3. Brody quotes a physician as stating, "Just because you make a person's hormone profile more youthful does not mean you will arrest or reverse aging." In a well-developed essay, respond to the following question: "To what extent should scientists experiment with the natural aging process?" Your essay can move beyond the issue of hormone therapy.

HEALTH CARE ONCE AGAIN

The Washington Post

■

The following editorial from *The Washington Post* examines the issue of health-care reform. Access to health care for all United States citizens has been a priority in Congress for some time, yet it continues to stir heated debate among politicians, insurance companies, hospitals, physicians and other medical professionals, and patients. Questions of cost and quality still remain unanswered. Although many people hope for compromise, according to the writer of this editorial, "Someone ends up either getting less or paying more." While reading this piece, think about the kinds of reform you would like to see in the health-care system. What works well now, and what needs to be changed? What lessons, if any, might we learn from other countries' health-care systems?

■

1   It's back. The ill-fated No. 1 issue from the last U.S. Congress, health care reform, threatens to become the consuming issue in this Congress as well. The driving force is the commendable Republican commitment to move toward a balanced budget. It is a difficult goal to achieve in the best of circumstances; the Republicans have made it more so by proposing to cut taxes while putting military spending and Social Security off limits. Those two categories, plus interest on the debt, are more than half of all spending. The giant health insurance programs, Medicare and Medicaid, are the largest targets left, about one-third of all the remaining spending and the fastest-growing major share. As the Republicans themselves have begun to warn, the budget cannot be balanced unless they are controlled.

2   The difficult question, politically as well as substantively, is how. The problems are different for Medicaid and Medicare. Medicaid programs are run by the states within broad federal limits; the federal

139

government then pays a little over half of what has been a rapidly rising cost. Congress could limit the annual increase in the federal contribution; block grants are a device that has been discussed. That
would help to solve the federal budget problem, but not the underlying problem of providing health care to the poor. Medicaid even now
covers only about half the poor.

3   A broad cap or spending constraint could be imposed on Medicare
as well, but that, too, would be only a first step. Because Medicare is
an all-federal program, Congress would also have to figure out how to
fit the care within the cap. Now it mainly seeks to control costs
directly by setting reimbursement rates. For Medicare patients there
is a system of federal health care price controls by another name. No
doubt there will be attempts to tighten these, as well as to raise the
share of costs that patients themselves must bear.

4   That is one approach; the alternative, to which Republicans, and
some others, tend to be philosophically drawn, is to rely more on the
marketplace and competition to hold down costs. Instead of paying
for health care directly, the government might begin to give
Medicare recipients vouchers with which to buy insurance. Providers
and managed care companies would then compete for their business
on the basis, at least in part, of which could provide the broadest coverage at the lowest price.

5   There is talk as well, among some budget-cutters, of structuring
Medicare so that above certain income levels the benefit would begin
to decline. The political problem, however, is that all these steps create losers. Someone ends up either getting less or paying more. Doctors, for example, feel threatened by managed-care companies that
limit not just what they are paid but how they must practice.

6   Newt Gingrich, the speaker of the House, told an audience of doctors the other day that there will be hearings on the subject of managed care. It is a major issue and a worthy topic. It is also an illustra-
tion of what happens when you set out to cut the budget. You end up
willy-nilly having to restructure parts of the health care system as well.

DISCUSSION QUESTIONS

1.   In small groups, discuss what you know about the issue of health-care
      reform. Who are the interested parties? What are the main concerns
      of the interested parties? You might make a chart to illustrate these
      concerns and the responses that the different groups of people have
      to them. Be prepared to share your findings with the whole class.

2. The writer of this article notes that the need to balance the federal budget has put increased pressure on the funding of Medicare and Medicaid. Many people in Congress warn that the budget cannot be balanced unless these two government-funded health insurance programs are controlled. To what extent should funds that are used to provide health care for needy individuals and the elderly be cut from the federal government's budget?

3. According to the article, "Providers and managed care companies would . . . compete for . . . business on the basis, at least in part, of which could provide the broadest coverage at the lowest price." What do you perceive as the advantages and disadvantages of this approach?

4. Do you think the federal government has an obligation to provide access to reliable health care to all United States citizens? Why or why not?

WRITING ASSIGNMENTS

1. Research the problems that are currently troubling the health-care system in the United States. Then write a report that describes the nature of one of these problems and any attempts being made to resolve it.

2. Imagine a roundtable discussion among the following participants: an insurance company executive, a hospital administrator, a member of Congress, a medical student, a physician, and a small-business owner. They are to discuss the following question: "What should be done to improve health care in the United States?" Write a paragraph for each participant that explores what response he or she might have to this question.

3. Write an exploratory essay that responds to the following question: "How can we ensure that all United States citizens have adequate health care?" Be sure to include supporting details and examples to support your ideas.

4. Write a personal narrative about an experience you had with your health-care system. Your narrative should describe in detail what happened and what you learned from the experience.

CHAPTER FIVE WRITING ASSIGNMENTS

1. The articles in this chapter discuss a variety of health-care concerns. Interview a health-care professional. Write the interview in a question/answer format as in the article "Q&A: Fading Ecology Movement's Identity Crisis" in Chapter Six. The interview should focus on the health-care issues your interviewee thinks are of most concern to people today. The articles in this chapter can help you prepare a guide to use during the interview. However, you need not limit your interview to the health-care subjects covered in this chapter.

2. The selections "If You Can't Lose Weight, You Can at Least Learn to Like Yourself" by Daniel Goleman and "Can Hormones Turn Back Clock?" by Jane E. Brody are both what media professionals might call human-interest stories. Such stories are intended to spark the curiosity of readers and provide interesting and potentially useful information. For these reasons they are thought of as newsworthy. Find another health-care issue that could be considered a human-interest story. Then write a news story about the subject in the same style as the Brody and Goleman reports. You might begin by taking some notes on the writing styles of these two examples. How are the topics introduced? How are ideas developed? Are many quotes used?

3. Choose a health-related issue that has an international focus (such as smoking, malnutrition, or war-related illness). Your topic should not be too broad. Write an informative report that explores the history of the issue, including specific examples and details to support your ideas. Be prepared to present your report to the class.

4. Write an argumentative paper that responds to the following question: "Is health care a human right as opposed to a privilege?" Support your opinions with specific details and evidence.

CHAPTER SIX

Coexisting with Mother Earth

Concern for the environment is not new to the 1990s. As early as the turn of the century, President Theodore Roosevelt followed a policy of conservation of natural resources during his years in office (1901–1909). In the 1960s, the ecology movement sparked renewed interest in the environment. Conservation initiatives such as recycling, which were started in the 1960s but not widely practiced, are now common practice for many people and communities. Unfortunately, however, our environmental problems are far from resolved. In fact, they seem to have become worse. As the articles in this chapter will demonstrate, realities of the modern world such as urbanization and war are leading us further away from a path of sound environmental practice.

In the first selection of this chapter, "A Forgotten Ecological Disaster," Donatella Lorch reports on the effect that deforestation of the Kibira Forest in Burundi is having on the chimpanzees and other wildlife. The Kibira Forest has shrunk by 50 percent since the 1960s. In addition to being plagued by poachers, the chimpanzees are now quickly losing their natural habitat. The deforestation problem has been further complicated by the movement into northern Burundi of refugees from the Rwandan civil war. Needing firewood, these refugees have found a ready supply in the Kibira Forest. The continued deforestation has uprooted wildlife, and conservationists predict loss of topsoil, drought, and floods. However, Lorch reports that one group, the Jane Goodall Institute, is working hard to save these chimpanzees and educate the people of Burundi about the need to preserve the Kibira Forest.

Moving from land to sea, Reginald Dale in "There Aren't Plenty of Fish in the Sea" illustrates that there is also tremendous concern about the conservation of our world fisheries. In his commentary, Dale writes about the plundering of the world's commercial fish stocks by fishing fleets that ignore regulations imposed to conserve fisheries. Dale points out that "the fundamental problem is the overcapacity of the world fishing fleet." Although governments continue to subsidize the growth and maintenance of their fishing fleets, the fish stocks are quickly becoming depleted because conservation initiatives are not being properly enforced. As Dale asserts, "There is no point building ever bigger, better ships if there are no fish left to catch."

In "Europe's Floods of 'Sins and Failures,'" Rick Atkinson examines the devastation left by "superfloods" throughout Europe, especially Germany and the Netherlands. Although the floods have been partially blamed on unusually heavy winter rains, meteorologists theorize that the flooding is also due to urbanization, modern farming practices, poor flood-plain management, and, possibly, global warming. Since urban areas and farmland do not absorb water readily, these regions are ripe for flooding. In addition, the channeling and straightening of the Rhine River to improve navigation for barge traffic has rendered the riverbanks more susceptible to flooding. Although innovations resulting from urbanization are viewed by many as progress, the consequences of tampering with nature without consideration for the future can be devastating.

Paul R. Epstein and Ross Gelbspan in "Changing Climate: A Plague Upon Us" add support to the theory that dramatic climate changes are the result of urbanization. Their commentary explores the link between man-made greenhouse gases, resulting from fossil-fuel emissions, and alterations in global climate patterns. According to Epstein and Gelbspan, these extreme weather conditions also create ideal conditions for the spread of disease. As they note, "Extreme weather conditions affect marine, plant and human health by affording opportunistic species fresh terrain and generating new bursts of activity. The drying up of ponds concentrates microorganisms, while floods contaminate clean water. Droughts encourage locusts and rodents; floods foster fungi." Although the urgency of this problem is apparent to many people, Epstein and Gelbspan warn us that time is running out and action needs to be taken.

The various environmental concerns addressed in this chapter are brought together in the chapter-concluding interview by Ken Shulman of environmental activist Luis Sepulveda. The interview explores the current direction of the environmental movement. Sepulveda suggests that the ecological movement has become splintered by divergent goals and political motives. He feels a return to civil disobedience is needed in order to see any progress made towards environmental reform.

A recurrent theme throughout these selections is the imperative for change in the ways we view and treat our natural resources. As you read this chapter, consider what we, as both individuals and communities, must do to create a better environment for ourselves as well as future generations.

A Forgotten Ecological Disaster

Donatella Lorch

New York Times Service

■

Since 1989, the Jane Goodall Institute has been dedicated to studying chimpanzees. In this selection, Donatella Lorch reports on the efforts of the institute to rescue the chimpanzee population in the central African country of Burundi from poaching, capture, and extinction. Baby chimpanzees are sold as cute pets, only to be caged and chained for spectators' amusement. In addition, lack of forest preservation is slowly destroying Kibira Forest, the natural habitat of the chimpanzee. Although the Burundi government says that it is committed to forest conservation, these efforts are not top priorities in a country that is reeling in the wake of the Rwandan civil war and is itself on the brink of war. As you read this article, think about how the sometimes fragile relationships among humans, animals, and their shared habitats can be kept in balance.

■

1 Bujumbura, Burundi—The infant chimpanzee was tied to a pole in a windowless, padlocked mud hut. Its owner told employees of the Jane Goodall Institute, who were posing as buyers, that he had found the creature and was trying to sell it for several hundred dollars.

2 The orphaned chimp was rescued by the institute's Burundian workers, who now care for it, along with 18 other chimps rescued from captivity. They have named the baby Bahati, which means Lucky in the Kirundi language, because it survived.

3 But there is little chance that Bahati will ever be able to be returned to the central African forests where it was born, conservationists say. The workers believe that the chimp's mother and as many as 20 other adult chimpanzees in her social group were killed to capture the infant.

4   Poaching is only one of the forces conspiring against Burundi's chimpanzee population. Their habitat is also slowly disappearing. Their home, the Kibira Forest, has shrunk by about 50 percent since the 1960s, conservationists say, and they expect an ecological impact—loss of topsoil, drought, and floods—that will be as troubling for the people of Burundi as for the wildlife.

5   "Without a forest here in Burundi, there is no life for Burundians," said Aly Wood, co-director of the Goodall Institute. "The Kibira is its own watershed. Without it there is no rain, no water, no crops, no life. We have to start teaching this in first grade."

6   Though the government says it is committed to forest conservation, it is hardly functioning, Western diplomats say. Indeed, there seems little chance that conservation efforts will get a high priority in a country on the brink of civil war.

7   The opposition, dominated by the minority Tutsi tribe, is demanding the overthrow of the government, which is led by a member of the Hutu majority. Tensions in the capital were palpable this week on the eve of a general strike in which opposition militants plan to set up barricades in an effort to paralyze the city.

8   Hundreds of thousands of refugees from last year's ethnic carnage in Rwanda, now living in camps in northern Burundi, have compounded the deforestation problem, felling trees for firewood. But even in quieter times, the environmental pressures on Burundi have been relentless.

9   With more than 260 people per square mile, Burundi is the second most densely populated country in Africa. More than 90 percent of Burundians are farmers, and they have been cutting away at the forest to increase their land.

10   Officials say the symbiotic relationship between animal, forest and man is often lost on the Burundian farmers who see the animals as predators that destroy their crops, and who are unaware of the importance of a watershed.

11   Ms. Wood says that forest preservation must evolve as a grass-roots effort, emphasizing education. But much of what the Goodall Institute wants to do looks like a wish list.

12   The institute, founded in 1989 by Jane Goodall, the naturalist who has devoted her career to studying chimpanzees, wants to create a controlled habitat in the forest for the chimpanzees here, a place where visitors could go to see the chimpanzees, as with the lowland mountain gorillas in Rwanda and Zaire. But it has a budget of only $35,000 a year.

13   Until mighty feats of fund-raising and political transformation are achieved, the institute must care for its orphaned chimps.

14   In a walled-in courtyard, the younger chimpanzees play, scream at intruders and climb on any visitor who gets too close. But the 10 adults and five adolescents are either caged or chained.

15   All of the chimpanzees in the compound were captured in the wild as infants, when they are easily sold as cute, cuddly pets. But when they grow into adults they can be dangerous. Adult males weigh about 110 pounds (50 kilograms), can easily rip flesh with their canine teeth and have the strength of five men, the institute's workers say.

16   Like Bahati, the other chimpanzees have sad pasts. Fifteen-year-old Poco spent 10 years in a cage over a mechanic's shop, placed there to attract business, before he was handed over to the institute. Uruhara, 5, was so neglected and malnourished that he had lost almost all of his hair. Akela, 6, was handed over by the owner of a local hotel five years ago, along with three other chimpanzees that he kept in cages to amuse guests.

17   Ms. Wood said the institute was trying to raise money to ship the adult chimps under its care to Kenya, where they would live in a large controlled habitat instead of cages.

18   "Our intention is to build our own sanctuary—get them out of cages and out of chains," she said.

DISCUSSION QUESTIONS

1. Reread the opening paragraph of this article. Why do you think the writer chose to begin with this story? What effect does this anecdote have on you as a reader? What are some rhetorical reasons for beginning the article in this manner?

2. Lorch quotes Aly Wood, the codirector of the Goodall Institute, as stating that "The Kibira is its own watershed. Without it there is no rain, no water, no crops, no life. We have to start teaching this in the first grade." Expand upon Wood's statement. Why is the Kibira its own watershed, and why should children learn this concept at such an early age?

3. Lorch writes that "Hundreds of thousands of refugees from last year's ethnic carnage in Rwanda, now living in camps in northern Burundi, have compounded the deforestation problem, felling trees for firewood." Can you think of other environmental hazards caused by war?

4. Lorch cites Burundian officials who say that "the symbiotic relationship between animal, forest and man is often lost on the Burundian farmers who see the animals as predators that destroy their crops, and who are unaware of the importance of a watershed." Can you think of any similar scenarios in which people do not recognize the long-range damage certain practices may have on the environment even though short-range needs call for a certain practice? In small groups, discuss situations with which you are familiar that parallel the Burundian problem. Be prepared to discuss your findings with the class as a whole.

5. Why do you think the author of this article has chosen the title "A Forgotten Ecological Disaster"? Speculate about its potential meanings.

WRITING ASSIGNMENTS

1. Lorch writes that the Kibira Forest has shrunk by about 50 percent since the 1960s. Write an informative report that details the slow erosion of this forest and its impact on wildlife as well as humans. You will need to consult outside sources before writing the report. Be prepared to present your report to the class.

2. Lorch quotes Aly Wood, the codirector of the Goodall Institute, as stating that "forest preservation must evolve as a grass-roots effort, emphasizing education." Why is education so crucial for this problem? Write an essay that explains the importance of education in ecological endeavors. Your essay should include examples beyond the Burundi crisis.

3. Write a dialogue between a Burundi farmer, a Burundi government official, and a member of the Goodall Institute. The topic of your conversation is "How to Coexist with Nature." When writing the dialogue, be sure to take into consideration the different priorities, attitudes, and motives of each participant. You may want to write this dialogue as a collaborative effort with classmates and then perform it in front of the class.

4. The Goodall Institute's wish list includes creating a controlled habitat for the uprooted chimpanzees in which they could live freely and safely. However, budgetary restrictions at this time prevent the creation of such a habitat. Write a letter to the Goodall Institute in which you offer suggestions intended to help them achieve their dream.

THERE AREN'T PLENTY OF FISH IN THE SEA

Reginald Dale

International Herald Tribune

■

In this commentary, Reginald Dale discusses the plight of the world's fisheries. At the hands of shortsighted government officials and unscrupulous fishermen who plunder this resource, the world's fish stocks are rapidly diminishing. Dale reports on the growing tension between Canada and nations such as Spain and Portugal over violations of rules intended to conserve fish stocks. In an effort to prevent the plundering of the northwest Atlantic fisheries, a Canadian fisheries protection vessel blasted warning shots at and seized a Spanish trawler off the coast of Newfoundland for violation of fishing regulations. Although the legality of such an action has been questioned, it seems that Canada has given the international community something to think about. As Dale comments, "If some countries get away with cheating, there will be no incentive for others to abide by the rules. That is a recipe for disaster in which everyone loses." As you read this selection, think about how this "recipe for disaster" might be prevented, as well as the likelihood of its prevention.

■

1   WASHINGTON—The four warning shots fired by a Canadian fisheries protection vessel off Newfoundland last month were a welcome sound. Whether the shots were technically illegal is far less important than the message they conveyed: Something must be done to stop the plundering of the world's fisheries before it is too late.

2   Overfishing is rapidly devastating one of the planet's major natural resources. According to the UN Food and Agriculture Organization, 70 percent of the world's fish populations are at risk, or already in decline.

But the shortsightedness of governments and the greed of fishermen are preventing the necessary disciplines from being imposed.

3   Rather than condemning Canada for seizing a Spanish trawler that was hard at work destroying some of the northwest Atlantic's last remaining commercial fish stocks, other nations should be congratulating the Canadians for giving international opinion a much-needed jolt.

4   In fact, Canada is winning the propaganda war that has erupted over its action. It's easy to see why. Spain has a richly deserved reputation for aggressively breaking rules designed to conserve stocks and ensure fair shares of the catch for other fishing nations.

5   Europeans who have suffered at the hands of Spanish fishermen, notably in Britain and Ireland, are cheering on Canada for resorting to the kind of decisive remedy that they feel their own governments—and the European Union authorities—have failed to apply.

6   On the contrary, the EU has not only allowed Spain and Portugal to overfish the Atlantic but it has encouraged them by subsidizing the operations of new high-tech vessels with giant nets that sweep the ocean depths like monstrous vacuum cleaners.

7   The European Commission has made matters worse by trying to rally the EU behind a member state, which, in the eyes of most reasonable people, is clearly in the wrong. EU solidarity should not be automatically available to any member government that demands it, regardless of the circumstances.

8   Spain has further forfeited sympathy by pettily retaliating against Canadian travelers—by imposing new visa requirements—and by hysterical warnings that the very credibility of the EU is at stake.

9   Canada is far from innocent. It has massively overfished the northwest Atlantic, too. But it is finally doing something about it. If it has been obliged to act outside its territorial limits, that is because nobody else is going to stop the devastation.

10   As world fish stocks decline and modern fishing fleets expand, there will be more such disputes over fish and ships. Such is the emotive and political power of those who make their living from the sea that governments will be tempted to blindly back their own fishermen.

11   If some countries get away with cheating, there will be no incentive for others to abide by the rules. That is a recipe for disaster in which everyone loses.

12   Agreeing on new conservation measures in the northwest Atlantic is only a first step. Much tougher enforcement is needed, inside the EU as well as internationally. Unfortunately, there are as yet no effective international procedures to deal with ships left uncontrolled by the countries where they are registered.

13   But the fundamental problem is the overcapacity of the world fishing fleet—and the huge sums being spent on supporting and expanding it. The FAO estimates the combined annual loss of the world fishing industry at around $54 billion, much of it covered by government subsidies.

14   Governments would be better off working together to phase out the subsidies and cut the fleets down to size. There is no point building ever bigger, better ships if there are no fish left to catch.

DISCUSSION QUESTIONS

1. What everyday myth does the title of this article implicitly refute? Could this title apply to other resources? If so, which ones? Do you think most people think our world resources are limitless?

2. Dale writes that "the shortsightedness of governments and the greed of fishermen are preventing the necessary disciplines from being imposed." Why do you think governments are often shortsighted? What prevents them from seeing the big picture?

3. Dale writes that "Governments would be better off working together to phase out the subsidies and cut the fleets down to size. There is no point building ever bigger, better ships if there are no fish left to catch." In what other areas of resource conservation might this philosophy apply? Do you think governments will listen to this viewpoint? Why or why not?

4. Dale reports that "there are as yet no effective international procedures to deal with ships left uncontrolled by the countries where they are registered." Consider what kinds of procedures and policies might be put into effect on an international level to help deal with uncontrolled fishing.

5. Dale writes, "If some countries get away with cheating, there will be no incentive for others to abide by the rules." Do you agree with this claim? Why or why not?

6. In small groups, discuss what else you think might be done to help conserve the world's fisheries on both national and international levels.

WRITING ASSIGNMENTS

1. The shortsightedness of governments and fishermen depicted in this article is not new. In the 1800s, whales were highly prized for their oil and other products. Whaling was an extremely profitable industry during this time. However, whales were hunted to near extinction. Laws regulating whaling were eventually put into effect. Write a paper warning against the dangers of abusing our fisheries using a comparison to whaling as a primary argument. You will need to do some research on whaling to help develop your argument.

2. Write an informative report that details the recent tension between Canadian and Spanish fishing fleets. Be sure to include the origins of this rivalry in your report as well as your predictions for future consequences and/or negotiations.

3. Dale writes, "Something must be done to stop the plundering of the world's fisheries before it is too late." Write a problem-solution essay that develops a plan for the resolution of this problem. You will probably need to do some outside research before developing your plan.

Europe's Floods of "Sins and Failures"

Rick Atkinson

Washington Post Service

■

In this selection, Rick Atkinson reports on the view that the floodwaters that ravaged communities across Europe, including much of the Netherlands and Germany, can be blamed on urbanization and farming practices. Land that has been urbanized or farmed does not absorb water as effectively as land in its natural state. Blame for these flood disasters has been passed back and forth among involved parties. Atkinson states that "Dutch officials have been particularly biting in their criticism of upstream Germany for a willy-nilly approach to watershed conservation, and neighboring governors within Germany have traded potshots over flood control procedures." However, what remains clear is that environmental reform is needed. As the environment minister for the German state of Rhineland-Palatinate asserts, "We've been raping nature for 40 years, and we've got to change that." While reading this article, you might think about the potential implications of this previous quotation. What does it to mean to "rape nature"? How can it be stopped?

■

1 BERLIN—As floodwaters continued to recede Thursday across most of Europe, communities from southern Germany to the Netherlands found themselves wondering how two "once-in-a-century" floods could hit the region within 13 months.

2 The rampage this week came as hundreds of thousands of people who live along the Rhine, the Moselle, the Main and other rivers had barely recovered from the devastating Christmas deluge of 1993. Damage from the two floods is likely to reach tens of billions of dollars.

154

3   Meteorologists suspect the catastrophic flooding is more than the result of unusually heavy winter rains. Rather, they theorize, a combination of urbanization, modern farming practices, navigation improvements and questionable flood plain management have rendered low-lying areas increasingly vulnerable.

4   Farmland and particularly urban areas do not absorb water as effectively as land in its natural state. Many experts contend that decades of squeezing European rivers, particularly the Rhine, into an ever tighter channel have made them unstable.

5   The Süeddeutsche Zeitung newspaper decried the "flood of sins and failures," and recriminations have flowed even faster than the water has ebbed.

6   Dutch officials have been particularly biting in their criticism of upstream Germany for a willy-nilly approach to watershed conservation, and neighboring governors within Germany have traded potshots over flood control procedures.

7   By virtue of size and geography, Germany has been both breeding ground and victim of the superfloods.

8   One-eighth of Germany lies beneath asphalt and concrete. Every day, according to Der Spiegel magazine, 90 more hectares (225 acres) is covered for streets, parking lots or other urban ventures. Widespread deforestation has also stripped the land of one of its most effective natural sponges. In addition, many farms are now crisscrossed with drainage ditches that effectively remove water from crop fields by dumping it immediately into rivers.

9   Another factor is the gradual straightening and channeling of the Rhine, which began in 1830. By removing bends and loops German engineers have given the river a greater capacity for barge traffic; they also made it a singularly effective conduit for massive volumes of water flowing into western Germany and the Netherlands.

10   At Karlsruhe in southwest Germany, for example, the Rhine crested at eight meters (25 feet) above flood stage only four times in the century before 1977; since then, the river has hit that mark 10 times, according to Die Zeit newspaper.

11   "This high water is partly manmade," Klaudia Martini, environment minister for the German state of Rhineland-Palatinate, said earlier this week. "We've been raping nature for 40 years, and we've got to change that."

12   One proposed solution is to create more polders—catch basins along rivers that can be used to divert rising waters before they rampage out of control. But such safety valves are extremely expensive

and are often resisted by local communities and farmers who do not want to see their fluvial plains converted into swamps. Moreover, as events this week demonstrated, even where polders exist there is often dissension over when and how to use them.

13   The European media have made much this week of the hypothesis that weather patterns have been insidiously affected by global warming. But many climatologists believe that evidence is too still too scanty to draw a direct link between evolving weather and the recent flood disasters.

DISCUSSION QUESTIONS

1. Speculate about the meaning of the article's title. What does it mean to you? Why do you think the writer of this piece chose to use it as a title? What rhetorical effect do you think it has?

2. Do you think that the floods described in this article are an isolated incident? Can you think of other similar incidents that have occurred in the United States or other parts of the world? Why do you think comparing and contrasting these natural disasters might be important?

3. The article makes the point that urbanization has put one-eighth of Germany "beneath asphalt and concrete." To what extent do you think nature should be compromised by urbanization and vice versa? Should all urbanization come to a halt for the sake of the environment? Do you think a compromise is possible? If so, what would it entail?

4. The article mentions that the unusual weather patterns may be the result of global warming but that the evidence is not sufficient to support this hypothesis. What is your opinion? Do you think the hypothesis is plausible? Why or why not?

5. Atkinson writes, "Damage from the two floods is likely to reach tens of billions of dollars." Can you think of any nonmonetary costs these floods may have produced?

WRITING ASSIGNMENTS

1. Atkinson quotes a German environment minister as stating, "This high water is partly manmade. We've been raping nature for 40 years, and we've got to change that." Write an exploratory essay that responds to the following question: "To what extent can and/or

should people change their routines for the sake of the environment?" You might begin by using a prewriting strategy such as clustering or mapping to think about the ways in which people and nature interact.

2. Write a cause-and-effect paper that details the causes and consequences of the European floods. Since there may be competing theories, you will probably need to synthesize the information and address which theories seem more plausible. The essay will require some outside research. Be sure to document your sources carefully.

3. Write a roundtable dialogue in which the participants are a farmer, an urban planner, a meteorologist, a member of the Environmental Protection Agency or an environment minister, and a student. The discussion topic is the following question: "How can we prevent future catastrophic floods?"

4. Write an expository essay that explores the potential meanings of the phrase "flood of sins and failures." Begin your essay by freewriting or clustering on this phrase. What does the phrase call to your mind? Support your opinions with details from the article as well as outside sources.

CHANGING CLIMATE:
A PLAGUE UPON US

Paul R. Epstein and Ross Gelbspan

The Washington Post

■

Dr. Paul R. Epstein is a physician with the New Disease Group at the Harvard School of Public Health and the Intergovernmental Panel on Climate Change. Ross Gelbspan has written on environmental issues for *The Boston Globe* and *The Washington Post*. In this selection, the two writers report on how man-made greenhouse gases are destabilizing global climate patterns, resulting in extreme weather conditions that help the spread of disease. Until recently, the significance of global climate change in the worldwide transmission of disease was not widely recognized. However, the unstable environments produced by the extreme weather are perfect breeding grounds for pests and pathogens, and scientists now feel that the unchecked burning of fossil fuels has begun to alter planetwide systems. As you read this article, think about how individuals as well as communities should respond to this information.

■

1   CAMBRIDGE, Massachusetts—Natural climate change has been with us for eons, but accumulating evidence suggests that man-made greenhouse gases are now beginning to destabilize global climate patterns, triggering extreme weather events and causing the migration of various life forms. One result is the spread of some diseases and the re-emergence of others.

2   Consider India. For much of last summer, temperatures had soared from their normal 26 to 32 centigrade (80 to 90 degrees Fahrenheit) and hovered around 52 centigrade. By fall, animal carcasses littered the plains; fleas multiplied in grain caches.

3   Above the baking landscape, rippling columns of air ascended, leaving low-pressure systems that lured in moisture-laden ocean air. Three-month monsoons bequeathed breeding sites for malaria, dengue fever and pneumonic plague. By the time the epidemics ran their course, as many as 4,000 Indians had died.

4   In the United States, long-range forecasts by the Climate Analysis Center of the National Oceanic and Atmospheric Administration show increased potential for conditions conducive to vector-borne disease. This summer may be ripe for the expansion of dengue fever in the American Southeast and the re-emergence of Eastern equine encephalitis in the Northeast.

5   The world has a chance to confront this new menace at the international climate convention under way in Berlin. It was convened to refine and implement the global climate treaty signed in Rio de Janeiro in 1992. The conference has an opportunity to reduce significantly the world's output of carbon dioxide and other greenhouse gases and thereby help control not only climate change but the resulting spread of disease.

6   The critical role of global climate change in the worldwide movement of many disease-carriers has received little attention. The process is simple. Weeds, rodents, insects, bacteria and viruses—known as R-strategists—rapidly reproduce and colonize disturbed environments. Larger, slower developing K-strategists such as predatory birds and animals are superior competitors under stable conditions, but they submit to the opportunists when their habitat is fragmented, polluted or altered by rapid climatic change.

7   Fossil records—"paleothermometers"—demonstrate that during warm epochs insects have proliferated and extended their range more swiftly than have plants. One indication of the current spread of climate-related disease can be seen in the migration of aedes aegypti mosquitoes, which carry dengue and yellow fever. Historically restricted by temperature to 1,000 meters (3,300 feet) in altitude, the mosquitoes now have been reported above 1,350 meters in Costa Rica and at 2,200 meters in Colombia. Malaria carriers are appearing at higher elevations in Central Africa.

8   These changes parallel the movement of plants to higher altitudes on three continents and the northward shift of California coastal marine species.

9   The movement of insects, rodents, microorganisms and weeds affects agriculture as well as humans. But predictions of favorable crop yields in North America under warming scenarios take no

account of plant pests and pathogens. Chemical control measures offer no comfort. The long-term use of pesticides to destroy proliferating pests cultivates genetic resistance and kills the fish, birds, lacewings and ladybugs that naturally regulate those populations.

10   Extreme weather conditions affect marine, plant and human health by affording opportunistic species fresh terrain and generating new bursts of activity. The drying up of ponds concentrates microorganisms, while floods contaminate clean water. Droughts encourage locusts and rodents; floods foster fungi.

11   The phenomenon called El Niño, the periodic eastward displacement of the Pacific's great warm water pool, is the most powerful known determinant of global weather patterns. Warm and cold El Niño events are associated with the deaths of large numbers of sea mammals; El Niño warm years are associated with upsurges of malaria globally, cholera in Bangladesh, hepatitis, diarrhea and dysentery in South America and encephalitis in Massachusetts.

12   We have entered the fifth consecutive year of anomalous conditions in the Pacific. Since 1877, no El Niño event had persisted beyond three years. Recent studies reveal enormous amounts of heat accumulating in the North Atlantic, Indian and Southwest Pacific depths. And—of vital concern—warm pools are collecting under polar ice sheets.

13   Warm water readily evaporates, increasing the atmospheric cycling of water. Warmer seas may further alter precipitation patterns affecting distribution of insects as well as marine life.

14   Harmful algal "blooms" are appearing with increasing frequency and variety. Last summer, algal blooms covered one-third of a heated Baltic Sea. Since 1991 a "red tide" has recurred annually in the Chilean Straits of Magellan.

15   Any effort to deal with climate instability must recognize its environmental and ecological impact, for aesthetic reasons but also to protect complex systems of biological controls over pests and pathogens.

16   The mounting physical and biological indications of climate change suggest that greenhouse gas buildup from the burning of fossil fuel (6 billion tons, or 1 ton per person, of carbon emitted annually) may have begun to affect planet-wide systems. And the progression may not be a straight line. Prolonged periods of climate "regimes" can change abruptly. Ice-core samples from Greenland indicate that the jump from the last Ice Age to the present hospitable "Holocene" state took not centuries, as once believed, but three to seven years.

17   Thus public perception must jump from debating "global warming" to understanding climate change, variability and stability. Will we read the signs of global change and react before the resilience of natural systems is exceeded? Or must we wait, as have earlier societies stricken by epidemics, to be transformed by them?

18   The World Health Organization, and the Centers for Disease Control and Prevention in Atlanta, need supplemental capacity to detect and respond to emerging diseases.

19   The global redistribution of infectious diseases may prove to be only one of the "surprise" areas of climate change. A fully integrated ecological risk assessment that included the spiraling losses in well-being, agriculture, development, tourism and insurance would suggest that the societal costs of not shifting from business as usual are far greater than we imagine.

20   This expanding potential disaster elevates the urgency for curbing consumption of coal, oil and timber—to slow the rate of climate change and allow time for life forms to adjust.

21   Protection of global health rests upon the efficient use of all resources. Ultimately our well-being depends upon our skill in duplicating the exquisite economy of photosynthesis by harnessing the sun to generate our energy needs.

22   Unfortunately, the outlook for substantial achievement at the Berlin conference does not inspire optimism. Divisions between the industrialized countries and the developing world threaten any real progress. So do ancillary disputes between the world's oil-producing states, which oppose any meaningful emissions limits, and its smaller island nations, which have a special vulnerability to unstable climate and are pushing for a 20 percent reduction in emissions by the year 2005.

23   Many European countries are pushing for hard targets and timetables by which to reduce climate-altering emissions, while the U.S. delegation is willing to subject any such goals to prolonged negotiations before they are ratified.

24   Unfortunately, the threat is all too real, and time in which to respond is short.

DISCUSSION QUESTIONS

1. In small groups, brainstorm about the causes of greenhouse gases. How are they produced? How might they be prevented? How easy do you think it might be to prevent the buildup of man-made greenhouse gases?

161

2. According to this article, what is the relationship between greenhouse gases and climate changes? Do you know of any other evidence that would support this connection?

3. In small groups, brainstorm about the various extreme weather conditions this article alludes to. What are some of the more recent weather events that have brought devastation to various parts of the world? Do you think there might be other causes for these conditions than those mentioned in this article?

4. In small groups, draw a diagram or map that illustrates some of the ecological relationships discussed in this article. The diagram could take the form of a flow chart or cluster or map—whatever the group determines to be most appropriate for the connections you want to illustrate. Be prepared to present your diagram to the class.

5. The authors of this article ask, "Will we read the signs of global change and react before the resilience of natural systems is exceeded? Or must we wait, as have earlier societies stricken by epidemics, to be transformed by them?" To which earlier societies do you think the authors are referring? How would you respond to the authors' questions?

6. At the conclusion of this article, the authors state that while European countries are ready to meet the challenge of reducing climate-altering emissions at the Berlin conference, the United States delegation needs time to negotiate. Speculate about what issues, in the view of the U.S. delegation, might need to be negotiated.

WRITING ASSIGNMENTS

1. Write a problem-solution paper that outlines a plan for reducing climate-altering emissions. The paper should be addressed to members of your immediate community and should contain practical advice individuals can use during their daily routines. You might want to consider submitting your essay to the school newspaper for publication. Alternatively, write to your congressperson and address this issue from a national and/or international angle.

2. Write an informative report that explains the cause-and-effect relationship of fossil fuel emissions, climatic changes, and the spread of disease. Your report should employ specific examples to illustrate this relationship. You may want to use secondary sources to help develop your report.

3. The authors of this article assert that "A fully integrated ecological risk assessment that included the spiraling losses in well-being, agriculture, development, tourism and insurance would suggest that the societal costs of not shifting from business as usual are far greater than we imagine." Write a causal analysis essay that explores the societal ramifications of climatic changes induced by greenhouse gases.

4. The authors of this essay state that the international conference on climate change in Berlin was beleaguered by divisions between industrialized and developing nations as well as other special-interest groups. Create a roundtable discussion of what you think might have been said at this conference by delegates of various nations. The roundtable should include at least six participants (three industrialized nations and three developing nations). Choose nations from different continents and regions.

Q & A: FADING ECOLOGY MOVEMENT'S IDENTITY CRISIS

Ken Shulman

International Herald Tribune

■

The following selection is an interview Ken Shulman conducted in Rome with writer and theater director Luis Sepulveda, a global environmental activist. In this dialogue, Sepulveda comments on the present state of the ecological movement. Claiming that it is in "a crisis of identity," Sepulveda thinks that one side views political activism as "marginal," while the other side "sees politics as the resolution of our problem." However, Sepulveda asserts that the answer to ecological problems will be found in "a return to militant activism, to civil disobedience." As you read through this article, think about whether or not civil disobedience should be employed to bring about environmental reform, and, if so, what form it might take and under what circumstances it might be appropriate.

■

1   Q. Is the ecological movement in difficulty?

2   A. More than in difficulty, I'd say it's in a crisis of identity. One part of the movement sees political activism as marginal, and the other part sees politics as the resolution of our problem. I am more tied to the Latin American form of environmentalism, which sees the root of the problem in the relationship between power and economy. The European ecologists tie the environmental movement more to the political process, with its inevitable deals and compromises. I find this unacceptable.

3   Q. Was it a mistake to centralize the global ecological movement?

4   **A.** It was an error to centralize everything under the direction of London, to make decisions regarding vastly different situations across the globe in this one place. In Europe, the problem is defined as an effort to improve the natural environment.

5   In Eastern Europe, the problem is trying to contain a catastrophe. And in the Third World we have a situation on the brink of disaster. In the Amazon, for example, the problem is not simply the deforestation. People have to understand that if they want to stop the damage, they should not buy gold that is extracted from that region.

●

6   **Q.** In Europe, the Green parties seem to be losing their momentum.

7   **A.** Over the last four years, the ecological movement has lost nearly 400,000 members. I think the movement should try to be less sensationalist and to develop a global consciousness of the problem.

8   **Q.** Then it is a problem of direction?

9   **A.** The problem is that when an organization becomes too big, it becomes prey to the usual ills that plague all organizations.

10   **Q.** What is the answer?

11   **A.** The answer is a return to militant activism, to civil disobedience. The ecological movement was born out of the late 1960s as an evolution of the political protests around the world. Inspired by the spirit of revolution, a few people began to see the contradiction between progress and the quality of life. And they thought it might be possible to have a harmonious, rational progress without destroying the environment.

12   **Q.** Where do you draw the line?

13   **A.** The industrialized world devotes the better part of its energies to producing things that are not really necessary. Look how big a variety of stereo equipment and televisions you find on sale.

●

14   **Q.** Are you saying that the man on the street should sacrifice some of his comforts?

15   **A.** The man on the street can mount a resistance to the consumer mentality. It isn't possible to live without consuming. But that consumption does not have to be obsessive. Does he have to sacrifice certain things? I think so. We could certainly give up our production of arms. It comes down to redefining the concept of progress. Personally, I don't think that man's happiness depends on every person having a computer.

16   Q. What does his happiness depend on?

17   A. What is fundamental is a return to the normal activity of man. And the normal activity of man is movement. Why do we want to put an entire library into a computer? Why not walk to the library, to recover the time and rhythms of the library. The book we find there on the shelves is alive. We can touch it, turn the pages. Why do we want to watch television instead of going to the cinema? The cinema is a temple, a social necessity. So many of the things that are considered part of this progress are simply elements that increase man's isolation from his fellow man.

18   Q. Do you think you can convince people to give up their cars?

19   A. This will be very difficult. It is a question of political will, of organizing public transportation and getting people to use it. There are people, lots of them, who would gladly give up their cars to give up neuroses that the car creates.

20   Q. Is Greenpeace through facing off with Japanese whaling ships in rubber rafts?

21   A. This, too, is part of the work. I've done this all over the globe. And it is always dangerous. When there is the press, or international observers, you know they won't try to run you down. But with no witnesses, it's a mortal game. I am 100 percent committed to this battle.

DISCUSSION QUESTIONS

1. In small groups, brainstorm on what you know about the ecological movement. You might first freewrite individually and then share your thoughts to create a cluster. Share your findings with the class in a wider group discussion.

2. Sepulveda thinks that the ecological movement is having an identity crisis. Elaborate on what you think he means. What is an identity crisis? Can a movement (as opposed to a person) have an identity crisis?

3. Reread Sepulveda's response to Shulman's first question. What do you think Sepulveda means when he asserts that "the root of the problem [is] in the relationship between power and economy"?

4. Why does Sepulveda think it was a mistake to centralize the ecological movement? Do you agree with him? Why or why not?

5. Sepulveda asserts that "the movement should try to be less sensationalist and to develop a global consciousness." What do you think he means by this statement? Do you think his assertion is well-founded?

6. Sepulveda thinks that the answer to today's ecological problems is to return to "militant activism, to civil disobedience." Do you agree with him? Why or why not?

7. Sepulveda argues that "The man on the street can mount a resistance to the consumer mentality." What do you think he might mean by this statement? How can people "mount a resistance to the consumer mentality"? What would be the advantages and/or disadvantages of doing so?

WRITING ASSIGNMENTS

1. Sepulveda asserts toward the conclusion of the interview that so many things that are considered part of progress only serve to "increase man's isolation from his fellow man." Sepulveda offers a few examples of this phenomenon, but can they be generalized to a trend? In an exploratory essay, respond to the following question: "To what extent does progress contribute to a person's isolation and/or alienation?"

2. Sepulveda states that "The industrialized world devotes the better part of its energies to producing things that are not really necessary." Do you agree or disagree with this statement? In a well-developed essay, respond to the following question: "To what extent does the industrialized world produce goods that are unnecessary?" Your essay should move beyond generalities by using specific details and examples to develop and support your arguments. You might begin with a prewriting exercise such as freewriting or clustering on this topic.

3. Sepulveda states that "over the last four years, the ecological movement has lost nearly 400,000 members." Why do you think this drop in participation might have occurred? Write a paper that offers potential reasons for this change. You will need to consult secondary sources in order to support your viewpoint.

4. Choose an environmental movement or organization such as Green-peace and write an informative report on their work. What are their origins? What have they done? Where are they going? You will need to conduct some research to complete this assignment.

5. Sepulveda asserts that he doesn't believe "man's happiness depends on every person having a computer." Shulman responds to this assertion with the question, "What does his happiness depend on?" How would you respond to this question? In an exploratory essay, respond to the following question: "What does a person's happiness depend on?"

CHAPTER SIX WRITING ASSIGNMENTS

1. Luis Sepulveda in "Q & A: Fading Ecology Movement's Identity Crisis" argues that "a return to militant activism, to civil disobedience" is necessary for environmental and ecological reform. Likewise, Reginald Dale reports in "There Aren't Plenty of Fish in the Sea" that a Canadian fisheries protection vessel fired shots that may have been illegal in order to protect a northwest Atlantic fishery from plundering. Both examples illustrate the view of some people that civil disobedience and a militant approach are an essential part of the environmental movement. What is your opinion? In a well-developed essay, respond to the following question: "To what extent should civil disobedience and militant action be part of the ecological/environmental movement?" Support your opinions with specific reasons. Develop your points with specific details.

2. Brainstorm about the environmental issues concerning your community at this time. Choose one issue and then write a report that both explains the problem and offers a plan for solving the problem. You may want to interview key persons involved with the issue. Use the information gathered from the interviews to help you develop your report.

3. Drawing upon at least three sources from the readings in this chapter, write an essay that explores the following question: "To what extent does industrial progress need to be balanced by environmental considerations?" Be sure to support your generalizations with specific details and examples from the readings.

The Sporting Life

Baseball, soccer, tennis, golf, basketball, skiing . . . the list goes on. People take great pleasure in being either sports participants or spectators, and the appeal of sports is international. We hear about or watch European soccer and basketball championships, French cycling races, or Japanese baseball. Sports fill a large portion of daily newspapers and television and radio newscasts. However, sports news is not simply game summaries and statistics. Sports news often covers controversial issues such as race relations and civil war. The selections chosen for this chapter all concern sports-related news items that ask us to think critically about the world of sports.

The chapter opens with an article by Rob Hughes entitled "What They Really Need Is a Round Ball." In this selection, Hughes examines how soccer could play an important role in improving race relations in South Africa, and he suggests sending Brazil's world-champion soccer team to South Africa, noting that the Brazilian team is "a champion of multiracial expression on the playing field."

In another selection about soccer entitled "A Sport Courting Disaster," Hughes reports on the conflict between soccer players and the boards that govern European soccer. According to Hughes, European soccer players are not given the same rights as other employees. Jean-Marc Bosman, a Belgian soccer player, brought a case before the courts in which he contested a soccer club's right to retain a player for trade purposes even after the expiration of a contract. Bosman's one wish is that all soccer players enjoy "the same right of all workers to seek employment anywhere within the community provided they are not bound by a mutual contract."

In the United States, there is also strife between players and team own-ers. In an article titled "Hall of Fame Inductees Sound an Alarm for Base-ball," Ira Berkow writes about a warning that baseball legends Mike Schmidt and Richie Ashburn sounded when they were inducted into the Baseball Hall of Fame in Cooperstown, New York. Making reference to the baseball strike, which shortened one of the best seasons in recent years, Schmidt and Ashburn urged players and owners to work out their differences. They warned that if the tensions and poor attitudes continued, fans would lose respect for this national pastime.

Moving to the international sports arena, in an article entitled "From Basketball to Politics," Christopher Clarey examines the tensions that erupted between teams from Greece, Croatia, Lithuania, and Yugoslavia during a European basketball championship. Although Yugoslavia no longer exists as one nation, there is a "Yugoslavia" team composed of players from Serbia and Montenegro. The Croatians and Serbians are former country-men divided by a civil war, and strong emotions on the court were difficult to control. In a blatantly political gesture, the Croatians walked out of the arena as the Yugoslavs were about to receive their gold medals.

The chapter concludes with a lighter piece entitled "When Fashion Moves into the Sports Arena." Mary Blume explores how sports figures are currently being used to promote fashion. Blume reports that the operator of a Paris modeling agency, Marilyn Gauthier, has started to employ sports figures in glamour shots, insisting that "Athletes are today's heroes, like rock stars were in the '80s." Although Gauthier claims she is the first to think of combining fashion and sport, Blume recalls that, more than twenty years ago, the New York Jets quarterback Joe Namath "posed fetchingly in women's panty hose in a brilliant ad campaign."

As you read these selections, you might think about why sports can make such interesting news for many people. Why do people enjoy sports so much, and why are they so interested in sports-related news? What do you think attracts people to sports issues?

WHAT THEY REALLY NEED
IS A ROUND BALL

Rob Hughes

International Herald Tribune

◼

In the following selection, Rob Hughes asks whether or not South Africa should promote soccer rather than rugby as a national sport. In accordance with the Mandela government's "rainbow" message of racial equity, a multiracial South African rugby team played host to the Rugby World Cup. Yet, as Hughes reports, there are many empty seats at rugby matches. Rugby was the game favored by the white Afrikaners who ruled South Africa for so long; the four-fifths "nonwhite" majority in South Africa has always preferred soccer. According to Hughes, soccer has a history of promoting racial equality on the playing field, and he cites many black youths who have had very successful soccer careers. He adds that even while Mandela was incarcerated, "the predominantly black soccer association in South Africa defied apartheid's governors and welcomed whites among its teams." As you read Hughes's commentary, consider to what extent sports can help promote causes such as racial equality. Why do you think sports playing fields might be an ideal place to help such causes? What specific factors involved in sports might promote or discourage racial equality?

◼

1 LONDON—Are they running with the wrong ball in South Africa? The vibes from Cape Town promote sport—apartheid's tool for too many wretched years—as a symbol of change, a force toward togetherness. And the Mandela government rightly grasped the first opportunity that came its way to host an event such as the Rugby World Cup.

2 Whatever color we are, whatever code we pursue, we can follow the president's "rainbow" message. But, away from Newlands stadium,

we notice empty seats at the games, and this, in a country of 40 million people reportedly so euphoric, invites questions.

3   *Is* the ball the right shape? The oval rugger ball has passed, for four decades, exclusively through Afrikaner hands, white hands. Nelson Mandela, in common with the four-fifths of the populace who are non-whites, preferred soccer.

4   Now it would be idiotic to insist that South Africa should have waited for soccer's World Cup. That, given the politics, the finances, and the need for a dozen first-class stadia as well as an infrastructure to accommodate and move millions of visiting fans, would not have been possible until the next century.

5   However, it is neither too soon, nor too late, for Mandela and Steve Tshwete, his minister for sport and recreation, to set the round ball rolling for the majority of South Africans. One call from the president to Brazil's sports minister would likely do the trick. Brazil, the world champion of soccer, also happens to be in a class of its own as a champion of multiracial expression on the playing field. Its sports minister, none other than Pelé, has few heroes but Nelson Mandela is certainly one of them.

6   Think of the lift to people in the townships, think of the pride and the sense of belonging a visit by Brazil's team would bring. The match would not advance the housing program, or solve the need for schools and hospitals, but in the deprived masses it might light a spark of pride. Soccer, no matter how scintillating the rugby over the next few weeks, would be something for *them.*

7   And why stop at Brazil? Next, call the Netherlands. Call Ajax, the new conqueror of Europe.

8   Last Wednesday, as Mandela prepared his speech to the world (and as he spoke of his disappointment that the Springbok team is all white), the Amsterdam team dethroned AC Milan in the Champions' Cup final. Ajax has as many blacks as whites. Its dressing room after the big match in Vienna flowed with champagne being drunk by players who look too boyish for alcohol.

9   Patrick Kluivert, for example. Young, gifted and black, he scored the only goal of the final. And got the ball from Frank Rijkaard. They are two of a kind. Both Amsterdammers, both of Surinam stock. Kluivert, 18, is on the threshold of a brilliant career; Rijkaard, 32, is retiring.

10   They provide an insight into the generational game that has revived Ajax. For obvious reasons, Rijkaard rather than Johan Cruyff has been the catalyst for recruiting talented black youngsters to Ajax. Kluivert got not only the pass but his inspiration from this man. Kluivert was 7 when he joined the Ajax training school. His European

Cup medal will be kept beside a photograph of himself as a mascot for the team, taken on the pitch by Rijkaard.

11   The story turns full circle. Not only for Kluivert but for Edgar Davids, for Clarence Seedorf, for other black Amsterdam youths whose triumph will probably lead them away to the money pot of Italian clubs.

12   Rijkaard did that. He won two European Cup medals with Milan before returning to pay his dues to Ajax. Now, as the team's coach, Louis van Gaal, contemplates who he can sell to perpetuate the youth plan and to help pay for the new Ajax wonder-stadium, Rijkaard leaves with a plea: "Not Kluivert, not yet. He is too young to go to Italy, he will develop better by staying with Ajax."

13   What will be will be. But do you detect a parallel between the stories of Ajax and Springbok rugby?

14   A large element to the freedom of movement within Ajax's success has roots in the former Dutch colony in South America now called Surinam. Once a slave colony. The Afrikaners who ruled South Africa, and whose game is rugger, also descend from Dutch settlers. They might find, once the profits from this World Cup are channeled down to former no-go areas of their country, that blacks pass the ball around at least as well as they have done. For the joy of sport, the fulfillment of it, is that we are all brothers under the skin.

15   Those pushing rugby must first prize the round ball of the overwhelming majority of black kids. Their cause will be helped by the sight of Jonah Lomu, quite the most thrilling physical specimen of the Rugby World Cup thus far, who is of Tongan extraction. Nevertheless, there are a score of South Africans, black and white, chasing the rainbow of soccer rewards abroad.

16   Lucas Radebe is an example. Originally from Bophuthatswana, then of Soweto's Kaiser Chiefs, he now belongs to Leeds United in England. So why shouldn't England, the mother country of soccer, also send a team to play a mini-tournament in South Africa? Just as Ruud Gullit, another Dutch-Surinam player, pledged himself to freeing Nelson Mandela from Robben Island, so there are like spirits in England who would leap at a request to play for the new non-racial ideal.

17   What a tournament, what a party it could be: Brazil, Holland, England, South Africa and either Ghana or Nigeria, whose talents have already shown what Africa can achieve on the global stage.

18   There are compelling reasons to make haste with such games. One is to recognize that, even while Mandela and Tshwete were captive, the predominantly black soccer association in South Africa defied apartheid's governors and welcomed whites among its teams.

175

19   Second, if it is left too long the Europeans might be left behind. Soccer is like a fever: it is indiscriminate, but it flourishes where the temperature is highest and resistance is weakest.

DISCUSSION QUESTIONS

1. In small groups, discuss what you know about apartheid. What is its history? How would you describe it? What do you think its relationship to sports is? Make a cluster or brainstorming diagram to represent your thoughts. Be prepared to share your ideas with the rest of the class.

2. Hughes writes that "The vibes from Cape Town promote sport—apartheid's tool for too many wretched years—as a symbol of change, a force toward togetherness." How might sports serve as "a symbol of change, a force toward togetherness"? How could sports also be used as a tool of apartheid?

3. Hughes writes, "Think of the lift to people in the townships, think of the pride and the sense of belonging a visit by Brazil's team [soccer's world champion] would bring. The match would not advance the housing program, or solve the need for schools and hospitals, but in the deprived masses it might light a spark of pride." Explain how pride could help the people of the townships. What is the benefit of increased pride?

4. Throughout this article, Hughes suggests that South Africa should pay more attention to soccer rather than rugby. Why does he feel this way? Do you think his opinion is valid?

5. Hughes concludes his article with the statement, "Soccer is like a fever: it is indiscriminate, but it flourishes where the temperature is highest and resistance is weakest." What do you think he means here? Why do you suppose he ends the article in this manner?

WRITING ASSIGNMENTS

1. Write an exploratory essay in which you respond to the following question: "To what extent can a sport such as soccer help to solve racism and prejudice?" Be sure to support your opinions with specific examples and details.

2. Write an informative report that explains the relationship between South African apartheid and sports. How did apartheid affect people's participation in sports? How did it affect fans? How has this relationship between sports and apartheid evolved in recent years? Be sure to support your main points with specific details.

3. Research the life story of one of the athletes mentioned in this article. Then write a short biography of the athlete's sports career. How did it begin? Where is it headed? Be sure to develop your biography with specific details.

A SPORT COURTING DISASTER

Rob Hughes

International Herald Tribune

■

In the following selection, Rob Hughes reports on two court cases that contested the belief that professional soccer can be self-governing in the European Community. Jean-Marc Bosman, a Belgian player, challenged the right of soccer clubs to retain players for trade purposes even after their contracts have expired. Under the Treaty of Rome, Bosman was in the right. According to Hughes, Bosman's goal was simple: "The right of all workers to seek employment anywhere within the community provided they are not bound by a mutual contract." Hughes also gives an account of three small Welsh soccer clubs that sought damages from the Football Association of Wales for being forced to play in a league they did not wish to be in. According to Hughes, the soccer federation apparently forbids clubs and club members "to seek justice in a court of law against their federation *even if that country's law allows the federation's decisions to be contested in a civil court.*" While reading this article, you might think about sports stars as people who have rights. Why do you suppose organizations want to maintain a level of control over their players that reaches beyond the legal system?

■

1   LONDON—Can sport live within the law of the land? That may seem a strange question, stranger still in Europe, where professional soccer has operated legally for more than a century. Yet the higher the commercial stakes, the greater the conflict between common law and the quasi-rules that govern soccer.

2   The very fabric of the sport, the belief that soccer can be self-governing, will be threatened in two courts this month. In Luxembourg, at the European Court of Justice, a very determined Belgian player is

to challenge the rights of clubs to retain players beyond their contractual agreement, or to sell them for million-dollar fees.

3   Should Jean-Marc Bosman win his case—and under the Treaty of Rome he is likely to do so—the end of soccer financing as we know it is nigh. Backruptcies, even of clubs that are institutions, will ensue; some individual players will become as rich and as footloose as the top American professional athletes; many others will be sacrificed, out of the sport, out of a job.

4   Bosman versus "The Game" is the test case that has been coming since the European Community was formed. His claim is a simple one: The right of all workers to seek employment anywhere within the community provided they are not bound by a mutual contract. Soccer administrators across the continent—indeed, throughout the world, for Europe is the buying mecca of soccer—are running scared.

5   From UEFA to Madrid, from Milan to London, the general secretaries with vested interests are pleading that the European Court of Justice heed the history of their sport. They ask, in effect, that the judges recognize soccer as a special case, a work pool separate from the common sea of European markets.

6   Bosman regrets the trouble he has caused. A quiet man, he was pushed into a rebel's cloak because of the way the system exploited him. Having captained Belgium's national youth team, having played half a dozen times for the Belgium B side, he was 25 when his club sought to retain him on a quarter of his previous wage at the end of his contract in 1990.

7   When Bosman refused, and asked to leave, RC Liege exercised its option under Belgian federation rules to demand a trading fee of four times the fee it paid for him. That effectively put him off-limits to buyers, or at least made him an unattractive proposition. Still, two French teams did bid for Bosman. Neither could meet RC Liege's price, so, at 27, his athletic prime wasting away, he became a renegade, playing in the Indian Ocean resort of La Reunion.

8   The strain broke his marriage but not his will. After years of toiling through the Belgian courts, he is now on the steps of the European Court, seeking $450,000 damages from RC Liege, the Belgian FA and UEFA, who "prejudiced his right to free circulation" in soccer.

9   The player and his lawyer believe all transfer fees—the money paid by one team to another to trade in human potential—are illegal. "I want players to be free at the end of their contract to work where they want in Europe, the same as people in other walks of life," says Bosman.

10   A simple wish, but with potentially ruinous consequences for an industry that has enjoyed, from Day 1 of the EC, a gentleman's agreement to operate outside the Treaty of Rome.

11   For five years no one in soccer has been in Jean-Marc Bosman's corner. Now, as his day of judgment nears, they flock to him. The men of power to whom $450,000 is one night's takings, the politicians canvassed by those men of power, even the trade unionists, knock on his door and say don't do it. Maybe he will, maybe he won't. There is talk of an out-of-court settlement, of the Belgian federation or someone else paying Bosman the $450,000 to drop his crusade.

12   Meanwhile, three small clubs in Wales are scheduled to go to the High Court in London on March 13, seeking $900,000 damages for the loss of their rights to trade in their home towns.

13   Newport AFC, Colwyn Bay and Caernarfon are suing the Football Association of Wales for restraint of trade and breach of contract. The association sought to force the clubs into playing in a new Welsh league while they preferred a higher grade of soccer and the higher profits from playing across the border in English leagues.

14   The FAW exiled them, forbade them to play even home matches in their own stadiums. A petty dispute, you might think, and so it was until FIFA attempted to arbitrate. The clubs are a week from the court of law, and now in breach of FIFA statutes.

15   For article 57 of those statutes makes it a sin for clubs or club members to seek justice in a court of law against their federation *even if that country's law allows the federation's decisions to be contested in a civil court.*

16   By that criterion, Jean-Marc Bosman is out of order. The Welsh clubs are out of order. And soccer is a long way from the playing fields. We are entering corridors where the only winners will be the big wigs of the law itself, the lawyers and barristers happy to take soccer's surplus cash.

17   It will end in tears. But then, so could the "beautiful game," as Pelé called it.

18   Last weekend, in Scotland, five men of soccer met at Turnberry, a location famous for the gentle game of golf. There, at the 109th annual meeting of the International Football Association Board, those five betrayed the oldest rule in soccer's book.

19   It is a game of two 45-minute halves. The ethos of soccer lies in the players' ability to pace themselves over that time; continuity is of the essence, and some of FIFA's recent rule changes were made precisely to ensure this continuity.

180

20   Now Graham Kelly, Jim Farry and Alun Evans, the chief executives of the English, Scottish and Welsh federations, together with FIFA's president, João Havelange, and its general secretary, Sepp Blatter—have agreed to experiment with two-minute "timeouts."

21   These American-style breaks in play can be called twice in either half by either team. FIFA says the coaches want them, but many of us suspect that television wants them more—as commercial breaks. There should be a law against it.

DISCUSSION QUESTIONS

1. Why do you think Hughes titled this article "A Sport Courting Disaster"? What rhetorical effect does the headline have on you as a reader?

2. Hughes opens the article with the question, "Can sport live within the law of the land?" What is your opinion? Can you think of any other sports besides soccer that have compromised the law of the land? Support your ideas with specific examples.

3. Hughes writes that Bosman's "claim is a simple one: The right of all workers to seek employment anywhere within the community provided they are not bound by a mutual contract." What do you think of this goal? Do you think sports figures should have the same rights as all other employees?

WRITING ASSIGNMENTS

1. The article refers to the Treaty of Rome. Write an informative report that explains what the purpose of this treaty is. The paper will require you to do some outside research. Develop the report with specific details and facts. Be prepared to present your findings to your fellow students.

2. Imagine that you are a member of the jury in the Jean-Marc Bosman case. Write a dialogue between another member of the jury and yourself in which you argue for or against Bosman's case. You may want to do some more research on this case before writing the dialogue.

3. Write a paper in which you respond to the following question: "To what extent are athletes treated fairly by club owners?" Your essay may deal with soccer exclusively and/or use other sports. Use specific examples and details to support your opinions.

HALL OF FAME INDUCTEES
SOUND AN ALARM FOR BASEBALL

Ira Berkow

New York Times Service

■

In the following selection, Ira Berkow reports on the induction ceremony of former Philadelphia Phillies heroes Mike Schmidt and Richie Ashburn into the Baseball Hall of Fame in Cooperstown, New York. During the ceremony, both Schmidt and Ashburn noted that, as a result of the baseball strike, game attendance was down and fans were unhappy with the behavior of both players and owners. Schmidt commented that fans' respect for the game is in sharp decline. Yet more than 25,000 people showed up for the induction ceremony in Cooperstown. As Berkow notes, "it is clear that there remains in America a hunger and yearning for baseball." As you read this article, think about what you felt during the baseball strike. Do you remember it? What feelings can you recall? Do you agree that fans have lost respect for the game?

■

1   COOPERSTOWN, New York—It was a day when all should have been right with the world, and with baseball in particular. The sun was bright and a spirited crowd, a sea of red caps in sprawling Clark Field, was there to honor the two Philadelphia Phillies, Mike Schmidt and Richie Ashburn, being inducted into the Baseball Hall of Fame. Yet a note of alarm was struck. By Schmidt and Ashburn.

2   "The game," Schmidt said Sunday, "has reached a crossroads. Take a look at the empty seats in ball parks and the empty ball fields in playgrounds. It concerns me, and for those in baseball, it should scare you."

3   "Let's get this mess straightened out," Ashburn said. "We're here without an agreement between players and owners. We're here without a commissioner. I can't believe this."

4   The backlash of the players' strike last August that motivated the owners to shut down one of the best seasons in recent memory, to draw a curtain on the playoffs and World Series, has soured fans to an extent that, it seems, has not made an appreciable dent with those who run the game, or run in the game.

5   "The passion, humility and respect" for the game and its fans, said Schmidt, is in perilous decline. Today's "look-at-me, in-your-face attitude of players, supported by television, is highly suspect."

6   The backlash has been felt in Cooperstown itself, this serene, almost make-believe 19th century village in which the lovely fiction that baseball was invented here is harmlessly perpetrated. Attendance at the Hall of Fame is down 13 percent this year. This, combined with a 20 percent drop in major league attendance and drops in television ratings, should, as Schmidt said, scare the pants off those who earn their living from it.

7   It hasn't seemed to. The owners still believe they can strong-arm the players into accepting their unacceptable demands. The players, in too many cases, still feel that they can abuse the fans with impunity.

8   Schmidt called for the players and owners to sit down and come to an agreement on their contract so that fans can root for their teams. And he urged that they agree on an independent commissioner.

9   That, of course, is almost humorous. The last thing the owners want is an independent commissioner. Every time a commissioner acts independently they throw him out, from Happy Chandler to Fay Vincent. Which is why they're overjoyed with Bud Selig, whose first priority is not to the world of baseball but to his little fiefdom in Milwaukee.

10   For the third straight year, or every year that the owner of the Brewers has been interim commissioner, he has not had the time to show up for the Hall of Fame induction ceremonies, one of the highlights of each season.

11   (It should also be noted that the de facto commissioner of the players, Donald Fehr of the union, was not in attendance, either.)

12   Despite these "tough times for baseball," as Schmidt termed it, the crowd of an estimated 25,000 to 28,000 was the largest in the 56-hear history of the event. "And here are no fireworks, no giveaways," said Ashburn. "It is just fans coming here for the game of baseball."

13   For all the goofy romance attributed to fields of dreams and fathers playing catch with sons, there is a thread to the game that reaches from observers like Walt Whitman and Mark Twain to, well, to a lot of pops and kids, today—still.

14   During the some two hours of the ceremonies, which included inductions of Leon Day, a Negro leagues pitcher; Vic Willis, a turn-of-the-century ace for, primarily, the Boston Beaneaters and the Pittsburgh Pirates, and William Hulbert, a baseball pioneer, the fans sitting and standing under the sea of red caps cheered readily.

15   It got particularly loud when Schmidt urged that Pete Rose should be in the Hall and when Ashburn spoke of the fans' needs. Ovations also were rendered when any of the other 30 Hall of Fame members, from Feller and Musial to Reese to Reggie, were introduced.

16   And if this day in Cooperstown was any indication, then it is clear that there remains in America a hunger and yearning for baseball.

17   The question, as advanced by Schmidt and Ashburn, was: Is anybody listening?

DISCUSSION QUESTIONS

1.   In small groups, discuss what characteristics of baseball attract fans to the sport. Why is it so appealing to so many people? Why has it endured? Will it endure? Make a brainstorming map or cluster to illustrate your thoughts. Be prepared to present your ideas to the class.

2.   Berkow writes that "The players, in too many cases, still feel that they can abuse the fans with impunity." Do you think that Berkow's claim is valid? If you are a fan of baseball, what has your experience been? Do you think there has been an attitude change on the part of players since the strike?

3.   Reread the first paragraph of this article. What is its rhetorical effect? In what ways does it prepare you for what follows?

4.   The baseball players struck over salaries and perks. What is your opinion of the salaries that professional athletes are paid? Do you think they are underpaid or overpaid? Support your opinion with specific reasons and evidence.

WRITING ASSIGNMENTS

1. Research the baseball strike of the summer of 1994. Then write a report that examines the history of the strike and its outcome. Use specific details and facts to develop your paper. Be prepared to present your findings to the class.

2. Berkow writes, "For all the goofy romance attributed to fields of dreams and fathers playing catch with sons, there is a thread to the game that reaches from observers like Walt Whitman and Mark Twain to, well, to a lot of pops and kids, today—still." Write a paper that explains what Berkow means by the phrase *a thread to the game*. What is that thread? How can it be defined? Use specific details and examples to illustrate your explanation of the phrase.

3. Berkow mentions "field of dreams," Mark Twain, and Walt Whitman—all references to creative endeavors on the subject of baseball. Find a creative work—a poem, a song, a film, a story, a painting—that focuses on baseball. Then write a critique of the work. How does the creative piece strike you? How well does it represent the sport? What particular aspects of baseball does the work emphasize or romanticize or downplay? Be sure to support your opinions with specific details and facts.

FROM BASKETBALL TO POLITICS

Christopher Clarey

New York Times Service

■

Although Yugoslavia has been torn apart by civil war between Serbians and Croatians and no longer exists as a nation, there is nevertheless a "Yugoslavian" basketball team. All of the players on this team are from Serbia and Montenegro; there are no players from Croatia. The following article by Christopher Clarey comments upon the political tensions that surfaced during the European basketball championships. At the close of a tumultuous tournament, the Croatians, once former countrymen of the "Yugoslavs," walked out of the arena during the awards ceremony just as the Yugoslavs were about to receive their gold medals. As one player stated, "Sports and politics should not go together." As you read this article, consider this comment. Do you agree with it? Could sports and politics ever mix? Can you think of other situations when sports and politics have been thrown together and produced negative results?

■

1   ATHENS—Midway through the European basketball championships, Vlade Divac said, "Sports and politics should not go together."

2   He was not the only player to say so during the relatively tranquil last week of competition. But on the night the tournament ended in Yugoslavia's 96-90 victory over Lithuania, there was no escaping politics.

3   First the Lithuanians briefly walked off the court with two minutes to play because of the refereeing, then the third-place Croatians walked off the medal stand and out of the arena just before their former countrymen, the Yugoslavs, were to receive their gold medals.

4   As the flags rose and a small marching band tried to play the Yugoslav national anthem, the Greek crowd booed the winners, just as they had booed them for much of the game. The jeers drowned out the anthem, just as politics ended up drowning out the basketball.

5   "I'm disappointed about everything," said Divac, the Yugoslav's center who plays for the Los Angeles Lakers.

6   It was the sixth European victory for a team called Yugoslavia, but this title was won by players from only Serbia and Montenegro, in their first major tournament since the lifting of a three-year ban from international competition.

7   Under different circumstances, post-game discussion would have centered on the overall quality of Sunday night's final and the several remarkable performances.

8   The most remarkable was that of Yugoslav point guard Alexander Djordjevic, who got a tournament-high 41 points and made 9 of 12 3-point shots.

9   The Lithuanian guard Sarunas Marciulionis scored 32 points and was named the championships' most valuable player. Center Arvidas Sabonis, who is bound for the National Basketball Association, got 20 points and eight rebounds, although fouling out with five minutes to go.

10   And it was in those last five minutes that the trouble began. Already unhappy with the officiating, particularly that of the American referee George Toliver, the Lithuanians were enraged when Toliver called an offensive foul on forward Saulius Stombergas with two minutes left and Yugoslavia ahead, 87-83. According to people near the bench, Sabonis then made a lewd gesture at Toliver and the team was given its technical foul.

11   The Lithuanians walked out, and Sabonis even indicated that he would pay any fine incurred out of his own pocket. But then they returned, and the three free throws gave the Yugoslavs a seven-point lead.

12   "We weren't brave enough," said their coach, Vladas Garastas. "We should not have come back on."

13   Garastas and Marciulionis, however, were certainly bold in the post-game news conference, insinuating that Borislav Stankovic, the secretary-general of basketball's governing body FIBA, has influenced the tournament schedule and officiating in favor of his fellow Yugoslavs.

14   "Basketball in Europe hit the bottom tonight," Marciulionis said. "This wasn't basketball anymore . . . The problems are much, much deeper."

15   The Greek fans, certainly not pleased that the Yugoslavs had eliminated their team in the semifinals, were clearly in agreement. Throughout the second half, they rained disdain on FIBA and when the game ended they changed their chant to "Lithuania is the champion."

16   The Yugoslavs were left to celebrate in a largely hostile environment, and not all of them behaved magnanimously.

17   Predrag Danilovic, a future member of the Miami Heat, ran behind one basket, faced a group of jeering spectators and grabbed his crotch.

18   "I think it was not a good thing he did," his coach, Dusan Ivkovic, said later.

19   Shortly thereafter, with their bronze medals still around their necks, the Croatians stepped down from the podium and left the arena. The blatantly political gesture was in stark contrast to the tenor of the Croatians' largely apolitical comments throughout the tournament.

20   "It was pretty sad," said Florian Wanninger, a FIBA spokesman. "We had some hints that there might be some problems, and we will react because what they did is against regulations. I can't tell you how but we will react."

21   None of the Croatians stayed around to discuss it, but the Yugoslavs certainly made their feelings known.

22   "It was stupid," Danilovic said. "My team would never have done that."

DISCUSSION QUESTIONS

1.   In small groups, discuss what you know about the former Yugoslavia and its dissolution. What happened? How were the people affected? Create a brainstorming map or cluster to help you focus your thoughts. Be prepared to share your ideas with classmates.

2.   The opening paragraph of this article contains the line, "Sports and politics should not go together." To what extent do you agree or disagree with this statement? Are there any occasions when sports and politics might work together? Support your opinion with specific reasons.

3.   One of the players in the tournament stated, "This wasn't basketball anymore . . . The problems are much, much deeper." Speculate about these problems. How deep are they? What forms do they take?

4.   What characteristics of competitive sports such as basketball make them vulnerable to political agendas? Can you think of other examples of sports events or figures that have become politicized?

WRITING ASSIGNMENTS

1. Write an essay that responds to the following question: "Can sports and politics ever mix?" Be sure to support your main ideas with specific examples and details. Use a prewriting strategy such as clustering or brainstorming to help you get started. You may also want to do some outside research.

2. A FIBA (international basketball's governing body) spokesperson said of the trouble at the tournament, "We had some hints that there might be some problems, and we will react because what they did is against regulations. I can't tell you how but we will react." Write a letter to FIBA that expresses how you think the basketball association should respond to the incident. Your letter should use specific details and facts to make your point.

3 Write a roundtable discussion in which players from the Lithuanian, Greek, Yugoslavian, and Croatian basketball teams discuss the following question: "Is it possible for sports to remain apolitical?" The roundtable discussion should refer specifically to the game discussed in the article as well as other appropriate sports examples.

WHEN FASHION MOVES INTO THE SPORTS ARENA

Mary Blume

International Herald Tribune

■

In this selection, Mary Blume reports on the use of sports figures to promote fashion. Marilyn Gauthier, who operates a Paris modeling agency, has recently started a division called Marilyn Sports, which she is promoting with sports figures such as boxer Evander Holyfield. She claims that she is the first to think of sports in terms of fashion. However, Blume points out that more than twenty years ago, Joe Namath, the New York Jets quarterback, "posed fetchingly in women's panty hose in a brilliant ad campaign." Gauthier insists, "Athletes are today's heroes, like rock stars were in the '80s." Gauthier's one unanticipated problem is juggling an athlete's training schedule with fashion shoots. As you read this selection, think about why you think fashion and sports are being mixed. What is the appeal of mixing the two seemingly separate worlds? Have you seen any advertisements that have used this strategy? If so, how have you been affected?

■

1 PARIS—When Evander Holyfield unexpectedly lost a 12-round decision to Michael Moorer last year, a Parisienne named Marilyn Gauthier was at the Las Vegas ringside, less concerned with the fight's outcome than with Holyfield's gleaming body. She'll be back in Las Vegas this weekend when Holyfield fights again, her mind not on heavyweight titles but on fashion shoots.

2 Gauthier runs a Paris model agency and has recently opened a section called Marilyn Sports.

3 "I was the first to think of sports in terms of fashion," she claims. The first in France perhaps, but in the United States about 20 years

ago Joe Namath, the New York Jets quarterback, posed fetchingly in women's panty hose in a brilliant ad campaign.

4   "Everyone here loves the idea of using athletes but still France is way behind," says Marilyn, who is known by her first name and speaks mostly in fashion Franglais. "Here they just think of using them for male deodorants."

5   Marilyn isn't thinking in terms of million-dollar sponsoring contracts but, more modestly, of endorsements and glamour shots.

6   "A *sportif* can wear *un smoking*," she insists.

7   One of her athletes is Kelly Slater from Florida.

8   "People think he can't do anything off his surfboard," she says, "but he is sublime."

9   Marilyn has the usual complement of female models—including Kate Moss and Carla Bruni—and lissome males whose broody expression may be caused by the fact that typically they earn about 30 percent less than the girls. She has only eight athletes so far, most of them titleholders in their specialties.

10   "Athletes are today's heroes, like rock stars were in the '80s," she insists.

11   The advantage they have over professional male models is that, like Jean Galfione, the cute blonde European champion pole vaulter who has already strolled down a catwalk, they are stars and therefore, in the hallowed French expression, *médiatique*.

12   Holyfield was the first to sign, after six months of negotiation.

13   "He has an extraordinary body because he was a middleweight who built himself up, you can count the muscles. I really feel *un feedback* from the female editors I deal with."

14   Everyone knows that women these days are eager observers of pecs and delts and that the male body sells. Even in the recent British TV production of "Pride and Prejudice," the idea of making Mr. Darcy into a sex object, with a swimming scene thrown in, has been credited with attracting a record audience of 10 million viewers.

15   Marilyn doesn't care much for basketball players' bodies, but has one on her roster because in France basketball is newly *médiatique*. Nor do soccer players charm her, but with the World Cup only three years off she reckons they are the coming thing. Swimmers and fencers are often beautifully made but are not *médiatique*.

16   Tennis players all seem to be indentured to Mark McCormick and so do the star golfers, but Marilyn doesn't care for golf anyway.

17   Her own sporting activity has been confined to French boxing, which involves a lot of rude kicking, and kung fu.

18   "I only like doing violent contact sports, the others are *très boring* for me."

19   In addition to the fashion press, Marilyn these days reads the sports paper L'Equipe and attends every sporting event that she can.

20   She has one female ice-skater on her list—"she is pretty enough to do a cosmetics ad"—but concentrates on men.

21   One thing she didn't foresee is that athletes' training schedules do not always permit them to be at fashion's call. And she hasn't yet faced discussing body hair or facial blemishes with her new charges.

22   "I haven't dared. But usually," she hopefully suggests, "because they are personalities they are accepted for themselves."

23   Not by everyone. Asked while passing through Paris if he would like to snap a beefy athlete, the photographer Helmut Newton promptly replied, "Not me, though I love muscles." He did for one shoot have a mountain climber scale the façade of Monaco's Hôtel de Paris, but of course chose an abseilling woman.

24   Acceptance not having been easy, Marilyn's first step has been to plant magazine articles to make her athletes even more *médiatique*. Holyfield has done nicely with photographs in the company of Johnny Hallyday and Jean-Paul Belmondo ("the American boxer is the actor's idol," the caption read) and got a fair amount of attention when a fashion photographer posed him on a sofa covered with roses, including a rosebud anklet. But Joe Namath he is not.

25   The female editors loved the stories, Marilyn says, though so far advertisers haven't bitten.

26   Well, fashion may be the roughest noncontact sport around, but as we all know, it isn't if you've won or lost, but how you've played the game.

DISCUSSION QUESTIONS

1.   In small groups, discuss why you think fashion and sports are being promoted together. What specifically are the effects of using this technique? Make a brainstorming map or cluster to help you illustrate your thoughts. Be prepared to present your findings to the whole class.

2.   What do you think the French mean by the term *médiatique?* How would you define it?

3.   Gauthier claims that "Athletes are today's heroes, like rock stars were in the '80s." Do you agree with her statement? Why or why not?

4. Blume writes that acceptance of the use of athletes in the fashion world has not been easy. Why do you think some people may have a hard time accepting the use of athletes in the fashion world?

5. Blume concludes her article with the line, "Well, fashion may be the roughest noncontact sport around, but as we all know, it isn't if you've won or lost, but how you've played the game." Why do you think Blume has chosen to end her article in this way? What rhetorical effect does this conclusion have upon you as a reader?

WRITING ASSIGNMENTS

1. Find an advertisement that combines the worlds of sports and fashion. Then write an analysis-critique of the advertisement. Is the ad persuasive? What are the elements of the ad and how do they work together? What rhetorical effect does it have upon you? Does it ask you to do or feel anything in particular? Be sure to use specific details to support your general claims. Remember to include the advertisement with your essay.

2. Write a proposal for an advertisement that combines fashion with sports. Your proposal should include a rationale for the advertisement as well as a full description of how the ad would be presented and the effect you hope to produce. Be sure to use descriptive language to develop your plan.

3. Write a definition paper of the word *médiatique*. What meanings do you think this word conveys? Be sure to illustrate your thoughts with specific details and examples.

CHAPTER SEVEN WRITING ASSIGNMENTS

1. Several of the articles in this chapter concern the relationship between sports and politics. Drawing on information from this chapter as well as other sources, write an essay that addresses the following question: "To what extent can sports influence political and/or societal issues?" Develop your paper with specific details and facts.

2. Write a paper that explores the following question: "What specifically attracts people to sports events?" Your paper can cover a broad spectrum of sports but should include specific details and examples to support your main points.

3. Choose one sport that interests you. Then write an informative report that details the origins and history of the sport. Develop your report with specific details and facts. Be prepared to present your report to the class.

4. Write an analytical paper that responds to the following question: "In what specific ways do sports affect our lives?" Begin your writing process with a prewriting technique such as clustering or freewriting and be sure to support your opinions with specific evidence.

CHAPTER EIGHT

Living in a Technological World

It is hard to imagine life without the technology we have all grown so accustomed to. Only twenty years ago, virtually nobody had a personal computer. Now, 35 percent of all households have at least one computer. CD-ROMs and the World Wide Web have replaced the printed version of many encyclopedias and other reference sources. Children play computer games instead of board games. We can bank at an ATM or by phone rather than going to the bank. Information can be faxed around the world within minutes. Indeed, the list of technological inventions grows daily. This chapter brings together articles that examine only a few of the many technological innovations that affect our lives every day.

The chapter opens with an article entitled "The Web: Out of the Lab and Spun Around the World" in which Barry James reports on the development of the World Wide Web and gives us a glimpse of its future applications. Originally conceived of as a vehicle for scientists and researchers to share data around the globe instantaneously, the Web was developed at the European Laboratory for Particle Physics by Tim Berners Lee, a networking expert, and Robert Caillou, a documentalist. However, the Web is quickly moving from the world of the research laboratory to the world of the living room. In "Saving Money on the Web," Laurie Flynn introduces us to Web uses that several businesses are now employing in their customer service department. Federal Express, for example, now offers a Web site to customers for tracking purposes. For many companies, the Web provides a more economical alternative to having large phone banks.

One of the latest networking inventions is an emerging technology called the M-bone (multicast broadcasting), which is making the Internet a broadcasting medium. Peter Lewis, in "A Two-Way Virtual Street: Internet Broadcasting Goes Interactive," discusses how this form of broadcasting goes a step beyond conventional broadcasting since it allows viewers and listeners to become broadcasters, too. While traditional broadcasting allows one site to transmit to many, multicasting enables many computers to broadcast to each other simultaneously. However, the technology is still in developmental stages, and since special hardware and software are needed, M-bone is still limited primarily to scientific and research facilities that have the necessary high-capacity hardware.

Technological innovation is also being used to help deter credit card fraud. Barbara Wall's article, "In the War Against Credit Card Fraud, a Technological Arms Race," reports on how credit fraud has been somewhat curtailed by technological deterrents such as CRIS (cardholder risk identification), a system that employs a global network to produce risk scores on each transaction. The new system seems to be working at present; however, Richard Martin, editor of Cards International, warns, "As fraud detection methods become increasingly high-tech, card fraudsters are employing more sophisticated methods to dupe the industry."

Although technological development seems to be paving the information superhighway for a more streamlined lifestyle, this technology is passing some people by. The chapter concludes with an article entitled "In the Information Age, a New Set of Have-Nots" by Nicholas Negroponte, author of Being Digital and director/founder of the Media Laboratory at the Massachusetts Institute of Technology. In this selection, Negroponte comments on a group of Americans, "the digitally homeless," as he calls them, who are very often well-educated, affluent, middle-aged adults without a clue about the computerized world. Unlike the younger generation who have grown up with this emerging technology, many adults find it difficult to adjust to a computerized lifestyle.

As you read through this chapter, you might start to think about how a computerized lifestyle affects you. What aspects of computerization are taken for granted? What would life be like without computers? Specifically, how has the quality of our lives changed with the amazing growth of computer technology?

THE WEB: OUT OF THE LAB AND SPUN AROUND THE WORLD

Barry James

International Herald Tribune

■

In the following piece, Barry James reports on the origin, impact, and future of the World Wide Web. Although the Web has become a fairly common term in a relatively short period of time, many may not know that it was born in Geneva, Switzerland, at the European Laboratory for Particle Physics (also known by its French initials as CERN). The Laboratory was originally charged with investigating the Big Bang theory but took a detour to develop the Web. According to Laboratory officials, the Web has increased Internet traffic by 350,000 percent, and its uses have moved far beyond what scientists at CERN ever envisioned. While reading this article, think about the ways in which the Web may have already changed the way you live. What implications does the Web have for your future?

■

1   GENEVA—The European Laboratory for Particle Physics, which was set up to investigate the Big Bang at the beginning of space and time, set off a significant explosion of its own by inventing the World Wide Web, an intuitive way of using computers that is powering the phenomenal growth of the Internet.

2   Laboratory officials said traffic on the Internet increased 350,000 percent last year as the cyberworld discovered the ease of using the Web.

3   If the Internet is the information superhighway, the Web is the equivalent of the trucks that carry the mail. It carries, in fact, the digital equivalent of the entire works of Shakespeare every second. The growth is likely to become even more exponential once users

discover that they can use the Web to make phone calls all over the world for the price of a local call.

4   Despite this runaway success, the particle physics laboratory—known by its French initials as CERN—is handing over the development of the system to a new collaborative project headed by the Massachusetts Institute of Technology and the French National Institute for Research in Computer Science and Control.

5   Jacques Altaber, one of the CERN officials responsible for early Web development, said the organization had given up responsibility for the system because it needed to get on with its main business, which is building a $2.5 billion 21st-century particle accelerator that will be used to unravel some of the deeper mysteries of the beginning of the universe.

6   Before letting go of the Web entirely, CERN organized a conference bringing together educators, scientists and journalists to show off the latest advances in what Mr. Altaber called potentially one of the biggest revolutions in the history of communication, including the invention of printing and the telephone.

7   Two CERN specialists, Tim Berners Lee, a networking expert, and Robert Caillou, a documentalist, came up with the idea for the Web in 1989 because the organization needed a way to transmit data quickly in house and to thousands of physicists on both sides of the Atlantic.

8   Britain's science minister, David Hunt, who opened the Web conference, said, "This exciting invention came from the needs of physicists in universities and institutes all around the world who needed to share instantaneously the data from CERN's enormous experiments to understand the fundamental workings of nature."

9   "It was only later that the educational, commercial and cultural significance of the World Wide Web was appreciated," he said, "and I am sure we have by no means come to an end of its possible applications."

10   Mr. Berners Lee and Mr. Caillou based the Web on hypertext, an existing technique for storing and viewing multidimensional documents. In hypertext, any highlighted item on a computer monitor, whether it is text, a graphic, a sound or a moving image, can be summoned with the click of a key or a mouse.

11   The user does not have to know how a computer works, how the Internet works or where the information comes from.

12   Providing the connection is good, a Web user can "surf" among thousands of networks almost as easily as switching from one computer window to another.

13   In what Mr. Altaber said is a way that is both "democratic and Darwinian," the Web is rapidly becoming the Internet's operating system, driving out older techniques that require users to type arcane commands.

14   Because the Web makes it easier for people to get onto the Internet as well as to browse through it, Mr. Altaber said, it is "becoming a tool for all sectors of a modern economy and society. It is an obvious tool for any organization or company operating on a global basis."

15   According to its co-inventor, Mr. Caillou, the Web is the exact antithesis of the top-down planning that governments and large organizations prefer. "Its users said, 'Let's see how it works. Later on we can figure how to standardize it,'" Mr. Caillou said.

16   The biggest threat to the Web, he said, "is that a single company will grab it and run away with it, then enslave it to their de facto standards." He said that 1995 would be the decisive year for the Web. Either it will remain freewheeling and decentralized, or it will become increasingly fragmented as commercial interests gain control.

17   "I don't want to name any names," he said, "But you shouldn't oblige the population of Soweto to buy software from a company in California."

18   Mr. Caillou suggested that if controls were needed on the unruly Internet it should be placed under the responsibility of the United Nations for the benefit of mankind, rather than letting it fall under the control of commercial interests or governments. "We have to keep it open and universal," he said.

19   Although it is no longer directly responsible for the Web, CERN, the world's leading center for particle physics research, will remain one of its biggest and most innovative users. For example, it is designing its future Large Hadron Collider—a highly complex, 27-kilometer (16.6-mile) chain of vacuum tunnels, superconducting magnets, particle accelerators and gigantic detection chambers—almost entirely on the Internet.

20   The scores of institutes and companies involved in the project send their designs over the Web to be incorporated into the master plan at the organization's headquarters. If any part has to changed, the dimensions of the entire project are automatically reconfigured and the revised designs are sent back to the manufacturers, again across the Web.

21   The underlying structures are being fleshed out into a virtual reality replica of the collider to enable scientists and engineers around

the world to visualize the finished project, inside and out. When perfected, the model will enable engineers to work out such problems as winching a 200-ton magnet down a 60-meter shaft and then aligning it to a tolerance no thicker than a human hair.

22 The Web is developing in all kinds of ways that its inventors never envisaged. "Who could have guessed 10 years ago," Mr. Hunt said, "that particle physics research would lead to a communication system which allows a farmer on a remote Scottish island to get instantaneous information from Australia on the latest sheep-breeding techniques; or which would allow every school to have the biggest library in the world inside a single computer?"

23 In Norway, Borre Ludvigsen gets more than 3,000 calls a month from around the world after putting his family home on the Web in order to teach himself how to become a "communications architect."

24 A Swiss high-technology company, Lightning Instrumentation, saw its turnover increase 15 percent in four months after it put a server on the Web for the price of a few newspaper ads.

25 Joe Breen, the head of editorial publishing at the Irish Times, said his newspaper is on the Web because it is "something journalists could understand; at last they sighted a realistic migration path from print to screen, utilizing their knowledge of editing, design and content."

26 Although he said the newspaper had not yet figured out a way to make money out of the project, the enthusiastic response from Irish émigrés from Tokyo to Toronto indicates that the newspaper has an unsuspected worldwide audience.

27 Human nature being what it is, the Web attracts the bad as well as the good. Its graphic possibilities, for example, make it possible to send pornographic pictures around the world as easy as designs for a particle collider, posing unprecedented problems of legislation and jurisdiction.

28 Trotter Hardy, of William and Mary Law School in Williamsburg, Virginia, said a couple who put pornographic pictures on a computer bulletin board in California were tried and found guilty of obscenity in Tennessee in what is likely to be one of the first of many such cases between states and countries with different ethical codes.

29 The growth of the Web will become even more explosive once the European telecommunications industry is freed from the shackles of state-owned, monopoly telecommunications companies.

30 David Williams of CERN's computing and networks division cited enormous cost disparities between America and Europe, and within Europe. For example, a leased line from London to Paris costs 23

times as much as a line to Edinburgh, the same distance. A leased line in Switzerland costs 90 times more than a line over an equivalent distance in the United States.

DISCUSSION QUESTIONS

1. The title of this article is "The Web: Out of the Lab and Spun Around the World." Why do you think the author has chosen this title? Why do you think the inventors of the World Wide Web chose that name?

2. James states that "The Web is developing in all kinds of ways that its inventors never envisaged." He then described various ways the Web is being used. In small groups, brainstorm about the ways you think the Web might be employed. What ideas do you have for its use? Be prepared to share your ideas with the class as a whole.

3. James writes that "According to its coinventor, Mr. Caillou, the Web is the exact antithesis of the top-down planning that all governments and large organizations prefer." What do you think is meant by this statement? How is something not top-down? What are the benefits of not being top-down in the context of the Web invention?

4. James quotes Mr. Caillou, coinventor of the Web, as fearing that one company will take control "and run away with it, then enslave it to their de facto standards." What do you think Caillou means with this statement? What are the potential ramifications of a single company taking control of this innovation?

5. The article explains that the vast potential of the Web has attracted some bad influences. James writes that "Human nature being what it is, the Web attracts the bad as well as the good. Its graphic possibilities, for example, make it possible to send pornographic pictures around the world as easy as designs for a particle collider, posing unprecedented problems of legislation and jurisdiction." Explore the nature of these problems. Do you think it will be possible to regulate the use of the Web? What kinds of regulations might need to be put in place? What other sorts of misuses do you think the Web might fall prey to?

WRITING ASSIGNMENTS

1. The coinventor of the World Wide Web, Robert Caillou, has suggested that control of the Web might be placed under the auspices of

the United Nations so that it will not fall under the control of commercial interests or governments. Caillou asserts, "We have to keep it open and universal." Write a paper that explores the following question: "To what extent should the United Nations become involved in the governing of the Web?" Your paper should consider the specific role the United Nations would be able to play in this endeavor and the feasibility of such a scenario.

2. If possible, experiment with the Web. Spend some time finding out what it has to offer. Then write a narrative paper that details your experiences. What happened? What did you learn from the experience? How will you use the Web in the future? It does not matter if this will be the first time you have used the Web or if you are an experienced Web "surfer." Your task is to create an interesting narrative of your experience.

3. Write a process analysis paper that explains to a novice how to use the Web. If you have not used the Web before, this will be an opportunity for you to learn. You should be as specific as possible, using examples and details to illustrate the process.

4. Write a proposal for a new use of the Web. The focus of the proposal is entirely up to you. However, your proposal should contain a detailed explanation of the use, a rationale for the use, and a description of likely users.

SAVING MONEY ON THE WEB

Laurie Flynn

New York Times Service

■

In the following selection, Laurie Flynn offers a report on the potential the World Wide Web has for saving people and business money. More businesses are now using the Web to automate their handling of customer service since a Web site is much cheaper to operate than phone banks. Federal Express, for example, offers a Web tracking service that allows people to log onto a Federal Express home page. Customers can then fill in the appropriate information on the computer screen and their package status report will be relayed to them. The article shows how the Web's usefulness is beginning to reach far beyond being the world's largest data library. As you read "Saving Money on the Web," you might think about what you would like to see the Web be able to do in the future.

■

1   NEW YORK—The Internet's World Wide Web, a great repository of data, has yet to become that great market. But right now a number of innovative service-oriented companies are using the Web not to make money but to save some—not nickels and dimes either, but possibly millions of dollars.

2   For companies ranging from overnight package deliverers to banks, the Web is the place to offer technology-savvy customers a new convenience: automated service. In the process, these companies are finding that having a Web site is a lot cheaper than operating customer phone banks.

3   Federal Express Corp., for one, delivers more than 2 million packages each day and at any given moment needs to determine the status of a large number of them.

4   Since last November, customers have been able to log onto the Federal Express home page on the Web. After calling up on a computer screen a package-tracking form, a customer types in his or her bill-tracking number.

5   Within minutes, the Internet server, or search system, hooks up with the Federal Express computer in Memphis, Tennessee. That computer finds the information and sends back a status report on the package.

6   In May alone, Federal Express customers tracked 90,000 packages through the Web site. Internet tracking has become one of the most cost-effective ways to track packages, said Robert Hamilton, manager of electronic commerce marketing for the company. He declined to quantify the savings, saying only that they were "significant."

7   Some expenses are involved in setting up a Web site—mostly software-designer fees and contracting with an Internet provider to make the physical connection to the network. But the cost of package-tracking on the Web is minimal.

8   Federal Express has already cut tracing costs by having major clients use software to link up with the Federal Express tracking computer. These customers remain connected through a private network, which Federal Express maintains.

9   According to Sally Davenport, a company spokeswoman, 60 percent of the package-tracking now is done through automated means. The rest has to be handled by service representatives at the Federal Express call center in Memphis.

10   United Parcel Service of America Inc. has also begun to offer package tracing through the Internet. Since its Web site was set up May 19, customers have tracked 35,000 packages through it, said Steve Heit, network-access development manager for UPS, which is based in Atlanta. Although the site was not set up to save money, Mr. Heit said, it clearly is less expensive than other tracking methods.

11   That businesses are using the Web to offer automated customer service is a sign that the Internet may finally be entering its second phase—going from being the world's largest library of data to being a provider of crucial services. The third phase might come next year, as companies begin to offer customers the use of the Internet for financial transactions.

12   Computer and software companies, of course, were the first to discover that the Web could help them save money and improve service. Customers can more easily get technical support and software revisions or corrections. For the companies, the Internet is a low-cost alternative to phone banks.

13   Hewlett-Packard Co. uses a Web site to distribute revisions to its Unix operating system and additions to its printer software collection. Andrew Old, a Hewlett-Packard spokesman, said the company expected "substantial" savings from the Web site.

14   Similarly, Apple Computer Inc. makes software updates available to customers through its Web home page. All that a user has to do is to get to Apple's Web site and click on highlighted text describing the software he or she wants to acquire. The computer, using the Internet's file transfer program, issues a request to download the program.

15   "Customer service is the easiest payback model," said Paul Callahan, an analyst with Forrester Research Inc., a market research company in Cambridge, Massachusetts. "It doesn't involve any financial transactions, which avoids the biggest pitfall of the Internet right now—security."

16   Development of security measures is well under way, even though Mr. Callahan estimates it will be 18 months before the Internet can be considered secure—that is, before there is a widely adopted procedure to prevent credit card numbers from being intercepted and used fraudulently. Nonetheless, some companies planning to do business on the Web say that a secure system will be in place as early as the end of this year.

17   Until the security mechanisms are in place, the banking industry is offering a limited form of customer service on the Web. Wells Fargo & Co. of San Francisco gives customers Internet access to transaction histories in their checking and savings accounts, as well as to their current balances.

18   For account information alone, the Wells Fargo site is reached each day by about 2,000 customers who might otherwise have called a customer-service representative to discuss their accounts.

19   Several financial institutions, including Chemical Banking Corp., Bay Bank and Bank of Boston Corp., already offer or plan to offer electronic banking services over secure private networks. But so far, only Wells Fargo offers Internet access.

20   Wells Fargo views its Web site as a warm-up act for the full-featured on-line services that customers will eventually demand.

DISCUSSION QUESTIONS

I.   The article suggests that convenient and inexpensive customer service has become a great money saver for businesses. Can you think of other ways people and businesses could save money using the Web?

2. What connections can you make between this article and the selection entitled "In the War against Credit Card Fraud, a Technological Arms Race"? Does the Web provide new avenues for credit card fraud? Do you see a way to prevent this type of fraud?

3. Flynn makes the point that one of the biggest pitfalls of the Internet is lack of security. Beyond financial concerns, in what other ways could the Internet be a security risk? Do you think there might be some disadvantages to using the Web for customer service? Can you envision any problems that would make telephone service preferable?

WRITING ASSIGNMENTS

1. Write an essay that explores the advantages and disadvantages of using the Web as a method of customer service. Begin your writing process by brainstorming about what you expect from good customer service. Your essay should come to a determination about the future of customer service on the Web. In other words, do the advantages outweigh the disadvantages or vice versa?

2. Interview someone whose business depends heavily on good customer service. The focus of your interview should be about the extent to which the business owner thinks the Web can help his or her business. Be sure to create an interview guide before conducting the interview.

A Two-Way Virtual Street: Internet Broadcasting Goes Interactive

Peter H. Lewis

New York Times Service

■

In the following article, "A Two-Way Virtual Street: Internet Broadcasting Goes Interactive," Peter H. Lewis reports on an emerging technology designed to turn the Internet into a broadcasting system. Multicasting allows groups of computers equipped with special hardware and software to share text, audio, and video. Unlike unicast communication, in which one computer communicates with another, and broadcast communication, in which one computer communicates with many, multicast communication permits many computers to communicate simultaneously among themselves. The M-bone is the multicast backbone of the Internet. Although multicasting is still limited primarily to scientific and research facilities, it has tremendous potential. While reading this article, you might think about the ways in which multicasting could change our lives and daily routines.

■

1   NEW YORK—The view from Steve Deering's office is spectacular.
2   "I'm sitting here right now watching the space shuttle hovering near the Russian space station, listening to live audio from the Russian ship," said Mr. Deering, a computer scientist at Xerox Corp.'s Palo Alto, California, research center.
3   The window through which he watched the space ballet Monday was the screen of a desktop computer, attached to the global web of computer networks known as the Internet. And the means by which he watched and heard the space rendezvous was an emerging technology called the M-bone, which is turning the Internet into a broadcasting medium.

4   Indeed, whether it's watching the astronauts on the shuttle or the Rolling Stones on tour, more people are experimenting with the M-bone these days. But unlike conventional broadcasting, the M-bone allows viewers and listeners to be broadcasters themselves. Practitioners call this "multicasting." (The M-bone is the Internet's multicast backbone, which functions as a network based on the Internet's framework).

5   Mr. Deering, a principal developer of the technology, said the M-bone could become a sort of global video telephone system that allowed groups of people—not just individuals—to share voice, data and images over the Internet.

6   Because the M-bone has been in use only since 1992, however, and because using it requires special hardware and software, only 1,500 of the estimated 70,000 networks that make up the Internet have been set up as M-bone hubs.

7   As a result, it remains to be seen whether the M-bone will evolve into an Internet-based network connecting businesses and homes, or whether it is merely a limited prototype for the so-called information superhighway that is supposed to be built by telephone and cable TV companies to carry interactive audio, video and text services.

8   Already, some corporate researchers have begun using the M-bone as a fairly inexpensive alternative to teleconferencing systems and even to business travel. And since it employs the Internet's existing physical structure, which often leads to office desktop computers, many businesses are already equipped to explore uses for multicasting.

9   Scientists, meanwhile, use it to monitor live video and data signals from robot submarines on the ocean floor. Engineers scattered around the world use the M-bone to collaborate on complex projects, employing interactive so-called white boards that allow them to share notes and drawings on-line.

10   Medical students in Britain and Sweden can watch as a surgeon in San Francisco performs an unusual operation, asking the doctor questions as the procedure takes place.

11   Speeches by President Bill Clinton and Newt Gingrich, the speaker of the U.S. House of Representatives, have been carried live on the M-bone, along with performances by an assortment of musicians.

12   Mick Jagger of the Rolling Stones opened the first major cyberspace multicast concert by saying, "I wanna say a special welcome to everyone that's, uh, climbed into the Internet tonight and, uh, has got into the M-bone. And I hope it doesn't all collapse."

13   The M-bone did not collapse, but the astute Mr. Jagger had alluded to the biggest drawback of multicasting, which is the limited bandwidth—or data capacity—of the existing Internet.

14   Audio and video signals consume enormous amounts of bandwidth—far more than simple text does. And some researchers fear that widespread use of the M-bone could clog the Internet and interfere with more common services, including electronic mail.

15   Because multicasting is still experimental and not well-known outside the scientific and academic communities, voluntary guidelines have been sufficient so far. M-bone users typically ask permission from one another before scheduling a multicast session, allowing those who want to tune in to do so, and those who do not to keep their data spigots closed.

16   There is also an informal agreement to be sparing when using the feedback capabilities. Because of bandwidth concerns, for example, Mr. Deering and other shuttle-watchers have not been permitted to talk with the U.S. astronauts and Russian cosmonauts. And some other multicasts are restricted to low-quality video or audio-only communications, as a courtesy to others downstream.

17   The steady increase in computing power and the continuing trend toward high-bandwidth networks could ease the current barriers to widespread M-bone use.

18   Meanwhile, Internet bandwidth capacity is being expanded rapidly to meet growing demand by businesses for such services as the World Wide Web. And an increasingly popular type of high-speed telephone service known as ISDN, or integrated services digital network, is offering high-capacity Internet links to commercial and residential computers.

19   Even without the M-bone, multicast applications are now possible on internal corporate computer networks, the kind that link personal computers within a building. But the M-bone, because it is built atop the Internet, can reach far beyond local networks to millions of computers scattered in more than 150 countries. There are M-bone links today in Russia, as well as at the McMurdo Sound research station in Antarctica.

20   Multicasting has obvious appeal for Internet-connected schools, for linking remote offices and for playing new generations of interactive computer games. Music companies are eyeing the M-bone as a way to distribute new recordings, including music videos.

21   But potential is one thing, reality another. Multicasting is still limited primarily to scientific and research organizations that have high-

capacity phone lines and powerful computer work stations using Unix—a complex type of software found mainly in scientific and engineering communities.

22   And while multicasting capabilities are being built into newer networking equipment, it still requires no small amount of software and technical expertise to configure a new network to use it.

23   Businesses may be wary of holding sensitive seminars or business meetings on the M-bone because it is no more secure than the notoriously insecure Internet. And what would seem the obvious security solution—using data-encryption software to transmit multicasts in secret code—is thwarted by U.S. government policies barring the export of data-encryption technology.

24   And any dreams of beaming video commercials and face-to-face sales pitches over the Internet are tempered by the reality of the existing audience.

25   "Most people get on the M-bone from work, and most of the workers who are on the M-bone are not consumers," said Dave Hayes, a network specialist at the Jet Propulsion Laboratory in Pasadena, California.

DISCUSSION QUESTIONS

1. Why do you think Lewis chooses to begin this article in the manner he does? What theoretical effect does this opening statement have on you as a reader?

2. What is M-bone, and how does it differ from unicast and broadcast communication?

3. In small groups, brainstorm about the potential advantages and disadvantages of M-bone. Use clustering or mapping to help you explore your ideas. Be prepared to share your thoughts with the whole class.

4. Lewis writes of M-bone that "potential is one thing, reality another." What do you think he means by this statement?

5. What do you think is the likelihood of M-bone becoming an everyday household item? Support your opinion with specific reasons or evidence.

WRITING ASSIGNMENTS

1. Write an informative report that details the background as well as the future plans for M-bone. How was it developed? What is its

potential? How could it change the way we communicate? Your report should go beyond the information presented in the article by Lewis. Thus, you will need to consult secondary sources.

2. Write a proposal to request the acquisition of M-bone for your school. The proposal should address the ways in which M-bone could benefit the school community, including students, faculty, and staff. Your proposal should be as specific as possible, so you will need to include details and examples that demonstrate how M-bone will benefit the school.

3. Interview a person who has experienced M-bone firsthand or knows about it. You might begin by asking the computer consultant at your school for information. Be sure to make an interview guide before the interview.

4. Write a cause-effect paper that explores the ramifications of the new M-bone technology. Think about the various areas of our lives that could be affected by M-bone technology. How could this technology change our lives? You might begin this writing project by creating a cluster that illustrates these changes.

IN THE WAR AGAINST CREDIT CARD FRAUD, A TECHNOLOGICAL ARMS RACE

Barbara Wall

International Herald Tribune

■

In this selection, Barbara Wall examines efforts being made by credit card companies to combat fraud. Recently, companies such as Visa, MasterCard, and American Express have begun programs to curb the rampant credit card fraud that continues to cost the industry millions of dollars. The newest innovation, CRIS (cardholder risk identification service), is now being used by Visa. With this system, a global computer network will produce a risk score for each transaction. When a score exceeds a predetermined purchase limit, the bank that issued the credit card is alerted, and the cardholder is contacted to verify the authenticity of the transaction. Although these devices have cut down significantly on credit card fraud, criminals are simply becoming more sophisticated in their attempts to commit credit card fraud. As you read this article, consider why this problem has become so prevalent.

■

1   In the battle against card fraudsters, Visa has introduced a new high-tech electronic device that aims to spot fraud within hours of the transaction taking place and long before the fraud is actually reported.

2   The "cardholder risk identification service," or CRIS, will use the information supplied by Visa's global computer network to generate a risk score for each authorized transaction. If the score exceeds a predetermined threshold, a warning message is sent to the card issuing bank, which then checks the authenticity of the transaction with the cardholder. The system has just been introduced in Spain, following a successful trial period in the United States, where fraud savings of over $23 million were recorded.

3   CRIS is one of a number of initiatives employed by Visa to reduce fraud. MasterCard, meanwhile, has invested a small fortune in "smart card" technology, with a view to creating the ultimate in fraud-proof plastic. A spokesman for MasterCard says that chip technology is the best means of fighting card crime. Other issuers have experimented with holograms, photographs and additional personalized identification devices.

4   This activity seems to be doing the trick. Visa card fraud in Europe, the Middle East and Africa dropped by more than 26 percent in 1994, meaning that fraud counted for only 0.07 percent of total sales volume. MasterCard, American Express and Diners Club also reported a significant drop in worldwide card fraud, though the companies admit that they cannot afford to be complacent.

5   Last year card fraud cost around £165 million ($258 million) in Britain alone. Richard Martin, editor of Cards International, a trade journal for the industry, says that the card market it just too lucrative for fraudsters to abandon without a fight.

6   "As fraud detection methods become increasingly high-tech, card fraudsters are employing more sophisticated methods to dupe the industry. Counterfeiting, which demands a great deal of skill, continues to foil card issuers, and the word is that this category of card fraud is increasing," he said.

7   Last year MasterCard reported a 66 percent increase in counterfeit fraud. Although Visa's counterfeit fraud fell 15.5 percent in the first quarter of 1994, Robert Littas, vice president of risk management and security for Visa concedes that it remains a major problem, accounting for at least 10 percent of all Visa card fraud.

8   "In many counterfeit rackets the fraudsters work with dishonest merchants. Imprints of customers' cards are passed on to the counterfeiters for a fee. Once the fraudsters get hold of the imprints it is relatively easy to manufacture dummy cards," Mr. Littas said. "Even the magnetic strip on the back of the plastic can be duplicated, though this demands a great deal of skill."

9   "The problem is acute in tourist resorts," Mr. Martin said, "especially in regions where electronic authorization remains a relatively new concept. Major trouble spots include the Far East—most notably China—and some of the popular Mediterranean holiday destinations."

10   He warns that the more prestigious the card, the greater is the risk that it will attract unwelcome attention. "The virtual unlimited spend on some of these cards acts as a powerful magnet," he said. "Fraudsters are also aware that bearers of prestige cards are generally

subject to less scrutiny than standard cardholders when flexing their plastic in retail outlets."

11   While the banks must shoulder the cost of counterfeit fraud, the cardholder is often held responsible for losses incurred prior to a card being reported lost or stolen. Banks in Britain and the Netherlands limit cardholder liability to 150 Ecus (about $185). However, according to BEUC, the European Consumer's Association, certain banks in France, Portugal, Belgium and Spain will hold the client fully responsible for losses if the personal identification number (PIN) has been used in the fraudulent transaction, even in cases where no gross negligence is involved.

12   Reports of fraud occurring at automated teller machines is a source of growing concern amongst banks and law enforcement agencies. "Although violent crimes—where cardholders are forced to reveal the PIN under duress—are not that common, ATMs have become the principle mode of cash withdrawal these days and organized criminals are continually looking for new ways to compromise the system," said John Newton, a police officer in London who specializes in card fraud-prevention techniques. "As soon as one loophole is plugged, another one opens up."

DISCUSSION QUESTIONS

1. Why do you think Wall uses the phrase *technological arms race* in the title of this article to describe the fight against credit card fraud? What effect does the phrase have on you as a reader?

2. In small groups, speculate about the reasons why credit card fraud has become such a prevalent crime. Until now, what has made it such an easy crime to commit? What attracts criminals to this type of crime?

3. In small groups, discuss ways you think credit card fraud and counterfeiting can be prevented. What can individuals do? What can banks, card companies, and shop owners do to stop this sort of criminal activity?

WRITING ASSIGNMENTS

1. Write a column for your school newspaper that both informs people about the increase in credit card fraud and offers individuals practical advice for its prevention. Your essay should include specific suggestions people can use to avoid becoming a victim of this crime. You

may want to interview police officers and other security personnel about what prevention strategies they recommend.

2. Write a causal analysis essay that explores the reasons why credit card fraud has become such a popular crime. What specific aspects of our society and daily routines make credit card fraud such an easy crime to commit?

3. Write an essay in which you speculate about the long-term effects of credit card fraud on our society if it continues to grow. You might start your essay by discussing this question with people in some way connected to this issue (for example, shop owners, police officers, credit card holders).

IN THE INFORMATION AGE,
A NEW SET OF HAVE-NOTS

Nicholas Negroponte

The New York Times

■

In this selection, Nicholas Negroponte, author of *Being Digital* and founder of the Media Laboratory at the Massachusetts Institute of Technology, puts an interesting twist on the term *have-nots*. Negroponte suggests that the new set of have-nots are affluent, middle-aged, and often highly educated Americans who have found themselves either in the slow lane of the information superhighway or not on it at all. On the other hand, the post-MTV generation is using computers "for everything from homework to games to dating." Negroponte recommends that if you are in the "have-nots" groups, you should latch on to your child or grandchild and ask for help. While reading this article, consider how computer technology affects your life. What computerized activities do you participate in every day? Is your use of computer technology different than that of your parents, grandparents, or other people of your parents' generation? Have you ever had the experience of helping someone older than you learn how to use a computer?

■

1   CAMBRIDGE, Massachusetts—When Newt Gingrich spoke of buying laptop computers for needy Americans, critics promptly dismissed the idea as silly.

2   But it is not silly at all.

3   It raises a question that does not seem to have occurred to those who brushed aside his suggestion as a case of offering cake to the starving: Just who are the needy? Who are the have-nots?

4   Most Americans over 30, rich or poor, have been left out of the digital world. Even though 35 percent of households have at least one

216

personal computer, and home computers will represent 70 percent of PC sales this year, adults tend to use them for such specific purposes as word processing, simple accounting and business applications that allow them to work at home.

5   Children, on the other hand, use them for everything from homework to games to dating. Plenty of adult Americans are computer-illiterate. Fewer and fewer 10-year-olds are. None are, if you count Nintendo and Sega—as I do.

6   Two forces are working at once. Parents feel obligated to prepare their children by buying them a home computer, just as my parents felt obligated to buy an encyclopedia. This includes 30 percent of households with children and less than $30,000 of annual income. Children, meanwhile, find that computers are at that wonderful intersection of playing and learning and that they can take over and control the digital world without parental intervention. It can be their own medium, not someone else's.

7   Together, these two forces helped push the sales of personal computers ahead of television for the first time last year. By the year 2000 I believe that as many homes will have a computer as have a television. In fact, many Americans will be watching television in the upper-right-hand corner of their PC screens.

8   Who are these people? They are the post-MTV generation, who are finding that there is more entertainment on the Internet than all the "networks" combined.

9   They meet, play and even get married in cyberspace, a land that has no material bounds or geographic limits. The boy next door may be 10,000 miles away.

10   Weightless, sizeless, colorless bits, those 1s and 0s that travel at the speed of light, are the DNA of a wired society of on-line people. And the ones who know how to navigate it—the *digerati*—are, for the most part, the young.

11   Conversely, many affluent and middle-aged Americans are suddenly have-nots. Paradoxically, the elderly, especially widows and widowers, are turning to computers and on-line communities.

12   Seniornet(at)aol.com is growing at almost 10 percent a month.

13   The digital revolution, blind to wealth, has left many powerful people behind—and, increasingly, nations too.

14   Consider two countries with roughly the same population, Germany and Mexico. More than half of all Germans are over 40. More than half of all Mexicans are under 20. Which country is in a position to benefit more from the digital revolution in a world where a computer will cost less than a bicycle by the year 2000?

15   As developing nations install new telecommunications systems, they will leapfrog over First World countries with older ones. Already, Thailand has more cellular telephones per capita than the United States.

16   The combination of starting from scratch and having a young population can be a major asset.

17   Back in the United States, the average age of an Internet user is 23 and rapidly dropping. In the digital era, these people are the haves.

18   The have-nots—the digitally homeless, the truly needy—are the large number of older, middle-class Americans, often highly educated, who couldn't tell a CD-ROM from the World Wide Web.

19   If you are in this group, and if you have a child or a grandchild between, say, 10 and 15, ask him or her to help you get started.

20   That's how I do it. We have a lot to learn from the young.

DISCUSSION QUESTIONS

1.   Why do you think the author began the article with the anecdote about Newt Gingrich's idea to purchase laptop computers for the needy? What do you think of this proposal?

2.   In small groups, brainstorm about how you use computers in your everyday lives. Create a cluster to illustrate their uses. Be prepared to present your findings to the whole class.

3.   What do you think the author means by the term "the *digerati*"? What do you think the term means?

4.   Negroponte writes that "The have-nots—the digitally homeless, the truly needy—are the large number of older, middle-class Americans, often highly educated, who couldn't tell a CD-ROM from the World Wide Web." Why do you think it is harder for these persons to integrate computers into their lives? Why do you think Negroponte suggests that adults wishing to learn about computers should ask their children?

5.   Negroponte asserts that "The combination of starting from scratch and having a young population can be a major asset." What do you think he means? Why do you think he makes this assertion?

WRITING ASSIGNMENTS

1. Write a comparison-contrast paper that explores some of the differences computers have made in your life as compared to your parents' lives when they were your age. Begin by prewriting on the various functions of computers in your life. Then think about how your parents performed these functions without computers. Interview your parents or people from their generation to get firsthand information. You need not include all the ways in which computers affect your life. You might even choose to develop one specific area such as entertainment or education.

2. Choose something that you do every day with a computer. Then write a process analysis paper (how-to paper) that describes the process involved; assume that your audience consists of computer novices. You might begin by going through the motions of the process yourself while taking notes. Your audience should be able to perform the computerized task after reading your instructions.

3. Negroponte writes that "Children . . . find that computers are at that wonderful intersection of playing and learning." Write an essay that explores the following question: "What does it mean to be at an 'intersection of playing and learning'?" Where, when, and how does this intersection occur? Be sure to use specific examples and details to illustrate your points and develop your opinions.

CHAPTER EIGHT WRITING ASSIGNMENTS

1. Write a research report that details the development of the World Wide Web. Where did the idea come from? How long did it take to develop? How does it work? What were some of the problems encountered during its development? These are a few of the questions that might be explored in your report. Your research should go beyond the articles in this chapter. Be prepared to share your findings with the class.

2. All the articles in this chapter examine ways in which computers have changed our lives. But has all this change improved the quality of our lives? In a well-developed essay, respond to the following question: "To what extent has computer technology improved the quality of our lives?" Be sure to support your general claims and opinions with specific details and examples.

3. Computers have become so much a part of our everyday routines that we probably take them for granted sometimes. Keep a computer journal for one week. In the journal, make an entry every time you use or come into contact with some form of computerized technology. Remember that computers are found everywhere—from supermarket checkout lines to automatic tellers to telephone number information. After one week, review your entries and write a report about the experience. What did you learn? Do computers touch your life more or less than you expected?

4. Imagine that a local charity is willing to donate a new computer equipped with the latest technology to worthy students. Part of the application process requires an essay written by the student. In two double-spaced pages, you are to respond to the following question: "How will you use the computer to enhance your education and reach your goals?"

CHAPTER NINE

Understanding the World Economy

A frost hits Florida and the price of citrus fruit goes up. Political upheaval leads to a complete reversal in the way a community of people live. War brings growth to one nation's economy and ruins another country's natural resources. The world economy is a complicated web of interrelated occurrences. It is not only affected by world events but also creates them. Both volatile and fragile, its stability can be thrown into turmoil by any number of events.

The selections in this chapter have been chosen to give you some insight into how the world economy functions and how it affects people. The chapter opens with an article that clearly demonstrates that dramatic economic changes can have an impact on the lives of many people. In "Privatization: Lessons of the East," Richard E. Smith reports on the growing pains Germany is experiencing as it transfers former East German state-owned businesses over to the private sector and as efforts to build a unified German free market continue. Since the privatization of businesses has produced widespread unemployment, social and political unrest have been increasing. Although some experts think the privatization has gone more smoothly than expected, those who are unemployed are skeptical about their futures.

Similarly, in a piece entitled "Russian Firm Learns to Navigate Free Market," Fred Hiatt and Margaret Shapiro explore the movement of Russian firms into the free market. In particular, the two journalists focus on Severnaya Verf ("northern shipyard"), a Russian shipyard, and the strategies it has employed to shift from a communist economy to the free market. Hiatt and Shapiro note that, although the transformation has been slow, stabilization has started and progress is occurring.

Clare Hollingworth, in "Twenty Years After, Vietnam Treads Softly," reports on the Vietnamese economy and the United States' return to Vietnam, not as adversaries but as investors in this growing market. As one Vietnamese official stated, "We need the Americans today to help us attract the capital so urgently required to modernize our infrastructure. . . . We also need their advice in establishing new industries as well as stock markets."

Related to Vietnam's developing economy is an article by Reginald Dale entitled "The Third World Is Shrinking Fast." In this selection, Dale examines the growth of many countries that once were considered part of the Third World but now have rapidly growing economies as a result of privatization and free markets. Dale states that "The clear-cut lines between rich and poor countries have been swept away . . . developing countries are no longer mainly scrabbling a hard living from subsistence agriculture and the exploitation of their commodities and raw materials."

The chapter concludes on an optimistic note with a selection entitled "Real Job Training Sets Plan Apart" in which Erik Ipsen looks at how one Scottish community has dealt with the problem of unemployment in a profitable manner. Instead of giving unemployment checks or offering job training that has no real future, Glasgow offers a program that trains people to make community improvements, and the workers receive wages for their services. The program is subsidized by the government but run by local businesses. As Ipsen asserts, "What the organization's trainee workers do is produce things—not holes in the earth to be filled in and dug again, not brick walls to be built and torn down—but permanent community improvements." The program not only helps the community but brings back the self-esteem of formerly unemployed people.

Clearly we are affected by economic trends and consequences every day. Whether we are buying groceries, making a major purchase, or looking for a job or a place to live, the economy affects our lives. While reading the articles in this chapter, try to make personal connections with what you are reading. Although many of the articles are about the economies of other nations, they raise universal questions that you might want to consider. How can we cope with unemployment? To what extent should nations help each others' economic situations? What effect does an unstable economy have on political and social concerns? And, finally, in what ways might knowledge of other people's economic conditions help a person in his or her daily life?

PRIVATIZATION: LESSONS OF THE EAST

Richard E. Smith

International Herald Tribune

■

In 1991, the Berlin Wall fell and a way of life that East and West Germans had known for three decades came to an end. Since that time, the privatization of East Germany's economy has been a crucial issue in Germany's reunification. The following article by Richard E. Smith reports on the growing pains Germany is experiencing as it transfers former East German state-owned businesses over to the private sector and as efforts to build a unified German free market continue. The Treuhandanstalt is the agency established to privatize the East German economy. In a period of a little over four years, the agency sold 14,000 industrial and commercial businesses and brokered approximately 1.5 million jobs. However, this privatization has come with an enormous price tag. Since privatization has become a priority, over one-third of the once fully employed East German labor force is now unemployed, causing much social and political unrest. As you read this article, consider the specific kinds of political, social, and emotional turmoil individuals and communities must undergo when asked to restructure their lifestyles.

■

1   BERLIN—When the headquarters sign of the Treuhandanstalt was ceremoniously taken down in December in Berlin's historic Alexanderplatz, there were few Germans who did not have a strong opinion about what had gone right and wrong in one of history's more remarkable economic experiments.

2   The agency that was entrusted with the privatization of East Germany's economy had in just over four years sold 14,000 industrial and commercial businesses, and has brokered guarantees of some 1.5 million jobs.

3   But such gigantic accomplishments were only achieved at massive cost. Over a third of East Germany's once fully and permanently employed work force had lost jobs, while lingering debt and clean-up costs of the area's bankrupt industry are expected to saddle German taxpayers for a generation.

4   Not surprisingly, postmortems are flooding party caucuses, the conference circuit, academia and the media.

5   Much of the debate falls in line with the predictable face-off between free-market enthusiasts and guardians of social welfare that raged throughout the life of the Treuhandanstalt.

6   Critics of the private-sector approach, furthermore, claim that East Germany has now become a mere annex to the West German industrial giant.

7   Supporters emphasize that the East has been transformed from a bankrupt and dead-end economy to the fastest-growing region in Europe, with a current growth rate of nearly 10 percent and state-of-the-art infrastructure making it one of the fastest lanes on the continent's information superhighway.

8   But as the dust clears, a few genuine lessons appear to be emerging from the German experience—a pioneer exercise with no real precedents—that might be instructive to far-sighted South Koreans or Taiwanese who may one day also find themselves with opportunities to vastly expand a domestic market overnight.

9   Looking back, perhaps the greatest surprise for many analysts was the degree to which both West German government and industry miscalculated the value of East Germany's economy.

10   Rarely was a country so heavily scrutinized and monitored as East Germany, the East Bloc's Silicon Valley and arguably ground zero for much Cold War tension. Not only did West Germany have its own well-staffed Ministry of Inner German Affairs, but East and West Germany shared many economic statistics, an anomaly in an era when much East Bloc economic information was classed as state secrets.

11   In spite of such interest and access, however, it has become clear that Bonn and the captains of Western industry vastly overestimated the market value of East Germany, much as the Central Intelligence Agency and other U.S. intelligence bodies seem to have fundamentally over-estimated the strength of the former Soviet Union.

12   The Treuhandanstalt initially assessed East Germany's industrial properties at a value of about 600 billion Deutsche marks ($430 billion), but that gold chest steadily shrunk over the next four and a half years to ultimately show a net deficit of around 250 billion DM.

13   Part of the problem was that the centralized bureaucracy could and did manipulate statistics in a variety of ways.

14   "Our nomenklatura defined a robot in such a way, for example, that even a milk machine could be included in the statistics for robots," Gerhard Schurer, former chairman of East Germany's State Planning Commission, said at a recent seminar.

15   Aside from creative industrial definitions, there was ample room for financial machinations with no one but the state to keep itself honest. "Credits would be drawn with great effort at one bank and the funds would be deposited at another bank in order to establish creditworthiness there," Lothar de Maiziere, the last prime minister of East Germany, was quoted as saying at the same seminar.

16   Even if such questionable practices had not been skewing the statistics, they were in any case highly fragile, since much of East German industry became redundant as soon as the Berlin Wall fell simply because it could never stand up to Western competition. Consider the value of a factory that made East Germany's antiquated Wartburg and Trabant cars, for example, as soon as consumers had the option of buying anything else.

17   Aside from the pitfalls of totalitarian statistics, a number of other lessons would probably appear to a future Korean policymaker—the inevitability of corruption with such massive amounts changing hands, the dangers of new bureaucracies replacing old ones and the social resentment that festers when power is so concentrated.

18   But, judging from their near mantra-like focus on one point, it seems clear that upper ranks of the Treuhandanstalt itself would highlight a single overriding lesson: The priority had to be placed on privatization rather than on saving jobs.

19   "Privatization is the best restructuring," said Birgit Breuel, the last president of the Treuhandanstalt, again and again when union and political leaders pleaded for a more gradual approach.

20   "The priority will continue to be the transfer of firms into private ownership," Detlev Rohwedder, Ms. Breuel's predecessor as president of the Treuhandanstalt, said in 1991. "That is the best way to marshal knowledge, new capital and new strategic goals in order to save a company and jobs."

21   This was the answer given, for example, to IG Metall, Germany's largest union, when it lobbied for the establishment of a sister organization to the Treuhandanstalt that would have helped restructure companies gradually and would have saved many jobs, at least for a while.

22   The Treuhandanstalt instead wanted to channel those resources as quickly as possible into the sector of the economy that was self-supporting, and this meant that speed was crucial in order to disarm critics by showing results rapidly.

23   "The more successful we are, the sooner we will disappear," Mr. Rohwedder said four years ago.

24   This did not mean that either Mr. Rohwedder, who was born and grew up in East Germany before migrating to West Germany and a career in business, or Ms. Breuel, who long was finance minister in a state bordering East Germany, was unaware of the pain of rapid privatization.

25   Long acquaintance with East German conditions made them in particular aware that the companies being dissolved or auctioned off by the Treuhandanstalt had social as well as economic responsibilities in the old regime.

26   Companies were often virtual communities unto themselves in East Germany with their own kindergartens, schools, libraries, clinics and summer guest houses on the Baltic Sea.

27   The armies of East Germans who found themselves on the streets were thus deprived not only of a paycheck but a base for their social lives.

28   Ms. Breuel never flinched from the basic principle, even when aggrieved leftist politicians started making a rebound in recent years as the voting power of hundreds of thousands of unemployed and underemployed made itself felt. Accusations of "slash-and-burn" and "sell-out" were rampant, and indeed Mr. Rohwedder's assassination in early 1991 has never been clarified.

29   Wolfgang Roth, long-time economics spokesman for the Social Democrats, said that the government was presiding over "a catastrophic development" that was creating "wide areas of de-industrialization."

30   With the stakes so immense, Ms. Breuel found it symbolically important to carry out the basic work quickly and then close the Treuhandanstalt's shop by her initial deadline, even though much work remains.

31   She even wanted the baton to be passed to private-sector bodies for the remaining work, but other views prevailed and four new state agencies have inherited various Treuhandanstalt functions.

32   Nevertheless, she clearly never lost sight of her working principle that privatization should be given absolute priority.

33   "Despite justified criticism in individual cases, the work of the Treuhandanstalt was successful," said Ingeborg Elisabeth Buhl, an economist with Deutsche Bank Research.

34 "Working under difficult conditions, including considerable political pressure, it privatized more quickly than could have been expected in 1990. The privatization has required enormous funds, but slower privatization would have been even more expensive for the taxpayer."

DISCUSSION QUESTIONS

1. What do you think Smith means when he states that "Critics of the private-sector approach, furthermore, claim that East Germany has now become a mere annex to the West German industrial giant"? What does it mean to become an annex of something? What are the social and political ramifications of perceiving oneself as being annexed?

2. Smith writes that much of the debate over the privatization of East Germany's economy "falls in line with the predictable face-off between free-market enthusiasts and guardians of social welfare." What do you see as the advantages and disadvantages of both sides?

3. According to Smith, supporters of privatization assert that the former East Germany has been transformed from a moribund economy to the fastest-growing region in Europe, with a "state-of-the-art infrastructure making it one of the fastest lanes on the continent's information superhighway." What connections can you make between this comment and the article in Chapter Eight by Nicholas Negroponte entitled "In the Information Age, a New Set of Have-Nots"? Why do you think the former East Germany has become "one of the fastest lanes on the continent's information superhighway"? What would Negroponte say?

4. Smith writes that "companies being dissolved or auctioned off by the Treuhandanstalt had social as well as economic responsibilities in the old regime. Companies were often virtual communities unto themselves in East Germany with their own kindergartens, schools, libraries, clinics and summer guest houses on the Baltic Sea." What are the benefits of this sort of community lifestyle in a work environment? Do you see any disadvantages? Do you know of other regions or nations where workplaces are organized in a similar fashion? Can you think of any work situations in the United States similar to the one described here?

5. The article suggests that the privatization of the East German econo-my occurred extremely quickly but with a social cost. To what extent do you think people's lives should be disrupted for the sake of a greater cause—in this case the development of a free-market econo-my in the former East Germany?

6. What do you think might be the significance of the title of this article? What are the "lessons"?

WRITING ASSIGNMENTS

1. Research the fall of the Berlin Wall. What led up to this historic event? What were the circumstances surrounding this event? Then write an informative report on this subject. Be prepared to share your findings with the class.

2. Write a causal analysis paper in which you explore the social and political ramifications of the privatization of East Germany's economy. You will probably need to do some reading beyond this article in order to obtain a broader perspective on this issue. Be sure to devel-op your ideas with specific examples and details.

3. Smith writes, "The armies of East Germans who found themselves on the streets were thus deprived not only of a paycheck but a base for their social lives." In a well-developed exploratory essay, respond to the following question: "To what extent do you think work worlds and private worlds should overlap?" Be specific in your response.

4. Smith writes of the East German economic transformation, "The pri-ority had to be placed on privatization rather than on saving jobs." Write a brief paper in which you explore the pros and cons of this line of thinking. Can you compare this situation to any other circum-stances in history when a similar sort of action was taken? What do you perceive to be the potential problems and/or advantages of this policy? Before beginning your paper, you may want to do some research.

RUSSIAN FIRM LEARNS TO NAVIGATE IN A FREE MARKET

Fred Hiatt and Margaret Shapiro

Washington Post Service

■

In the following selection, Fred Hiatt and Margaret Shapiro look at the navigation of Russian firms into the free market. Their article focuses in particular on one Russian shipyard's shift from a communist economy into the free market. Like many Russian firms, Severnaya Verf was a business that depended heavily upon military orders, employed a surplus of people, and took too long to complete orders. However, in three years, the shipyard has transformed itself by privatizing, creating spin-off subsidiaries, attracting foreign investors, and employing talented workers with initiative. Although the transformation is slow, progress is taking place. As you read this report, you might begin to think about the various sorts of difficulties countries entering the free market might encounter. In what specific ways must employer and employee attitudes about business and labor change?

■

1   ST. PETERSBURG—Few enterprises seemed more hopeless when communism died than the Severnaya Verf shipyard on the banks of the Neva River. Like thousands of companies across Russia, it depended on military orders, it employed too many people and it took far too long to produce anything.

2   But three years of life in the free market have begun to make a mark. Severnaya Verf—the name means "northern shipyard"—has privatized, spun off subsidiaries, attracted foreign investment and discovered talent and initiative in a work force that for years was told only to follow orders.

3 And in the last few months, the enterprise, like Russia's economy, achieved something remarkable: Its production slump stopped.

4 Recent statistics suggest that Russia's Great Depression has finally hit bottom. As hundreds of new and privatized companies adapt to a changed world, and with signs that inflation may be slowing, some experts predict a period of stabilization.

5 "The outlook is now better than at any time since the reforms began," said Richard Layard, a British economist who has advised the Russian government since it began dismantling the command economy in 1992.

6 "In principle, the level of production is stable," he said. "Once the economy reaches the bottom, then the recovery starts."

7 A March report by the government's Center for Economic Reform found that "industrial production in Russia has now bottomed out."

8 The bottoming-out raises hopes that Russia's long-feared explosion of unemployment may never materialize. It also suggests that the heavily militarized, heavily industrialized economy may be slowly creaking in a new, more consumer-friendly direction.

9 But an end to decline, even if sustained, does not mean things are rosy. Russian industry in September 1994 was producing only 51 percent as much as in December 1991, when Russia embarked on its free-market reforms, and by this January the figure had reached only 54.5 percent.

10 While some sectors have stabilized, others, especially those producing consumer products that cannot compete with imports, continue to collapse.

11 Moreover, Yegor T. Gaidar, the architect of Russia's reforms, cautioned that the apparent improvement stems partly from government money-pumping that also led to a monthly inflation rate of 18 percent in January.

12 The rate fell to 11 percent in February—still an annual rate of 350 percent—and is likely to drop farther this month.

13 "One can speak of economic stability only when the stabilization and early growth of industrial production coincide with a relatively low rate of inflation," he told the newspaper Vek.

14 But Mr. Gaidar agreed that the Russian economy was shifting, with the long-neglected service sector taking off.

15 From the start, reformers said that some slump in production would be necessary and even beneficial because the Soviet economy was so misproportioned.

16   "We have ceased producing lots of equipment nobody needs and making steel in excessive quantities," Mr. Gaidar said.

17   Some reformers also believe that official statistics somewhat exaggerate the slump, since many new producers try to stay out of sight of tax collectors and other officials.

18   Maxim Boiko, head of the Russian Privatization Center, said 14,000 companies had now been privatized.

19   "Now, a process of reconstruction is going on," he said. "Faster in some firms, and slower in others, but an intensive process is taking place."

20   Both the process and the roadblocks are fully in evidence at Severnaya Verf.

21   "We are struggling for our survival," said Vadim Volostnykh, 57, a third-generation shipbuilder and chief of the company's strategic-planning division.

22   "There are signs that the decline in production is over," he added. "But the current, low level of production is very unstable for us. Our fixed costs are as high as before."

23   A proud producer of navy destroyers since 1912, the company has watched military orders slump from more than 70 percent of its total business to less than 15 percent in five years—and the military does not pay even those bills, Mr. Volostnykh said.

24   To cope with such a blow, the shipyard began privatizing in the summer of 1992. It broke up into one holding company and eight subsidiaries, each with more maneuverability and a better chance to attract foreign investment than one giant company.

25   The yard's machine shop, for example, used to serve only the shipyard and other military shipbuilders in the area, fulfilling instructions from Moscow.

26   Now the shop is a company of its own, and its longtime foreman, Dmitri Komissarov, is chief executive, profitably making machine tools for mining enterprises in Russia and abroad.

27   A second spin-off, manufacturing kitchen sinks, has sold 30 percent of its stock to a Swiss company. A third, making furniture, is striking a partnership with a Danish company.

28   "The smaller they are, the quicker and better they adjust," Mr. Volostnykh said.

29   The overall strategy was sound enough to convince a German shipyard, Bremen Vulkan Verbund, to buy 14 percent of shares in the parent company in November 1993. The Germans have helped the yard

30   not with money but with know-how in novel areas such as marketing and applying for loans.

Yet the future remains highly uncertain for the shipyard. The total work force has declined from more than 9,000 to 6,300. No one was laid off, but many young workers drifted away to the new private sector, where wages exceed the shipyard's $100 monthly average.

31   The largest single subsidiary, the shipyard itself, employs half the workers. It hopes to maintain some military orders, to keep its technological edge, while building more cargo vessels.

32   And Severnaya Verf can build high-quality ships, Mr. Volostnykh said, proudly pointing to a model of a sleek, Sovremenny-class destroyer. The problem is that Asian competitors can build more quickly and flexibly, thanks to superior organization, not equipment.

33   Severnaya Verf thrived in an era when the longer a project took, the more money the enterprise would earn. Privatization has not led to radical changes in that work ethic, partly because workers and managers own a controlling share of stock, Mr. Volostnykh said.

34   That, too, is typical of companies across Russia, where the government had to yield to pressure from factory directors in order to win support for any privatization at all.

35   The result is not all bad, Mr. Volostnykh said. The shipyard enjoys "social stability, security and concord between employees and management," he said. Workers, even those nearing retirement age, like Mr. Komissarov, have adapted well, when given responsibility.

36   And in the near term, the shipyard—like Russia in general—had no choice: There was no cadre of better-trained managers waiting to take over, Mr. Volostnykh said.

37   "But employees are inefficient owners," he said. "They're interested in today's wages, not the long-term future."

DISCUSSION QUESTIONS

1. Consider the title of the article. What rhetorical impact does it have upon you as a reader? How effective do you think it is as a headline?

2. In small groups, discuss the similarities and/or differences you see between this article and another article in this chapter entitled "Privatization: Lessons of the East" by Richard E. Smith. Make a graphic representation of the similarities and differences to present to the class.

3. What particular strategies has Severnaya Verf used to facilitate moving into the free market? Why do you think these strategies may have helped this firm gain a stronger foothold in the free market? What problems does the firm need to overcome even with the use of these strategies?

4. The authors write that Severnaya Verf may be able to build state-of-the-art equipment and machinery, but that "The problem is that Asian competitors can build more quickly and flexibly, thanks to superior organization, not equipment." Speculate about how Asian companies organize their production. What strategies do you think they employ to be faster and more flexible?

5. The authors quote Vadim Volostnykh, chief of Severnaya Verf's strategic-planning division, as saying "employees are inefficient owners. They're interested in today's wages, not the long-term future." Do you agree with this view of employees? How well do you think profit-sharing and similar programs work?

WRITING ASSIGNMENTS

1. Write a paper that compares and contrasts the shifts of the Russian and East German economies into the free market. Begin the project by reading the article entitled "Privatization: Lessons of the East" in this chapter. Then make a brainstorming list that explores the similarities and differences. Be sure to support your main points with specific details and examples.

2. Write an informative report about the current state of the Russian economy. What is its history? How did it get to its present state? What are the predictions for the future? This project will require some outside research. Support your main points with specific details, and be prepared to present your findings to the class in an oral presentation.

3. A Severnaya Verf official is quoted in this article as stating that "employees are inefficient owners. They're interested in today's wages, not the long-term future." Write a paper in which you respond to the following question: "Can employees also be efficient owners?" Be sure to support your opinions with specific evidence and reasons.

TWENTY YEARS AFTER, VIETNAM TREADS SOFTLY

Clare Hollingworth

International Herald Tribune

■

In 1975, United States military forces were forced to withdraw from South Vietnam in what has become known as the fall of Saigon. Over twenty years later, the Vietnamese government is now hoping the Americans will return—but this time as investors in a growing economy. The following selection by Clare Hollingworth examines the keen interest Vietnamese government officials and businesspeople have in having Americans aid them in their economic endeavors. As one official has said, "We need the Americans today to help us attract the capital so urgently required to modernize our infrastructure and build new factories and mines. We also need their advice in establishing new industries as well as stock markets." While reading this article, recall what you have heard or remember about the Vietnam War. What opinions do you have about the United States helping the economic development of a former "enemy"?

■

1 HO CHI MINH CITY, Vietnam—A public holiday has been declared on April 28 to celebrate the 20th anniversary of "liberation"—when the Communists took over Saigon and South Vietnam and the Americans withdrew.

2 While the population here looks forward to a day without work and to organized festivities in the parks, there is obvious relief that no military parades are planned. No one wants to "offend the Americans."

3 Even in the capital, Hanoi, where a national military parade is being rehearsed, there is little enthusiasm for the celebrations.

4   "We need the Americans today to help us attract the capital so urgently required to modernize our infrastructure and build new factories and mines," an official said. "We also need their advice in establishing new industries as well as stock markets."

5   English is now the second language in the cities. The Vietnamese constantly refer to news they have heard over the VOA or BBC. A daily newspaper and several magazines are printed in English.

6   On the surface every encouragement is given to foreigners—Japanese as well as Europeans and Americans—to go into business, in what appears to be a progressive Asian country about to join the fast-growing "Little Tigers": Singapore, Hong Kong, Thailand and South Korea.

7   But there are snags. Ho Chi Minh City may look more like Bangkok every day, with Mercedes cars and Honda motorcycles creating enormous traffic jams. But there is still a good deal of petty thievery among the luxury shops and market stalls.

8   The greatest difficulties foreign businessmen encounter center on differences between North and South. One frequently hears that "the tail still wags the dog." Ho Chi Minh City lives its own life. Sometimes, on its own, it holds up entirely legal contracts which have been authorized in Hanoi.

9   *Doi moi,* or restructuring, is the current buzz word for economic reform. According to Nguyen Xuan Oanh, the Harvard-educated professor who originated the idea, the priority for Vietnam today is to maintain monetary and political stability. When this is done, he says, greater political freedom will be possible. Vietnam, like neighboring China, currently suffers from an inflation rate of 15 to 20 percent.

10   But the most serious problem Vietnam faces comes from the dissatisfied rural population. More than seven in 10 Vietnamese live in the countryside, where there is rising discontent. Twenty percent of peasants are unemployed and an additional 20 percent are underemployed. Most young rural workers dream of moving to the bright lights of the big cities.

11   The government in Hanoi hopes to increase its political clout in the region by joining the Association of South East Asian Nations in July. Leaders in Hanoi hope membership in the pro-American grouping will strengthen their hand in dealing with Beijing on the dispute over the Spratly Islands in the South China Sea, and other issues.

12   Meanwhile, although a small minority of bankers are skeptical about the future prosperity of Vietnam, most businessmen are trying to get a toehold in the country before rents rise to the levels of the other "Little Tigers."

13   "We shall soon be celebrating the American return to Vietnam," a
senior official claimed, raising his glass, "not their withdrawal."

DISCUSSION QUESTIONS

1. In small groups, discuss what you know about the Vietnam War. Make
    a brainstorming list or cluster with the information that you generate
    during your discussion. Additionally, prepare a list of three questions
    about the war that you would like to have answered.

2. Hollingworth writes that "English is now the second language in the
    cities." Read the article in Chapter One entitled "Courses in English
    Flourish in Vietnam." What role does language play in the economic
    development of a country? Why would knowledge of English be so
    important to the economic growth of Vietnam?

3. *Doi moi,* or restructuring, according to Hollingworth, is the current
    buzzword in Vietnam's economy today. What do you think is meant
    by the term *doi moi?* What to you think *restructuring* might mean?

4. Do you think there might be some similarities between the economic
    restructuring occurring in Vietnam and the economic changes occur-
    ring in the former East Germany (as discussed in "Privatization:
    Lessons of the East")? Why or why not?

5. Hollingworth writes that there are "snags" in the growth of Ho Chi
    Minh City as a progressive Asian city, stating that "there is still a good
    deal of petty thievery among the luxury shops and market stalls."
    How unusual is this activity for a major city? Does this sort of thiev-
    ery make more of a difference in a developing nation?

6. Do you see any irony in the last paragraph of this article? Why should
    the Vietnamese be celebrating?

7. What do you think general public opinion is in the United States at
    present about commerce with Vietnam? Support your opinions with
    specific evidence.

WRITING ASSIGNMENTS

1. Write a proposal for a business venture or investment in Vietnam.
    Include a description of the business and its desired outcomes, a
    rationale for the investment, and a method for meeting the proposed
    outcomes. Be prepared to present your proposal to the class.

2. Research the economic development of Vietnam since the end of the Vietnam War. Then write an informative report that details the economic road this country has taken since the end of the war. You will need to consult outside sources in order to develop your essay.

3. Hollingworth writes that "the most serious problem Vietnam faces comes from the dissatisfied rural population. More than seven in 10 Vietnamese live in the countryside, where there is rising discontent." Compare and contrast this situation with that of East Germany as presented in the article "Privatization: Lessons of the East." Write a paper that explains, at least in part, what the Vietnamese might learn from Germany. What issues need to be considered when planning a restructuring of a nation's economy? Try to be as specific as possible in your response.

THE THIRD WORLD IS SHRINKING FAST

Reginald Dale

International Herald Tribune

■

At a recent United Nations summit meeting, delegates spoke of the impoverished conditions in Third World countries and the need to provide relief for them. However, in his commentary, Reginald Dale explores the changing economic picture of the Third World and claims that "What used to be known as the Third World has virtually disappeared." According to Dale, "the rapid spread of free markets, privatization, and booming trade" has dramatically altered the economic situation of these countries for the better. Forty years ago, the Third World stereotype was that of subsistence farming and mining. Today, 60 percent of developing-country exports are manufactured products. Although Dale acknowledges that these countries still have widespread poverty, he points out that the United States does too, and that if we continue to supplement the pockets of fast-growing countries, we are "in effect letting those governments off the hook." As you read through this article, try to recall news items you may have heard about the economic conditions of some of the developing countries mentioned in this article. To what extent do you think Dale is correct in saying that these countries no longer need aid?

■

1   Washington—The United Nations summit meeting on social development this month was not merely an extravagant waste of time. It was also a striking anachronism. Most of the delegates—especially the representatives of private charitable bodies who flocked to Copenhagen—seemed to have come by nonstop time machine from the 1970s.

2   They appeared blissfully unaware of the biggest upheaval in the world economy of the past quarter century—parallel in scope to the

collapse of Communism. What used to be known as the Third World has virtually disappeared.

3   It is hard for development activists to accept this. Many of them have dedicated their lives to proselytizing about the hopeless plight of the world's poor countries and what the wicked rich should do to help them.

4   So the social summit was cast in the old terms of rich-poor conflict. The disquieting image of countless countries mired in poverty, hunger and debt still dependent on the good will of others for survival was once again cultivated.

5   That is a picture of a static world that no longer exists. Thanks to the rapid spread of free markets, privatization and booming trade, the old Third World has been overrun by dynamic change. The clear-cut lines between rich and poor countries have been swept away.

6   "International trade, capital mobility, communications and transportation have knit the developing world firmly into the industrialized world's economic structures," writes Susan Raymond of the New York Academy of Sciences in the magazine Economic Reform Today.

7   The only chunk of the globe that still looks like the old Third World is sub-Saharan Africa, and not all of that qualifies. Outside Africa, you have to look hard to find a traditional Third World country.

8   There are virtually none in Latin America or the Middle East, and not many in Asia. Burma, perhaps, might count, and Laos, Cambodia and Afghanistan.

9   Most of the former Third World is making unprecedented economic and social progress. Developing countries are forecast to grow 70 percent faster than industrial countries over the next decade.

10   Unlike the old Third World stereotype, developing countries are no longer mainly scrabbling a hard living from subsistence agriculture and the exploitation of their commodities and raw materials.

11   Manufactured products now account for 60 percent of developing-country exports, against only 5 percent 40 years ago. But food production this year will still grow twice as fast in developing as in industrial countries.

12   In education, health and life expectancy, the gap between rich and poor is narrowing. In many parts of the world fertility rates have passed their peak.

13   By 2020, according to World Bank projections, only six of the biggest 15 economies will be drawn from the ranks of today's industrial countries. (The forecast starts with China as No. 1, followed by the United States, Japan, India, Indonesia, and Germany. Then come Korea, Thailand, France, Taiwan, Brazil, Italy, Russia, Britain and Mexico.)

14   Of course, there are still countries that are disasters, such as Somalia and Rwanda, but they are exceptions. There is also widespread poverty. But a lot of it is in countries like Thailand or India that are otherwise doing very nicely.

15   There also is plenty in first-world countries like the United States. All of which means that former Third World countries must assume much more responsibility for their own societies.

16   If rich-country donors focus on pockets of poverty in fast-growing countries like Thailand, "we are in effect letting those governments off the hook," Ms. Raymond says. "These free economies and pluralistic societies are not problem children."

17   Unfortunately, far too many people still think they are.

DISCUSSION QUESTIONS

1. What do you think Dale means when he writes in the first paragraph that the United Nations summit was "a striking anachronism"? Why do you think he says the representatives of charitable organizations "seemed to have come by nonstop time machine from the 1970s"?

2. Dale writes that "Thanks to the rapid spread of free markets, privatization and booming trade, the old Third World has been overrun by dynamic change. The clear-cut lines between rich and poor countries have been swept away." Do you agree with his assessment of the Third World? Are the lines no longer distinct? Can you point to specific examples to either confirm or refute Dale's statement?

3. Dale writes that "Of course, there are still countries that are disasters, such as Somalia and Rwanda, but they are exceptions. There is also widespread poverty. But a lot of it is in countries like Thailand or India that are otherwise doing very nicely." If these countries are "otherwise doing very nicely," who do you think should have the responsibility for taking care of the impoverished? Do you think Dale is saying nothing should be done?

4. At the end of the article, Dale quotes Susan Raymond of the New York Academy of Sciences as saying, "These free economies and pluralistic societies are not problem children." What do you think she means by this statement?

WRITING ASSIGNMENTS

1. Write an informative report on the economy of a developing country such as Thailand. Your report should cover the economic growth of the country over the past few decades. What changes and developments can you find? Support your main ideas and points with specific facts and details. Be prepared to share your findings with the class.

2. Write a paper in which you address the following question: "Should developing countries receive aid from outside agencies or First-World countries?" Begin your writing process by using a prewriting strategy such as clustering or freewriting and be sure to support your opinions with specific reasons and evidence.

3. Write an exploratory paper in which you respond to the following question: "To what extent are the lines between rich and poor countries no longer clear-cut?" Begin your writing process with a prewriting strategy such as clustering or freewriting. Be sure to support your opinions with specific evidence.

4. Write an essay that explores the following question: "How can charitable organizations and countries such as the United States help developing countries assume more responsibility for their own societies?" Begin your writing process with a prewriting strategy such as clustering or freewriting. Be sure to support your opinions with specific details and evidence.

REAL JOB TRAINING SETS PLAN APART

Erik Ipsen

International Herald Tribune

■

The following article by Erik Ipsen reports on a Scottish job training program that goes beyond most such programs. According to Ipsen, the trainees being paid by Wise Group actually produce things. Instead of building unneeded brick walls, the trainees learn their trade by participating in community-improvement projects. These job training programs are being run by private companies under government contracts. Believing that unemployment problems are best dealt with at the local level, Britain has shied away from state-run quick-fix job counseling and training programs, opting rather for the job training that improves both the community and individual self-esteem. As you read this report, think about the underlying reasons why such training programs are having success. What elements make them successful? Are there similar sorts of programs in your community? Are these types of programs needed in your community?

■

1   GLASGOW—Amid the din of hammering and chiseling in vocational training Unit 46 of the Easterhouse Community College on Glasgow's east side, Gordon O'Regen has discovered his vocation.

2   "Cladding is what I want to do," said Mr. O'Regen, his back to a huge stack of yellow fiber insulating blocks that he was cementing to the wall of the classroom. "I love this work."

3   Strictly speaking, Mr. O'Regen, 23, doesn't have a job. Instead he is being paid by Wise Group, one of scores of private organizations in Britain financed by the government to help train the long-term unemployed and get them back into jobs.

4   Two points separate Wise from its peers. Half of its trainee-workers go on to find jobs—a success rate that outstrips the average by more than 50 percent. Second is the definition of its role, as something more than a mere means to an end.

5   "The difference for us is that we think there is merit in what we are doing right here and now," said Alan Sinclair, the group's founder and chief executive. "This is not just a springboard to a job."

6   Jobs are scarce in Glasgow. Unemployment stands as 15 percent, far above the national average of 9 percent. The industrial companies that once dominated the economy did not just downsize, they closed down. The Wise response is to treat what ails severely economically depressed areas with a mixture of training and job creation.

7   It is a prescription that the group has taken afield. In the east London borough of Newham, the 3-year-old Newham Wise has outperformed its parent, finding jobs for 60 percent of its graduates. Wise's first franchise, north of Inverness, opened last year.

8   "Their philosophy is that a lot more can be done than simple job training," said John Philpott, director of the Employment Policy Institute in London. "And it gets results."

9   What the organization's trainee workers do is produce things—not holes in the earth to be filled in and dug again, not brick walls to be built and torn down—but permanent community improvements.

10   After eight weeks in class, Mr. O'Regen will go into his community to install insulation on public housing projects. Other trainees are converting the rubble-strewn backyards of public projects into gardens with brick walkways and custom-made iron fencing.

11   "It has brought back a lot of pride to a community that used to pay its own way in this city," said Dave Hanratty, a community representative in Glasgow's down-at-the-heels Parkhead neighborhood. "Our local boys were the ones doing the work. It gives them an uplift, and it put them back into society as rent-paying workers."

12   In spite of the praise and even emulation won by Wise, it represents an increasing anomaly in Britain. In recent years the government has shifted resources into job counseling and away from job training even though 4 in 10 jobless Britons are long-term unemployed.

13   "In Britain there is a stronger feeling than on the Continent that the problem lies with the individual rather than with the structure of the economy," Mr. Philpott said. "That is why in Europe you see more of an emphasis on job training."

14   Underlying that hard line is an increasing conviction on the part of policymakers and academics that there exists a strong linkage

between generous jobless benefits and Europe's increasingly high level of long-term unemployment.

15   So Britain has inched increasingly toward the American model. It offers what some experts regard as punitive benefits programs. On average, those programs offer the unemployed among the lowest benefits in Europe relative to the wages they earned in their last jobs.

16   Like the United States and unlike many Continental countries, Britain eschews state-run training programs. Instead it has opted for programs run by local private companies under government contract in the belief that they represent tailor-made solutions to local conditions.

17   Wise is one of those. In Glasgow the collapse over the last 20 years of the traditional heavy industry base has left the city with one of the highest unemployment rates in the nation.

18   "A two-week career counseling course in self-improvement is not going to do a lot here," Alistair Grimes, Wise's controller, said. He is also dismissive of the government's standard six-month training programs.

19   "A quick fix is not what is needed," he said.

20   It is from the sprawling public housing projects that carpet the hillsides south and east of central Glasgow that Wise draws the bulk of its trainees. Roughly a third of them have been jobless for three years or more, and most of them lack a high school diploma. From that raw material the group has excelled at creating not just workers but also much needed community improvements.

21   "We pay them £2.8 million and in return get more than £2.5 million worth of work that we would have to pay someone else for," said Stephen Inch, head of economic development for the City of Glasgow, one of Wise's many financial backers. "On top of that, we get training for several hundred people."

22   Tackling long-term unemployment never entered into the decision to set up Wise 11 years ago. Instead it was created to help address the problem of the poor insulating in Glasgow's housing estates, which meant that a significant slice of meager family budgets went to keeping the cold out.

23   It turned out that the sort of low-skill, high-volume draft-proofing that was required proved ideal for the city's unemployed. Thus it was only via the backdoor that Mr. Sinclair realized that his program might provide one answer to Glasgow's unemployment problem.

24   The program starts with eight weeks of training in a range of activities stretching from horticulture and woodworking to word processing and catering. The program then runs for another 10 months of actual work experience.

25   Mr. Sinclair, 40, insists that one of Wise's greatest contributions is restoring its worker-trainees' self-esteem. It is a notion bolstered by the fact that the group typically pays its workers a union-agreed weekly wage of £115 ($184), twice what they would get on the dole. Most of the trainee-workers agree on the importance of self-respect.

26   "Many of the boys here have never worked in the building game, so that they can go on from here with a bit of experience and a bit of confidence," said Daniel Hall, as he laid paving stones as part of a team renovating a south Glasgow community garden. Mr. Hall, 47, who lost his job two years ago, added, "I am back in a routine again, so I am happy."

27   By blurring the definition between training and actual work, Wise has also helped to overcome one of the greatest hurdles of such programs, an uplifting answer to the question inevitably asked by all employers: When was the last time you had a job?

DISCUSSION QUESTIONS

1. Do you agree with the statement made in this article that "there exists a strong linkage between generous jobless benefits and Europe's increasingly high level of long-term unemployment"? Why or why not?

2. Ipsen quotes John Philpott, director of the Employment Policy Institute in London as stating, "In Britain there is a stronger feeling than on the Continent that the problem lies with the individual rather than with the structure of the economy." What is your opinion of this statement? To what extent do you think this statement holds true for workers in the United States?

3. According to Ipsen, Britain has opted for local training programs as opposed to state-run programs "in the belief that they represent tailor-made solutions to local conditions." To what extent do you believe in such a philosophy? Give specific reasons for your position.

4. Ipsen writes that "one of Wise's greatest contributions is restoring its worker-trainees' self-esteem." Speculate about the importance of this contribution. How does restored self-esteem affect the individual beyond the workplace? What does the restored self-esteem do for the individual? The family? The community?

5. Besides the response given in the last paragraph of this article, what do you think the benefits are of "blurring the definition between training and actual work"?

WRITING ASSIGNMENTS

1. Visit your local employment office. Take notes on what you observe and ask questions about employment and job training opportunities. Then write an informative report about the experience. What did you learn from the experience? What information can you share with others about the experience? Be prepared to share your experience with others in the class.

2. Write a paper that explores the relationship between self-esteem and work. To what extent is one's self-esteem connected with one's work? Use specific details and examples to support your opinions.

3. Write an essay in which you respond to the following question: "To what extent is unemployment the fault of the individual rather than economic conditions?" Support your opinions with specific details and evidence.

CHAPTER NINE WRITING ASSIGNMENTS

1. Write an informative paper that details the economic transformation of one former communitst country. Your paper should include information about both the positive and negative effects of the economic changes being made in this country. You might begin this writing project by creating a list of questions you want to ask about this particular country's economy. Then respond to those questions with a prewriting strategy such as freewriting or clustering. Be sure to support your main points with specific facts and details.

2. Write a paper that explores the relationship of language to economic growth. How are language and the economies of different nations intertwined? You might narrow the topic by looking at this question in terms of only a few nations. Use a prewriting strategy such as clustering to help you get started. Be sure to support your main ideas with specific details and examples.

3. Write a paper that explores the impact of war or civil conflict on one particular nation's economy (for example, Bosnia, Rwanda, or Ireland). You will need to do outside research in order to gather information for the development of this essay. Be sure to support your ideas with specific examples, details, and facts.

4. The United States has been both praised and criticized for its intervention in the economic affairs of other nations. Write an opinion paper in which you respond to the following question: "What role should the United States play in the economic development of other countries?" Although this is an opinion paper, your main points and ideas should be supported with specific evidence and details.

5. Write a problem-solution paper in which you discuss the problem of unemployment in the United States and offer potential solutions. What specific strategies might be used to curb unemployment? Begin your writing process with a prewriting strategy such as clustering. Be sure to develop your thoughts with specific details.

Fighting for Human Rights

Although we may live in a world of diversity, human rights and civil liberties should be considered a common thread that pulls us together. Ideally, these rights should not be subject to the laws of a particular nation but rather should be an inherent part of our humanity. Unfortunately, this ideal scenario is far from reality, and we can only work toward it through vigilance and perseverance. The selections in this chapter have been chosen to broaden your knowledge about the status of human rights in the world today.

The chapter begins with a brief editorial about the International Covenant on Civil and Political Rights treaty, which was signed by President Jimmy Carter in the 1970s and finally ratified during the Bush administration. Entitled "Rights: A Look at America," the editorial offers commentary about the first review the United States received from the United Nations for treaty compliance. The editorial stresses that the United States' participation in the review process helps to emphasize the message that all countries must be accountable for the policing of human rights.

The selection that follows takes a closer look at this treaty. In "Role Reversal for U.S. at Rights Hearing," Julia Preston reports on the many reactions to the United States' report on its compliance with the International Covenant on Civil and Political Rights treaty. The process of being reviewed was a complete role reversal for the United States since it is usually in the position of policing rather than being policed. However, as one member of the United Nations review committee stated, "People look to your country as a yardstick for justice and fair play."

We find a serious question about human rights in "Materialism and Greed Spurring 'Dowry Deaths.'" In this selection, Molly Moore exposes the continuing practice in India of dowry harassment. Moore explains that although demanding a dowry was outlawed in 1961, a new focus on material wealth has prompted a need for families to have more funds, which has led to an increase in the number of dowry payoffs being demanded. If a bride's family does not comply, the bride may be beaten, tortured, or even killed.

Further human rights violations can be found in the article by Stephen Buckley entitled "In Nigeria, a Scared Silence Reigns." In this piece, Buckley explores the violation of human rights being perpetrated by the Nigerian military government against innocent Nigerian citizens. In addition to closing down all newspapers, dismantling labor unions, and routinely arresting and murdering innocent victims, the military regime has also declared that "no act of the federal military government may be questioned henceforth in a court of law."

The chapter concludes with an article entitled "CIA Ignored Abuses in Guatemala" by R. Jeffrey Smith and Dana Priest. The authors of this article report that the Central Intelligence Agency and United States military personnel were responsible for the arming and training of anti-Communist military forces that allegedly killed more than 100,000 peasants. The probe into the connection between United States military intelligence and the Guatemalan anti-Communist military forces was initiated by Jennifer Harbury, an American citizen whose Guatemalan husband disappeared.

As these selections will show, the battle against human rights violations is far from over. Much work needs to be done before the human and civil rights of all people are protected at all times. As you read through these articles, you might consider two questions: What is a human right? And once we can recognize human rights, how can they be protected?

RIGHTS: A LOOK AT AMERICA

The Washington Post

■

The International Covenant on Civil and Political Rights is a treaty that was signed by President Jimmy Carter but was not ratified until the Bush administration. This treaty sets standards for human rights and allows the United Nations to review a nation's compliance with this treaty. The following editorial is a commentary on the review the United States received from the United Nations for its compliance with the treaty. Since many feel that human rights is "an area in which the United States can rightly and proudly claim to be a world leader," some Americans may have felt strange having an outside organization review the human rights record of the United States. However, the editorial makes clear that the United States' participation in this process helped to get the message across that all countries must be accountable for the policing of human rights and that this participation is simply an extension of the scrutiny human rights policies presently receive in the United States. As you read this selection, think about what should be considered a human right and how these rights can be protected. Why do you think there is so much discussion about human rights? Why do you think people might disagree about what is or is not a human right?

■

1   Some Americans do not like seeing the folks at the United Nations picking over the U.S. human rights record. Who are they to offer instruction in the finer points of an area in which the United States can rightly and proudly claim to be a world leader? The question arises from the first-ever review, now going on in New York, of American compliance with the International Covenant on Civil and Political Rights. This treaty was signed by Jimmy Carter but ratified only in the Bush administration.

2   The days are fortunately past when a human rights review at the United Nations could be expected to produce an extravaganza of Communist-

Third World demagoguery. In those days, beginning with the Helsinki Accords fashioned during the Ford administration, human rights were at the cutting edge of a global political and ideological struggle. Now the atmosphere is different, and the focus is on specific national performance. The United States is not being called on the carpet in New York. It is simply submitting itself to a routine review and taking the occasion to showcase the American record of full compliance with the covenant and the American system of civil liberties.

3   The purpose goes beyond self-celebration. It is to strengthen the American capacity to hold to a high standard those whose record falls short. American participation is part of a useful process of building the habit and expectation of accountability into the policing of human rights.

4   Advocacy groups have showed up in New York to complain about American human rights practices. One group called the United States "a world leader in executing juveniles." The attack stings—and is grossly exaggerated. But some states do allow executions for crimes committed by 16- to 18-year-olds, a practice many Americans oppose and contest in court. The same is true of U.S. policy concerning detained aliens seeking asylum. The strength of the United States is not that it is perfect but that its own citizens are constantly testing and challenging human rights policies with which they disagree. That goes on with or without the prodding of critical outsiders.

DISCUSSION QUESTIONS

1.   In small groups, discuss what you think is meant by the term *human rights*. What do you think are examples of human rights? How would something qualify as a human right? Make a brainstorming list and be ready to share it with the rest of the class.

2.   Speculate about what you think the author of this piece meant by writing that "human rights were at the cutting edge of global and political struggle." Can you point to any specific examples that might support your speculations?

3.   Do you agree with the author of this article that "American participation [in the review process] is part of a useful process of building the habit of expectation of accountability into the policing of human rights." To what extent do you think America's participation will help to strengthen this process?

4. The author of the article writes that "Advocacy groups have showed up in New York to complain about American human rights practices." Other than the ones mentioned in this article, what human rights violations, if any, are still present in the United States?

Writing Assignments

1. Imagine that you are a member of a review team assessing America's record of compliance with the covenant. Write a roundtable discussion of the review team's response to the following question: "To what extent are the human rights of United States citizens protected?" The roundtable should contain at least five participants of different genders and various economic and ethnic backgrounds.

2. Write an informative report that details the history and the content of the International Covenant on Civil and Political Rights. You will need to get a copy of the covenant as well as other information about its history to develop your report. Be prepared to present your report to the class in an oral presentation.

3. Write a definition essay that explores the meaning of the term *human rights*. What should be considered a human right and what should not? What guidelines can be established to help determine what might be a human rights violation? You might begin by examining clear cases of human rights violations and then looking for common factors in all the examples you review. Be sure to support your main ideas and opinions with specific examples and details.

ROLE REVERSAL FOR U.S. AT RIGHTS HEARING

Julia Preston

Washington Post Service

■

In the following selection, Julia Preston reports on the various reactions to the United States' first report on its compliance with the International Covenant on Civil and Political Rights. As the title of this article indicates, the process of being reviewed was a complete reversal for the United States, which usually is in the position of policing human-rights violations rather than being policed. Although the article quotes one Egyptian committee member as stating "People look to your country as a yardstick for justice and fair play," several human-rights activist groups such as Amnesty International criticized the United States for human rights violations. While reading this article, consider what role you think the United States plays in monitoring human-rights violations. To what extent is the Egyptian committee member's comment valid?

■

1   UNITED NATIONS, New York—The United States had to swallow a big dose of its own medicine when senior American officials came for the first time to defend their country's human-rights record formally before the United Nations.

2   A high-powered delegation including John H. F. Shattuck, assistant secretary of state for human rights, and Deval L. Patrick, assistant attorney general for civil rights, gave the United States' first report on its compliance with a key international human-rights treaty.

3   Rights experts chided the United States for endorsing the treaty only half-heartedly and keeping laws on its books that allow capital punishment for teenagers. Nongovernmental rights monitoring groups used the opportunity to unleash a barrage of criticism.

4   It was unusual role reversal for the Clinton administration, which prides itself on vigorous scrutiny of rights violations by other governments and has often used the United Nations to press its case against offending nations.

5   The United States ratified the International Covenant on Civil and Political Rights in 1992. Like every other signer, it must periodically report on measures it is taking to meet terms of the treaty.

6   Hearings are held by the International Human Rights Committee, an independent body that includes leading authorities on rights law. This week, the United States is presenting its first report.

7   Mr. Shattuck's statement called the United States a "work in progress" in its human-rights practices.

8   "Our system is not perfect," he said. But he added that the "essential genius" of the Founding Fathers lay in their creating a system through which injustices "could be addressed and rectified, through the will of the people, under the rule of law."

9   In an interview, he said that being part of the treaty strengthens the United States' hand in dealing with abusive governments. "We're in full compliance with the treaty and have a system of civil liberties that is a model for the rest of the world," he said.

10   Mr. Patrick presented a long list of legal actions the administration has initiated to enforce anti-discrimination laws.

11   Committee members were concerned about reservations the United States tacked onto the treaty when it signed. In one, it declared that the pact does not automatically become domestic law. The U.S. position is that American laws already meet the covenant's standards. As a result, the treaty cannot be used as a basis for action in American courts.

12   Omran Shafei, who is from Egypt, extolled the United States' overall record.

13   "People around the world look to your country as a yardstick for justice and fair play," he said. But he worried that the covenant would become "a dead letter" in this country because of the U.S. conditions.

14   Cecilia Medina Quiroga of Chile wondered whether the failure of the Equal Rights Amendment would put the United States out of sync with the treaty. Júlio Prado Vallejo of Ecuador asserted that California's Proposition 187, which limits benefits to illegal immigrants, had created "discrimination against Latin American minorities."

15   Human-rights monitoring groups were even more outspoken. The U.S. treaty adherence "is purely cosmetic and has no practical value for Americans," said Kenneth Roth, executive director of Human Rights Watch.

16   Amnesty International said that "allegations of torture and ill-treatment in jails and prison are widespread" and that "police brutality is widespread and persistent in many areas."

DISCUSSION QUESTIONS

1. In small groups, compare and contrast this selection with the article entitled "Rights: A Look at America." Although the two pieces deal with the same topic, their rhetorical approaches are significantly different. Make a brainstorming list that identifies the differences and similarities. Be ready to share your thoughts with the rest of the class.

2. Preston writes that "It [the review] was unusual role reversal for the Clinton administration, which prides itself on vigorous scrutiny of rights violations by other governments and has often used the United Nations to press its case against offending nations." What specific examples can you think of in which the United States has protested human-rights violations of other nations?

3. Preston writes that "Mr. Shattuck's statement called the United States a 'work in progress' in its human-rights practices." What do you think Shattuck meant by this statement? Why might the United States' human-rights practices be a "work in progress"?

4. Preston quotes Shattuck as stating that "the 'essential genius' of the Founding Fathers" was in designing a system that could address and rectify injustices "through the will of the people, under the rule of law." To what extent do you think Shattuck's viewpoint is valid?

5. Preston quotes an Egyptian committee member as stating, "People around the world look to your country as a yardstick for justice and fair play." To what extent do you think this statement is valid?

WRITING ASSIGNMENTS

1. Preston quotes Shattuck as stating, "We're in full compliance with the treaty and have a system of civil liberties that is a model for the rest of the world." Write a paper in which you address the following question: "To what extent do you think the United States serves as a model of civil liberties for the rest of the world?" Support your opinions with specific evidence and reasons.

2. Write an informative report on a particular human-rights violation that has been cited by human-rights monitoring groups such as

Human Rights Watch. Consider the following questions as you prewrite: "What was the violation? Why should it be considered a human-rights violation? To what extent were civil liberties violated? Over what length of time (or has) the violation occurred?" Be sure to support your main points with specific details and examples. This project will require some outside research.

3. Write a letter to the editor of your local newspaper or to your congressional representative about a human-rights violation that concerns you. Your letter should clearly state what the violation is and what you would like to see done about it. Use specific details and examples to develop your letter.

MATERIALISM AND GREED SPURRING "DOWRY DEATHS"

Molly Moore

Washington Post Service

■

In the following selection, Molly Moore examines the continuing practice in India of dowry harassment. Although demanding a dowry was outlawed in 1961, Moore explains that the growth of the Indian economy and the development of a consumer mentality has prompted an increase in the number of families of the groom demanding dowry payoffs from a bride's family. If the bride's family does not comply, the young woman might be beaten, burned, tortured, and even killed. Until recently, these dowry deaths for the most part have been ignored by the judicial system. As you read this article, think about the human-rights violations that go beyond the beatings and deaths these women must endure. How might certain attitudes toward women violate civil liberties?

■

1   NEW DELHI—For 20-year-old Asha, marriage was hell. Her in-laws, she wrote in impassioned letters to her father, berated and beat her and once spiked her milk with pesticide in an attempt to poison her.

2   Finally, according to her father, just after her third wedding anniversary, her husband's family gagged her, beat her unconscious and electrocuted her with a live wire. They bundled her bloodied body in a quilt, tossed it in the front yard and called her father to say she was unwell because of an accident.

3   "I knew instantly she had been killed," said the father, Gyan Chand, 54, a government employee. "It was a case of dowry death."

4   In an era when India is enjoying record economic advances and boasts the world's fastest-growing middle class, it is also experiencing a dramatic escalation in reported dowry deaths and bride burnings.

The rise of this ancient practice has been fueled by the intersection of the new age consumerism and Hindu tradition dating from medieval times.

5   Officials say families of every religious, social and economic background are increasingly turning to dowry demands as a means to escape poverty, augment wealth or acquire the modern conveniences they once never heard of but now see advertised daily on television.

6   The police say reported dowry deaths have increased 170 percent nationwide in the last decade, with 6,200 recorded last year. That is an average of 17 married women burned, poisoned, strangled or otherwise killed each day because of their family's failure to meet the dowry demands of the husband's family.

7   "We are becoming a very materialistic and consumer-driven society," said Sundari Nanda, who heads the New Delhi Police Department's Crime Against Women Cell. "For such a society, dowry becomes a way of betterment for those in the process of climbing up."

8   A dowry is the money and gifts a woman's family provides the married couple and the groom's family at the time of marriage. And in the nation's rush to embrace modernity, the demand for it has become a lever for extorting money and goods from a bride's family for years after the wedding. If her family does not comply, the wife is subjected to cruelty, physical abuse and death.

9   "Dowry is a form of theft legitimized by marriage," said M. J. Akbar, a newspaper editor. "It's economic bondage. And when the woman stops being frightened by torture, the only option is to burn her."

10   While law enforcement authorities said the increase partly reflected a greater willingness by women's families to report the deaths, they also said the statistics represented only a fraction of the actual cases believed to exist. They also do not include the tens of thousands of incidents of nonfatal dowry harassment and physical and mental abuse inflicted on wives by husbands and in-laws.

11   Dowry is perhaps the greatest force contributing to the oppression of women in India and elsewhere on the subcontinent. Originally intended as a way to provide for daughters in a culture where women are not entitled to family inheritances, the tradition has evolved into an insidious practice of bankrupting families and abusing women.

12   "In these times when dowry demands should become less and less, instead everybody wants more," said Somvati Singh Alewata, 33, the wife of an Indian soldier and a mother whose daughter was recently married. "We just ruin our lives because of dowry. You have to pay dowry, or nobody will agree to marry your daughter."

13   From the time of a daughter's birth, parents know their family will face years, sometimes generations, of debt to pay for her wedding and dowry, prompting the wide-spread practice of killing baby girls and aborting female fetuses.

14   If the daughter is allowed to live, the parents—believing they are only caretakers for the girl, who will eventually be given to her husband's family—consider her a burden and often give her less food, medical care and attention than her brothers. The bridegrooms' families believe in turn that they are entitled to hefty payments for accepting the burden of a woman.

15   In the United States, the average wedding costs $7,500, according to the Association of Bridal Consultants, a trade group. That is about one-third of the average annual per capita income in the United States. In contrast, even the poorest Indian families often spend more than $3,000 on a wedding. That is the equivalent of nearly 10 years' wages for the average worker. Often, the cost of the ceremony and gifts leaves families deep in debt into the next generation.

16   Many dowry harassment cases follow the pattern of Phoolvati and Bhim Singh's experience with their daughter, Santara, 19. As in most Indian marriages today, the family selected a groom recommended by friends. The boy was unemployed, but his parents were farmers, and he was the sole heir to their property.

17   "Nobody asked for dowry in the beginning," said Mrs. Singh, 65.

18   Mrs. Singh, a farmer and the mother of six children, was touched. She and her husband gave their daughter the gifts any family would give a young bride: jewelry, silver, a bed, a black-and-white television, an electric fan, a sewing machine. "I gave all this with my own heart's happiness," the mother said in an interview.

19   Following tradition practiced at all of India's social levels, the newlyweds moved into the home of the groom's parents in a village about 20 miles from New Delhi. Within six months, Santara's in-laws began harassing her to ask her family for money to buy a car. "Why don't you go home and get 50,000 rupees," about $1,600, Santara said her mother-in-law told her. "Otherwise, we'll throw kerosene on you."

20   A few months later she carried out the threat, Mrs. Singh said, and poured kerosene on Santara. Before she could strike the match, Santara ran from the house, hid in a neighbor's home and sent word to New Delhi for her mother to rescue her.

21   But Santara then faced another problem common to young brides who flee troubled marriages: In a culture obsessed with social appearances and family honor, her mother began putting pressure on

her to return to her husband and filed a case of desertion against Santara's husband, hoping the court would force the groom's family to take her back.

22   "I could not keep a married daughter with me," Mrs. Singh said. "There would be a stain on her honor because she has been deserted. It would mean more and more dishonor for me."

23   Six months ago, a judge ordered the groom's family to take Santara back with a stern warning: "Don't kill the girl or you all will be hanged." Santara is now back in her husband's village, and her mother said, "I'll wait one year and see if they behave badly."

24   In recent years, a growing number of women's organizations have begun working to educate women and help abused wives escape dangerous family situations. In New Delhi, some 150 shelters and homes for tortured and abused women have opened in recent years. Some organizations, like the Women's Vigilance Society, specialize in helping families negotiate the corrupt and often inept police and judicial systems.

25   Under a 1961 Dowry Prohibition Act, giving and taking dowry is illegal, punishable by jail and fines.

26   Even so, few cases make it to court and fewer result in prosecutions. Often the husband's family bribes the police to cover up dowry-related murders. By the time Gyan Chand, who works in downtown New Delhi, arrived in the village 20 miles outside the capital where his daughter Asha had been killed, the police had already declared the death accidental.

27   Neighbors told him about the Women's Vigilance Society, and he enlisted its help to force the police to bring charges against his daughter's in-laws and arrest her husband and mother-in-law. Although Asha was said to be the fourth case of dowry death in the village in as many years, it was the first in which the police filed charges.

28   "Even when charges are filed, the law is not much help for women," said Rajana Kumari, who heads the Women's Vigilance Society and has written a book titled, "Brides Are Not for Burning."

29   She added, "It can take eight to 10 years for a case to go to court."

30   Increasingly, some organizations, local governments and families are fighting the dowry system. In the southeastern state of Orissa, where the police say reports of dowry deaths have jumped 11-fold in the last decade, the government has proposed legislation that would limit the amount a family could spend on a wedding and gifts.

31   And although dowry continues to be pervasive even in urban, middle-class families, a small number of young, educated career men and women are refusing to accept or give dowry in their marriages.

32   In an unusually bold move that made headlines in New Delhi newspapers last fall, Minoo Duggal, 25, a teacher, and her father called off
her wedding to an army captain three hours before the ceremony was
to begin because the groom's family began making additional dowry
demands.

33   Although Miss Duggal's family said they had agreed during marriage negotiations to pay $7,260 for the wedding, along with gifts to
the couple and the groom's family, Miss Duggal's father said the
intended in-laws asked for an additional $3,225 the day before the
wedding.

34   With the party ready to begin its parade to the wedding hall, Miss
Duggal's family posted a notice on the doors announcing: "Today's marriage canceled due to heavy dowry demand. Inconvenience regretted."

35   But in Indian society, even this story does not have a happy ending.
Miss Duggal has been unable to find a husband, and family members
complain that her actions have sullied the family's name and jeopar-
dized future marriage prospects.

DISCUSSION QUESTIONS

1. According to this article, what is a dowry and why has the dowry
    become so popular once again even though it was outlawed in 1961?

2. The article states that M. J. Akbar, a newspaper editor, called dowry "a
    form of theft legitimized by marriage." What do you think Akbar means
    by this statement? What is your interpretation of the statement?

3. What is the relationship of family honor to the dowry system? To
    what extent do you think family honor contributes to the continua-
    tion of dowry harassment?

4. How do attitudes about women's role in society contribute to dowry
    harassment? What is the relationship between the subjugation of
    Indian women and dowry harassment? Do you think that if women
    were allowed the same rights as men in Indian society much of dowry
    harassment might disappear?

5. The article uses many examples to develop its points. What is the
    rhetorical effect of these examples? How did the use of so many
    examples affect you as a reader?

WRITING ASSIGNMENTS

1. The article mentions a book called *Brides Are Not for Burning* by Rajana Kumari. Find a copy of the book and write a summary-critique of it. Your critique should include a summary of what you learned from the book as well as an assessment of the book's ability to describe this societal problem. Be sure to develop your critique with specific details.

2. Write a letter of protest about the dowry system in India to a human-rights organization such as Amnesty International or Human Rights Watch. Contact the organization first. Some organizations will send you information about specific guidelines and addresses for writing these letters. Be sure to develop your letter with specific details and facts.

3. The article states that "Dowry is perhaps the greatest force contributing to the oppression of women in India and elsewhere on the subcontinent." Write a persuasive essay that defends and supports that statement.

4. Write an informative report about the history of the dowry system in India. When and how did it originate? What led up to the dowry being outlawed in 1961? Why is dowry harassment still occurring? Your paper will require some outside research. Be sure to develop your thoughts with specific details.

IN NIGERIA, A SCARED SILENCE REIGNS

Stephen Buckley

Washington Post Service

■

The following selection by Stephen Buckley explores the violation of human rights being perpetrated by the Nigerian military government on Nigerian citizens. According to Buckley, both TransAfrica and Human Rights Watch, two human rights organizations, have reported that human-rights violations have been common in Nigeria. General Sani Abacha's military government has been accused of the arrest or murder of many innocent Nigerian citizens. This government has closed nearly twenty newspapers and destroyed labor unions. In addition, the government decreed that "no act of the federal military government may be questioned henceforth in a court of law." Many Nigerians feel that their only hope at this point is international intervention. While reading this article, think about the types of international aid that might work best to stop this injustice. What forms of pressure from the international community do you think might make a difference?

■

1   LAGOS—General Sani Abacha's war against opponents of his military government has left an eerie silence over Nigeria.

2   After seizing power in late 1993, he dissolved state legislatures, banned political parties and prohibited government decrees from being challenged in Nigeria's courts.

3   He has crushed labor unions and shut nearly 20 newspapers and magazines. His security forces have arrested dozens of activists, killed scores of Nigerians in demonstrations and are accused of systematically oppressing the Ogoni ethnic group, which has criticized the government.

4   "What you hear is the silence of the graveyard," said Abdul Oroh, executive director of Nigeria's Civil Liberties Organization. "It is quiet here because people are angry and feel helpless."

5   Rampant human rights abuses were cited by TransAfrica, the Washington-based lobbying organization, and the U.S. government last month in announcing campaigns to press Nigeria's military rulers to restore democracy. A State Department report this year said General Abacha's government had shown "little respect for human rights" in 1994.

6   Many Nigerian activists say they support international sanctions against the regime in part because General Abacha has so successfully paralyzed opposition forces at home.

7   "There's such a pall of helplessness over the place that people feel like things can only get worse" unless the international community intervenes, said Sully Abu, former editor of African Guardian magazine, banned by General Abacha last August.

8   "These people don't care about public opinion here," he said of the regime. "If you don't agree with them, they blow your brains out or throw you in jail."

9   Over the part year, Nigeria's security forces have arrested hundreds of opponents, including prominent human rights activists and politicians, holding them from several days to as long as a year.

10 Moshood K. O. Abiola is still being held after his arrest last summer, when he declared himself president on the one-year anniversary of annulled elections that he reportedly won.

11 Chief Abiola's arrest prompted a six-week strike by oil worker unions that strangled the economy in Lagos and the country's southwest. The government responded by arresting several labor leaders, some of whom are still in jail.

12 Last month, the police detained a former head of state, General Olusegun Obasanjo, an act that for many activists captured the regime's disdain for opponents.

13 General Obasanjo, who led Nigeria from 1976 to 1979, is the only military leader to have relinquished power in favor of civilian rule. In recent years, he has been an outspoken critic of military dictatorships across Africa.

14 "Here is a man who had served this country honorably, and they just arrested him and put him away like a common criminal," said Frederick Fasehun, a medical doctor and longtime human rights activist.

15 Ibrahim Gambari, Nigeria's ambassador to the United Nations, defended his nation's government last week, saying it had "not oppressed anyone."

16 Activists and politicians have been arrested "because the survival of Nigeria is paramount," he said. "We had to maintain stability.

265

These activists wanted to make political points. They were not thinking about what is best for Nigeria."

17   Late last month, a report by Human Rights Watch/Africa accused Nigerian security forces of murdering and raping members of the 500,000-member Ogoni ethnic group in southern Nigeria. The Ogoni have alleged that pollution from oil wells on their territory has destroyed their farms, killed their fish and ravaged their health.

18   The report quoted unidentified soldiers admitting that they had raided Ogoni villages, shot residents and burned their homes.

19   Last year, the Nigerian police arrested Ken Saro-Wiwa, a prominent Ogoni activist, and charged him with murder. The U.S. State Department's human rights report said prison authorities had bound Mr. Saro-Wiwa in chains, denied him medicine for a heart ailment and refused to allow him to see his physician.

20   Mr. Saro-Wiwa is currently being tried, but many prisoners often wait several years for a trial. Activists and lawyers charge that the delays are part of a continuing attack on the judicial system and prisoners' rights by the military government.

21   The military has ruled Nigeria since a coup more than 11 years ago, and General Abacha was considered the real power behind his two predecessors as heads of state, General Ibrahim Babangida and the military-appointed civilian, Ernest Shonekan.

22   Last year, the government suspended writ of habeas corpus. It extended the time by which suspects must be tried from six weeks to three months, and it decreed that "no act of the federal military government may be questioned henceforth in a court of law."

23   In several cases, the government ignored court orders. After a federal court ordered the government to reopen a newspaper it had banned, the government closed it by decree. When a federal court told the government to release a human rights activist last November, the government shunned the ruling.

24   Tunde Babawale, a political scientist at the University of Lagos, said the government's crackdown had "brutalized the psyche" of Nigeria's middle class, long the source of the country's political dynamism.

25   "People are no longer shocked by what this government does," Mr. Babawale said. "People are indifferent. The government does what it does and gets away with it. Those who cannot go into exile must take refuge in silence."

26   Human rights activists, middle-class Nigerians and students say they believe outside pressure will be the catalyst that brings democracy back to the continent's most populous nation.

27   The U.S. State Department last month exhorted Nigeria's military to "quicken the pace of its stated efforts to return Nigeria to civilian rule" and called on the government to halt the "unwise practice of silencing critics of military rule."

28   TransAfrica promised a campaign of media advertisements and protest at Nigeria's embassy in Washington and called for a U.S. boycott of Nigerian oil. The United States buys 50 percent of the oil exported by Nigeria, Africa's biggest oil producer.

29   "I pray for" international sanctions, said Joseph Femiriye, a mechanic and driver in Lagos, Nigeria's largest state, with about 10 million people. "I know things will change when we get democracy. But these military people do not believe in democracy. They believe in guns."

30   "We applaud the pressure. It is very welcome," said Beko Ransome-Kuti, executive director of Campaign for Democracy, which represents about 25 organizations opposed to Nigeria's government.

31   "We know what role international pressure can play and has played in many countries in the past," the director said. "Up until now, the international community has been very passive here."

DISCUSSION QUESTIONS

1. What is the rhetorical impact of the article's title for you as a reader? To what extent does the title affect your reading of the article?

2. Buckley quotes Sully Abu, the former editor of the banned *African Guardian* magazine, as stating, "There's such a pall of helplessness over the place that people feel like things can only get worse." Why do you think people feel helpless when civil liberties are denied? What is being denied that creates this feeling of helplessness?

3. Buckley indicates in his article that many Nigerians feel the only way to restore civil liberties is through international intervention. What is your opinion? If you agree, what form should this intervention take? If you don't agree, why not?

4. Tunde Babawale, a Nigerian political scientist, asserts that the present Nigerian regime has "brutalized the psyche" of the Nigerian middle class. What do you think Babawale means by the phrase *brutalized the psyche*? Use specific examples to support your response.

5. The Nigerian ambassador to the United Nations has been quoted as saying that antigovernment activists were arrested "because the survival of Nigeria is paramount. We had to maintain stability. These activists wanted to make political points. They were not thinking

about what is best for Nigeria." If you were a member of the United Nations human rights review panel, how would you respond to this statement?

6.   Buckley writes that "the government does what it does and gets away with it. Those who cannot go into exile must take refuge in silence." What do you think are the positive and negative outcomes of "taking refuge in silence"?

WRITING ASSIGNMENTS

1.   Write an informative report about the abuse of human rights in Nigeria. Your report should go beyond the information given in the article, so you will need to do outside research. Be sure to develop your report with specific details and facts.

2.   Buckley quotes the executive director of Campaign for Democracy as stating, "We know what role international pressure can play and has played in many countries in the past. Up until now, the international community has been very passive here." Write a letter to your congressperson that argues for some form of intervention in Nigeria as a means of preventing further human-rights abuses. Your letter should make specific suggestions regarding the form this intervention should take. The letter should also provide persuasive evidence to convince your congressperson of the necessity for intervention. Be sure to include specific examples and details in the letter.

3.   Reread discussion question 5. Then write a written response to the ambassador's statement. What is your opinion of the statement? Is he justified? Why or why not? Be sure to support your opinions with specific evidence and reasons.

CIA Ignored Abuses in Guatemala

R. Jeffrey Smith and Dana Priest

Washington Post Service

■

In the following selection, R. Jeffrey Smith and Dana Priest expose the connection between United States military and intelligence activity in Guatemala and human rights abuses. As the authors of this article report, the Central Intelligence Agency and United States military personnel allegedly were responsible for the arming and training of Guatemalan anti-Communist military forces accused of killing more than 100,000 peasants. Although the message from the United States government at this time was to respect human rights, this secret relationship was undermining any care for human rights. The probe into this scandal was initiated through the persistence of an American named Jennifer Harbury, whose Guatemalan husband disappeared. While reading this article, you might consider the following question: Do you think covert operations that deny human rights will always exist? Why or why not?

■

1 WASHINGTON—Revelations about a CIA informer linked to two murders in Guatemala have helped exhume an embarrassing relationship between U.S. military and intelligence personnel and a Central American regime that is notorious for human rights violations.

2 While U.S. public attention was largely distracted by civil wars in El Salvador and Nicaragua, the CIA and U.S. military trained and equipped anti-Communist military forces widely believed to have killed more than 100,000 peasants during a decades-long insurgency, according to U.S. intelligence, military and diplomatic officials.

3 On several occasions, U.S. presidents, Congress and diplomats tried to pressure the Guatemalan military to respect human rights.

But this message was repeatedly undercut by the secret relationship between U.S. and Guatemalan intelligence and military officials, which persisted even while Washington was publicly scaling back its ties, U.S. officials and former diplomats now say.

4   "This has got roots that are very, very deep in terms of the how the station chiefs viewed their roles in the country," said a retired senior military official, who requested anonymity when speaking about covert CIA activities in Guatemala that other officials said were conducted with secret approval from at least six U.S. presidents.

5   "It created a real dilemma for fair-minded Guatemalan officers," who saw their colleagues continue to receive U.S. payments for information on leftist insurgents and drug traffickers, the official said. "It's difficult for the U.S. to say, on the one hand, you've got to promote democracy, stop corruption, not be venal," while at the same time, "on the surreptitious side, we're doing exactly the opposite."

6   "The situation just got out of control in Guatemala," he added.

7   A rare public hearing on the intelligence community's role in Guatemala is scheduled for Wednesday, when the acting CIA director, William Studeman, and the American spouse of a murdered Guatemalan guerrilla fighter are to appear before the Senate Select Committee on Intelligence.

8   President Bill Clinton ordered a governmentwide investigation of U.S. policy in Guatemala last week, after a congressman disclosed CIA ties to a Guatemalan Army colonel, Julio Roberto Alpírez, whom other CIA informants have linked to the killings of the guerrilla and of a rural innkeeper who was a U.S. citizen. A CIA informant from around 1988 to 1992, Colonel Alpírez received a CIA cash payment even after his links to the first of these murders became known to the agency.

9   The probe includes separate investigations by the Justice Department and FBI into an anonymous tip, which has not been substantiated, that U.S. documents relevant to the murders were being destroyed. On Friday, the Pentagon also launched a comprehensive inquiry into its own activities in Guatemala, including all of its military intelligence and counternarcotics operations there.

10   What sparked "the rainstorm," as the Pentagon spokesman, Kenneth Bacon, described it, was the persistence of one American, Jennifer Harbury, a lawyer who refused to believe U.S. officials when they told her they had no conclusive evidence about the disappearance of her Guatemalan husband, Efraim Bamaca Velázquez, a guerrilla fighter.

11   Ms. Harbury learned about the CIA connection to Colonel Alpírez two weeks ago from Representative Robert G. Torricelli, Democrat of

270

New Jersey, and her success has now provoked similar protests from more than two dozen other Americans who say they were beaten by Guatemalan military or paramilitary personnel, or have U.S. relatives who were murdered or abused there.

12   Besides Michael DeVine, the innkeeper slain and nearly decapitated in 1990, the victims include Dianne Ortiz, an Ursuline sister who was tortured and gang raped in 1989; Nicholas Blake, a journalist killed by Guatemalan paramilitary troops in 1985; and several human rights advocates, priests and nuns, a Peace Corps volunteer and others working with the poor who were killed.

13   "I don't need to know how they know, I just want to know what they know," said Samuel Blake, a Pentagon consultant who helped excavate his brother's remains in the Guatemalan highlands in 1992.

DISCUSSION QUESTIONS

1. What effect do the specific details and examples used in this article have on you as a reader? How do they help convey the authors' message? Which examples have the most profound rhetorical impact for you?

2. What do you think is meant by the term *rainstorm*, which was used by Pentagon spokesperson Kenneth Bacon?

3. What connection can you make between this article and the article in this chapter entitled "Rights: A Look at America"? In what ways might the two articles be related?

WRITING ASSIGNMENTS

1. Write an essay in which you respond to the following question: "Should the activities of the CIA be made public when human rights are involved?" Support your opinions with specific details and examples. Begin your writing process by brainstorming about the reasons why or why not it might be important to have this information.

2. Write an informative report about human rights violations in Central America. You may choose to limit your research to only one or two countries. Or you may write a longer report and investigate the topic for all of Central America. Your report will require outside research. Be sure to develop your points with specific details and examples.

3. Write an imaginary dialogue between a fictitious person in a similar position to that of Jennifer Harbury and that person's congressional representative. The purpose of the meeting with the representative is to inform him or her of the situation and to seek resolution. Since the characters are fictitious, you may add details that are not necessarily fact.

CHAPTER TEN WRITING ASSIGNMENTS

1. Many films have been produced that concern civil and human-rights abuses (for example, *El Salvador, Missing, Mississippi Burning*). View one of these films and then write a critique of the film that focuses on the film's representation of human-rights issues. Be sure to support your opinions with specific examples and details.

2. Choose a human-rights issue that you see as a problem in the United States. Research this issue and then write an informative report that details its history and present status. Be sure to develop your thoughts with specific details and examples.

3. Choose a human-rights issue that is a concern in your community. Research the issue and then write a letter to your congressional representative that explains the problem and requests help for a solution to the problem. Be sure to substantiate your claims with specific details and facts.

4. Volunteer to do some charity work for an organization that deals with human-rights violations. Then write a narrative of your experiences with the organization. Your narrative should do more than simply summarize your experience. It should also offer an account of what you learned from the experience.

5. Write an exploratory paper that addresses the following question: "To what extent can human-rights violations be eliminated around the world?" Your essay should explore specific strategies for eliminating human-rights abuses. You should consider how well these strategies will work and what the roadblocks might be. Be sure to develop your paper with specific details and examples.

A World of Diversity

Multicultural Readings in the News

Faun Bernbach Evans

NTC *Publishing Group*
Lincolnwood, Illinois USA

Contents

CHAPTER ONE

Educating Our People

Chapter Introduction

The concluding paragraph of the chapter introduction asks students to make connections with their own educational experiences as they read the articles in this chapter. When students personalize or connect the readings to their own lives, their understanding of the text can become that much richer. You might begin this chapter with a general discussion about students' attitudes toward education. The following questions can facilitate this discussion:

- What do you think are some of the most important educational issues facing young people today?

- In what kind of environment do you think people learn best?

- What do you think the purpose of education is? Has this purpose changed in the last fifty years?

- How do you think the schools and colleges in your community might be improved?

- What do you think you can learn from other nations about education? What do you think other nations can learn from your country?

When Peace Forms Part of the Curriculum
Thomas Fuller

DISCUSSION QUESTIONS

1. Try to get students to move beyond simple *yes* and *no* responses by asking them to define the terms *international cooperation* and *world peace*. What do these terms mean? How are they similar, and how are they different? How might international cooperation lead to world peace?

2. Answers will vary. You might get students to discuss the meanings of the words *classroom* and *laboratory*. You might also ask students to speculate about the nature of the international cooperation that might result from the seminars.

3. Answers will vary. When students share their responses with the rest of the class, you might have the class ask questions of each group. Why did the group choose this course? Why does the group think it is an important course or topic?

4. You might try to get students to draw upon their own personal experiences with friendship when responding to this question.

5. You might first get students to become more aware of how national allegiance manifests itself in their behavior and attitudes. Clustering or freewriting on the idea of national allegiance could help introduce the concept.

6. This is a fairly broad question. The work done in the small groups can be shared with the class as a whole. It can also serve as prewriting for an essay on this topic.

WRITING ASSIGNMENTS

1. This assignment can be tailored to the needs of the class. You might choose to stress the interview component of the assignment. You might also have students prepare the report as an article for prospective students.

2. This assignment is intended to emphasize strategies of argumentation as well as audience awareness.

3. Students will obviously need to have a good understanding of the term *international cooperation* in order to compose this essay. The brainstorming component of this assignment is therefore very

important. Students should have the opportunity to prewrite with classmates as well as on their own.

4. You may need to take students through the process of organizing a comparison and contrast paper. Several prewriting sessions that focus on students' educational experiences as well as their understanding of other types of education will probably be necessary.

Spanish School Offers a Place in the Sun for Learning
Barry James

DISCUSSION QUESTIONS

1. Students can use a variety of prewriting strategies such as clustering, mapping, and listing to assist them in responding to this question. Since the question has a few components, the use of small groups has been suggested, but a whole-class discussion might also be useful.

2. Answers will vary, but you should push the students to support their opinions with specific reasons.

3. The intertextual nature of this question attempts to get students to make associations with other material they have read. You might extend this question by getting students to compare these universities with others they have read about or are familiar with.

4. Answers will vary. Try to get students to support their answers with specific reasons and, if possible, evidence from the text.

5. This is a broad question. You might facilitate the discussion by drawing students' attention to specific events and trends in international affairs that might be affected by the work done at these universities.

WRITING ASSIGNMENTS

1. You may want to discuss the genre of biography as a preliminary activity for this assignment.

2. You might choose to give some background information on the causes and effects of the Spanish Civil War before assigning this topic.

3. You might consider presenting this assignment as a piece of writing that is intended to provide helpful information to interested peers and that has potential for publication.

Equality Means Progress, Says Swedish Minister
Keith Foster

DISCUSSION QUESTIONS

1. You might get students to consider the interviewing process and the importance of asking good questions. You could have students use the journalistic 5W questioning heuristic to analyze the types of questions being asked.

2. Answers will vary. Get students to think about educational topics in the news that affect their lives. See if students can see any similarities between their concerns and those of the Swedish.

3. You might bring up topics such as bilingual education or the "English Only Movement."

4. Answers will vary. You might have students brainstorm for examples that could illustrate Tham's statement. Then have them use those examples to determine a more universal response to the question.

5. You might first ask students to offer potential definitions for *progress* and *equality*. What are the connotations of these terms?

WRITING ASSIGNMENTS

1. Either in groups or alone, you might have students first brainstorm about potential interview subjects. Stress the need to plan interviews. Have students work in groups to develop interview guides.

2. You might introduce this assignment as an opportunity to learn about gender issues in another culture. Have students share their research with each other in peer groups. Alternatively, you might include an oral presentation component to this assignment by having students give brief oral summaries of their research.

3. Use the issues raised in response to Discussion Question 5 to get students started.

Courses in English Flourish in Vietnam
Kate Brown

DISCUSSION QUESTIONS

1. You can have the small groups share their thoughts and ideas with the whole class. You might supplement this discussion with other readings about the Vietnam War as well as your personal recollections. Spend a fair amount of time on the war before discussing the article. The students will probably need the background. If you have a small group of students, you might want to forgo the group work and have a general class discussion.

2. Answers will vary. If you have a multilingual and/or multicultural class, the discussion should be a rewarding experience. However, if this diversity is not available, you may have to spend more time on the last part of the question, which addresses the need for knowing foreign languages.

3. You might push this question further by exploring the perceived need versus the realistic need of knowing a foreign language. Why do some Americans think knowing a foreign language is not necessary, while others view knowledge of a foreign language as essential?

4. You might get students to think about other countries where the demand for English is important. What might the similarities be between these countries and Vietnam?

5. The question will probably work well in small groups. You might first get students to think about the nature of language in general. What are its properties and functions?

WRITING ASSIGNMENTS

1. This report will require some research. Have students share their research with each other in cooperative groups.

2. Most students have had some experience with a foreign language, even if it has been limited experience. Alternatively, you might have students write about their memories of acquiring their first language, although this task might be more difficult ultimately than the previous one.

3. Make sure that students prepare an interview guide before they interview anyone. Students should think about what they want to learn from the person they will be interviewing.

4. This assignment can be presented either as a short research essay or an opinion paper.

Broader Horizons in MBA Programs
Lawrence Malkin

DISCUSSION QUESTIONS

1. First try to get students to think about the qualities and characteristics of a symphony. Then coach them into making the metaphorical connection between a group of students and a symphony.

2. Answers will vary. You might get students to explore world events that might have influenced MBA program directors and designers to reconsider the curriculum.

3. Answers will vary. The small groups can share their responses with the whole class after the brainstorming session.

4. You might begin by getting students to consider the nature of their textbook. Why a multicultural textbook?

5. Alternatively, you might look at a specific business that is currently in the international news and have students consider how an MBA would be best prepared to handle the real-life business scenario.

6. Get students to think about specific current events as a means of exploring this question.

WRITING ASSIGNMENTS

1. The parameters of this assignment are up to you. It can be turned into a full-term research project or a shorter essay. Or you might have students do only one interview. Get students to work in groups on the questionnaire.

2. Use Discussion Question 6 as a prewriting prompt for this essay assignment.

3. Present this project as a report that will help students make informed decisions about business schools. The oral presentation component of

this assignment is designed to get students to consider an audience other than their instructor.

CHAPTER ONE WRITING ASSIGNMENTS

1. This assignment would work well as a cooperative learning project that might span a few weeks. You might have students look at curriculum plans from specific departments so that they get a feel for the type of information they will want to include (e.g., course descriptions, course rationales, course sequences, etc.).

2. This assignment will probably require a lot of prewriting. Use both small-group and whole-class brainstorming sessions to get students started.

3. Alternatively, you might get students to specifically address the relationship of language to business using the two articles to help them support their main points.

CHAPTER TWO

Understanding the Impact of the Media

Chapter Introduction

The concluding paragraph of the chapter introduction asks students to think about how the media affect them personally. Personalizing or connecting the readings to their own lives will facilitate a richer understanding of the text. You might begin this chapter with a general discussion about students' attitudes toward the media. The following questions are intended to facilitate this discussion:

- How do the media affect our relationships with family and friends?
- How do the media affect our consumption patterns?
- How do the media affect our thinking patterns?
- How do the media affect our self-image?
- How do the media affect our understanding of world events?
- What changes have you seen in the media over the last ten years?

Americanizing the Airwaves
Richard Covington

DISCUSSION QUESTIONS

1. This question is multilayered. You might approach it by first discussing the characteristics of television and radio as well as their similarities and differences.

2. You might first explore the potential meanings of the word *sophisticated*.

3. You might ask students to contribute examples of niche programming they have listened to.

4. You might look at the nature of hyperbole as it relates to this quote.

WRITING ASSIGNMENTS

1. This assignment would work well as a cooperative-learning activity. You might introduce this assignment by discussing the appeal of the most popular radio formats in your community.

2. Make sure that students support their opinions with details. Students may want to do some research on this topic since it has been a news-worthy subject.

3. Stress the analytical nature of this assignment so that you avoid having students simply summarize the sorts of advertisements broadcast by the radio station.

San Francisco's Loud Voice for the Right Sounds Off
John Tierney

DISCUSSION QUESTIONS

1. Answers will vary. You may have some students who disagree with this statement.

2. Again, answers will vary. Some students may disagree with the premise that conservatives are ignored by the mainstream media.

3. You might share with the class examples of left-wing newspapers so that a basis for comparison might be made a little more concrete.

4. Have students first explore the nature of "shock jock" radio before they attempt to make a comparison.

WRITING ASSIGNMENTS

1. Use Discussion Question 1 as a prewriting exercise for this assignment.

2. Students might want to listen to some of these shows to gain a more in-depth understanding of the format as well as specific details with which to develop their essays.

3. You may need to spend some time distinguishing between a summary and a critique. Film or theatrical reviews might serve as good examples of critiques.

Traditional Ramadan Radio Tales Give Egypt a Medium for Its Message
Chris Hedges

DISCUSSION QUESTIONS

1. You might approach this question by first exploring the differences between radio drama and television, film, or theater. Ask students about the relationship of one's imagination to the various media.

2. Have students think about particular films or television shows they have viewed. Why do they watch them? What do they like about them? Then have them connect their experiences to what they think radio-drama fans might experience.

3. Get students to consider what is pleasurable about reading before approaching the question.

4. Answers will vary. Getting students to first think about the effect of particular entertainment forms on their own culture might be a helpful approach.

WRITING ASSIGNMENTS

1. You might have students first perform a radio drama from a script that they have found at the library. Performing one of these scripts will give students a feel for the style and flow of a radio drama before they write their own.

2. You might try to get an audiotape of these radio dramas to play for the students. This activity would also be a good prewriting strategy for Writing Assignment 1.

3. As part of their research, you might also have students interview people who celebrate Ramadan.

There's No Business Like Business Shows
Erik Ipsen

DISCUSSION QUESTIONS

1. First have students think about what the appeal is of anything that is available twenty-four hours a day. Then have them apply their responses to business.

2. You might facilitate this discussion with specific examples. For instance, give a statistic and see how the students respond. Then give the same statistic with some context and see what their response is.

3. You might get them to first think about the sorts of advertisements found in magazines such as *Money* or *Fortune*.

WRITING ASSIGNMENTS

1. You might use part of the class time to show a videotaped news brief from a popular news show. Discuss the style and format of the news brief with the class before having them write.

2. This project probably will work best with local news events since students will have a better opportunity to research primary sources and interview people.

3. You might want to have students share their research with the class by presenting oral summaries or reports.

"New Age" Newspaper Hits the Headlines
William Glaberson

DISCUSSION QUESTIONS

1. Clustering in small groups or as a whole class will help students explore the meaning of the term *New Age*.

2. Students could bring in copies of different dailies to help facilitate this discussion.

3. You might bring up the concept of "What's in a name?" You could start by having students think about the differences between titles such as *domestic engineer* and *homemaker*. You might give students a list of titles

for various members of the school community and have them think of alternative titles (e.g., *instructor = course facilitator*).

4. In small groups, you might have students work on an advantages versus disadvantages list. Then have the groups share their responses with the entire class.

5. Have students think about other businesses that are controlled by market research and focus groups. Then have them consider whether newspapers are different.

WRITING ASSIGNMENTS

1. As a prewriting activity, you might have the class critique a newspaper. Have students break into small groups to critique particular sections. Then have the groups share their thoughts with the whole class. The class also can make an assessment of the whole newspaper based on their group critiques.

2. Have students prewrite in groups or alone on possible focuses for the interview. Freewriting and/or clustering would work well.

3. Spend some class time reviewing letters to the editor and editorials. Look at the rhetorical strategies employed by the writers of these letters and editorials.

4. This project will obviously be produced over the term, but, if scheduled well, the results should be rewarding for both students and instructor.

TV Advertising Alters Its Image
Joseph Fitchett

DISCUSSION QUESTIONS

1. Students may find that the article does not adequately explain the nuances of this technology and therefore may have further questions that they can try to answer using other sources.

2. Answers will vary. Get students to support their opinions with specific reasons.

3. Refer students to the article in Chapter Eight entitled "A Two-Way Virtual Street: Internet Broadcasting Goes Interactive" by Peter Lewis.

4. You first might have students cluster or freewrite on the term *visual reality*.

5. Answers will vary. This question might work best in small-group discussions.

WRITING ASSIGNMENTS

1. The prewriting questions offered with this assignment are suggested starting points. Have students brainstorm for further ethical considerations. The assignment needs plenty of prewriting and discussion.

2. Use Discussion Question 4 as a prewriting activity for this assignment.

3. You may need to spend some time clarifying the purpose of a rationale in a proposal.

CHAPTER TWO WRITING ASSIGNMENTS

1. You may need to guide students when they write their interview questions so that they elicit more than *yes* or *no* responses. Explain how certain questions are more open-ended than others.

2. Small-group prewriting work on this question will help students develop their thoughts.

3. You might begin this writing assignment with a class discussion about how print media and electronic media affect the students' lives on a daily basis. Developing a chart during this discussion that compares and contrasts the two forms of media will also be helpful to students.

4. This is a broad topic, so you will need to spend time helping students narrow and focus their topics in order to develop strong theses.

CHAPTER THREE

Contending with Violence around the World

Chapter Introduction

The concluding paragraph of the chapter introduction asks students to consider the nature of violence and, in doing so, to think about ways in which individuals as well as communities can help decrease violence. Try beginning the chapter by discussing the roots of violence with either the full class or in small groups. You might approach the discussion inductively by exploring specific examples of violence and then looking at similar characteristics among them. Students will then be able to make some generalizations about the root causes of violence. Once they have developed their own understanding of some possible causes, they may be able to propose potential solutions. The following questions are intended to facilitate this discussion:

- What are some recent examples of violence in your local community? In the global community?

- Is violence more prevalent in certain societies than in others?

- Are there certain factors or circumstances that always seem to lead to violence?

- Is violence more prevalent in today's society? If so, why? If not, why not?

Japanese Are Shaken by Shooting of Official
T. R. Reid

DISCUSSION QUESTIONS

1. The assumption on the part of the Japanese when they made this statement was that their society was safe. You will probably need to discuss the students' assumptions about the safety of their communities.

2. You first might want to discuss what is meant by the term *egalitarian society*.

3. You will probably want to discuss the current state of the gun-control controversy. You might ask students to research this debate and make oral or written presentations of their findings.

WRITING ASSIGNMENTS

1. Use Discussion Question 1 as a prewriting activity for this assignment.

2. You might have students focus in particular on the suspected perpetrator of the attack, a member of the Aum cult, and the motive behind the attack.

3. Use Discussion Question 2 as a prewriting activity for this assignment.

Paris Terror Attack Gives Up Few Leads
Marlise Simons

DISCUSSION QUESTIONS

1. A full-class clustering activity using the chalkboard or an overhead projector would also work well for this question.

2. Answers will vary. Before attempting to have a full-class discussion, you might have small groups explore this question.

3. You first might have students think of specific organizations or types of groups that typically claim responsibility for acts of terrorism.

4. You might create an advantages/disadvantages chart on the board to facilitate this discussion.

WRITING ASSIGNMENTS

1. As a prewriting activity, you might have peer groups make brainstorming lists of terrorist acts. Then have the groups share their ideas with the whole class.

2. As a starting point, you might have students explore the various approaches to terrorism that different governments and heads of state have taken (e.g., Israel, United States, the United Kingdom).

3. The assignment is two-pronged, asking students both to write a film critique and to assess the value of the film as a representation of terrorism. The assignment will therefore require a good deal of prewriting. You will probably want to show students samples of film critiques so that they get a feel for the style and purpose of the genre.

Agony of Killer's "Only Living Victim"
Debra West

DISCUSSION QUESTIONS

1. Answers will vary. Push students to support their responses with specific examples and evidence.

2. You might have students freewrite or cluster on the term *prerelease center*.

3. You might also ask students what their opinions are about paroling criminals convicted of violent crimes. Why or why not should such criminals be paroled?

4. You might involve students in a prewriting activity that has them make two lists, one for the rights of citizens and the other for the rights of convicts.

WRITING ASSIGNMENTS

1. Use Discussion Questions 3 and 4 as prewriting activities for this assignment.

2. You first might want to explore the various connotations of the word *rehabilitate*.

3. In small groups, have students explore the various problems of our correctional systems. Then have each group report its findings to the entire class.

4. Use Discussion Question 1 as a prewriting activity for this assignment.

Juveniles Fuel Soaring Violent Crime in America
International Herald Tribune

DISCUSSION QUESTIONS

1. Answers will vary. You might have students think about the relationship of familial, economic, and/or racial issues to this question.

2. Try to get students to go beyond simply citing incidents that support this connection. Rather, get them to explain why the connection exists (e.g., the need for drugs makes juveniles commit crimes they might not otherwise commit). Get students to expand on the relationship between drug addiction and crime.

3. Answers will vary. You might get students to recall some of the specific reasons politicians have used to both support and reject these programs.

4. Brainstorming on the possible connotations of the term *multiplier effect* before tackling the question will facilitate the discussion.

WRITING ASSIGNMENTS

1. Use Discussion Question 3 as a prewriting activity for this assignment.

2. Use Discussion Question 2 as a prewriting activity for this assignment. Stress the analytic nature of the assignment. Students will need to make specific connections and associations. Diagramming the connections may be useful.

3. You may want to have students interview law-enforcement officials as part of the assignment.

After Shooting, Los Angeles Man Becomes an Instant Hero
Seth Mydans

DISCUSSION QUESTIONS

1. Responses will vary. Have each group present its thoughts to the entire class so that students can receive multiple perspectives.

2. First have students speculate about the type of place Simi Valley might be to live. Ask them about the values and attitudes they think might be present in the town.

3. First get students to offer definitions of the term *vigilante hero*.

4. Responses will vary. Make sure students support their responses with specific reasons.

WRITING ASSIGNMENTS

1. Prewriting activities might include having students give oral summaries of articles they have read on the Goetz case, working in small groups to compare and contrast the two people, and/or working in groups to focus thesis statements.

2. You might consider showing the film *Falling Down* in class and then using the postfilm discussion as a starting point for the essay.

3. Brainstorm in small groups or with the full class for examples of race and ethnicity in criminal investigations. Get students to extrapolate generalizations from the specific examples.

4. Get students to focus on the concept of a *reasonable response* to a situation. What constitutes reasonable? Then have them support their opinion of Cohen's statement.

London's Longtime Loathing for Guns Begins at Last to Fade
William E. Schmidt

DISCUSSION QUESTIONS

1. The discussion can go in any number of directions, from Constitutional rights to cultural differences.

2. You should get students to consider how authority manifests itself without the presence of firearms. Have students explore the social and cultural contexts of the two countries as a first step to approaching this question. Students might also consider the issue of tradition as it relates to this question.

3. This question might work well first in small groups, with the groups later sharing their thoughts in a whole-class discussion.

4. The media and immigration are two separate issues. You might want to deal with them one at a time.

WRITING ASSIGNMENTS

1. As a preliminary activity, have students write a list of questions they want to answer when doing their research for this assignment. Have students share these questions with other members of the class.

2. As a prewriting activity, have one group of students cluster or freewrite on the role of the patrol officer. Another group should cluster or freewrite on the role of a bobby. Then have the two groups compare and contrast their ideas.

3. Use Discussion Questions 1 and 2 as prewriting activities for this assignment.

In Rural China, "Gold Lords" Challenge the State
Patrick E. Tyler

DISCUSSION QUESTIONS

1. You might also encourage students to distinguish between the 1849 gold rush as it has been glamorized by the movie industry and the realities of this historical event.

2. Responses will vary. Students might think about controls and regulations that could be established by the prospectors themselves.

3. You might get students to think about the relationship of lawlessness to the wilderness.

4. You might approach this question by first examining the excavation of other natural resources such as oil and coal.

WRITING ASSIGNMENTS

1. Use Discussion Question 1 as a prewriting activity for this assignment.

2. Use Discussion Question 2 as a prewriting activity for this assignment.

3. This assignment is intended to develop the students' audience awareness and reasoning abilities. You may want to review these concepts when introducing the assignment.

CHAPTER THREE WRITING ASSIGNMENTS

1. After assigning roles to the various participants of this roundtable, you may want to give them some time to brainstorm about their specific concerns. You will also probably need to act as a mediator of the roundtable.

2. Students can draw from the articles in this chapter as well as other sources.

3. The Reid and Simons articles are good starting points for this discussion, but students will probably want to do some more research.

4. As a prewriting exercise, have students brainstorm on this topic in small groups and then share their thoughts with the whole class.

CHAPTER FOUR

Living in a World at War

Chapter Introduction

The concluding paragraph of the chapter introduction asks students to consider the root causes of war and in doing so to think about how exploring the causes of war might help us better understand how to prevent wars. Try beginning the chapter by discussing the roots of war with either the full class or in small groups. You might approach the discussion inductively by exploring specific examples of war and then looking at any similarities. Students will then be able to make some generalizations about the root causes of war before attempting to propose any potential solutions. The following questions are intended to facilitate this discussion:

- What are some current examples of war?

- Are there certain circumstances that make an area particularly vulnerable to war?

- How has the nature of war changed in the last fifty years?

Dresden: "It Was How You Would Imagine Hell"
Alan Cowell

DISCUSSION QUESTIONS

1. Answers will vary. You might start a discussion about the use of quoted material to elicit emotional responses.

2. Answers may vary, but students will hopefully see the connection between the author's word choice and the city of Dresden.

3. This question will work well in small-group discussions. Have the groups share their responses with the class as a whole.

4. Although answers will vary, students should support their opinions with specific reasons. You may want to review with students some of the causes of the Second World War.

5. Answers will vary. This question would also work well as a writing assignment.

6. Answers will vary. You may want to address the concept of history being a lesson for the future.

WRITING ASSIGNMENTS

1. You will need to emphasize that the essay is to be more than a report of the historical event. In addition, students also need to explore the consequences of the firebombing.

2. Use Discussion Question 3 as a prewriting exercise for this assignment.

3. As a prewriting activity, you might have students in small groups look at magazine interviews to get a feel for the style and format. Have the groups share with the class their ideas about what types of questions might be asked in the interview.

War-Torn Nation Faces a Hidden Foe for Years to Come
Paul Taylor

DISCUSSION QUESTIONS

1. Responses will vary, but students should see the emotional and psychological consequences of such a trauma.

2. You might approach this question by asking students what the differences are between soldiers and civilians as targets.

3. Students should see the rhetorical impact of these examples. Emphasize that they can use a similar strategy in their own writing.

4. Try to get students to see the psychological consequences of this type of warfare.

5. Answers will vary. Common responses might include Middle Eastern or Central American conflicts.

6. Responses will vary. You might have students first freewrite on their own before discussing the question with others.

WRITING ASSIGNMENTS

1. You might have students share research findings by having them make oral presentations of certain articles to the class.

2. As a prewriting activity, you might have students freewrite on the conclusion of this article.

3. Discuss some of the rhetorical strategies used in this article that might be persuasive.

4. Use Discussion Question 2 as a prewriting activity for this assignment.

Hutu Chiefs Gearing for War
William Branigin

DISCUSSION QUESTIONS

1. Responses will vary. You might have students freewrite on their own before discussing this issue with their classmates.

2. Responses will vary. Common responses might include the Holocaust, the Khmer Rouge massacre of Cambodians, the war in Bosnia.

3. Have students think about other wars or conflicts when outside countries have supplied arms to aggressors.

4. This is a broad question; responses will vary. You might have students write on this topic.

5. You might make a chart of the similarities and differences among the conflicts. Try to get students to move beyond simple comparisons so that they can see how common patterns can lead to certain consequences.

6. Charting the types of involvement might be useful. Students may see that in certain cases the motivations are the same but the means are different.

WRITING ASSIGNMENTS

1. You might suggest that students create a time line of events leading up to the war.

2. Use Discussion Question 6 as a prewriting activity for this assignment.

3. As a preliminary activity, have students present to the class an annotated list of the various types of organizations involved in this work.

When Both Sides Stood Ready for Bacterial Warfare
Denis Warner

DISCUSSION QUESTIONS

1. Responses will vary. You might discuss the rhetorical strategy of hooking the reader with vivid imagery in an introduction.

2. Responses will vary. Students might focus on environmental, physical, psychological, and/or societal consequences.

3. Responses will vary. Students might compare and contrast the potential consequences of nuclear and bacterial warfare.

4. Again, a comparison to nuclear warfare might be useful.

5. You might approach this question by first having students consider what a *war against humanity* might mean.

6. Students should see the irony in General Umezu's imprisonment. You might get students to discuss the rhetorical impact of this information on readers.

WRITING ASSIGNMENTS

1. Use Discussion Questions I and 5 as prewriting activities for this assignment.

2. Use Discussion Question 2 as a prewriting activity for this assignment.

3. You might first discuss how description can be used to persuade. Use Discussion Question 2 as a prewriting activity.

A New Nuremberg Could Just "Break the Frozen Sea"
Anthony Lewis

Discussion Questions

1. Students should perceive the incongruity between what it seems the world *should have done* and the reality of what the world did.

2. You may first need to discuss the term *anachronistic* with students. Freewriting on this question first may facilitate discussion.

3. Clustering on the term *cleansed* should facilitate the discussion.

4. Responses will vary. Students should support their opinions with specific reasons.

5. Try to get students to see the rhetorical impact of the ice imagery.

6. You might create a brainstorming list on the board of the sorts of self-interests that might mute a response.

7. Responses will vary. You might introduce specific examples of times in which military personnel have said they were only following orders.

8. Responses will vary. Students should support their opinions with specific reasons.

Writing Assignments

1. Use Discussion Question 6 as a prewriting activity for this assignment.

2. This assignment requires a fair amount of analytic ability on the student's part. Prewriting activities that guide this analysis should be incorporated into the writing process.

3. Emphasize that students should develop their arguments by referring to specific acts of aggression.

4. Use Discussion Question 5 as a prewriting activity for this assignment.

CHAPTER FOUR WRITING ASSIGNMENTS

1. Encourage students to prewrite a fair amount before taking a stand. Peer-group discussions may also facilitate the development of a strong thesis.

2. You might encourage students to approach this question inductively by first looking at specific cases and then determining some common underlying causes.

3. You might give individual students specific research tasks related to this topic and then have them report back their findings to the whole class.

4. Students will need to make sure they have a focused thesis for this assignment. The temptation might be to give individual accounts of these civil wars without any synthesis.

5. Have students freewrite on this question and then share their thoughts in small peer-group discussions.

CHAPTER FIVE

Staying Healthy
around the World

Chapter Introduction

The concluding paragraph of this chapter introduction asks students to consider the relative importance of health issues around the world as well as the universality of these concerns. You might begin this chapter by getting students to see the universality of health concerns since good health is so crucial to our survival. Then have students discuss what they see as some of the most important global heath issues in the world today. The following questions are intended to help facilitate this discussion:

- Are the health concerns different today than they were fifty years ago? Twenty years ago?

- Do health concerns differ from nation to nation? Region to region? Community to community?

- Why might it be important to know about the health issues of other countries and regions?

- What do you think are the most important health concerns of today's society?

So Doctors Without Borders Is Leaving the Rwanda Refugee Camps
Alain Destexhe

DISCUSSION QUESTIONS

1. It would be a good idea to have students read "Hutu Chiefs Gearing for War" in conjunction with this article.

2. You might have students create a chart that lists the pros and cons of both options.

3. Responses will vary. You might look at the situation in Bosnia.

4. Responses will vary. Students should consider the relationship between nationalism and health-related issues.

5. Responses will vary. Small-group discussions will work well with this question.

WRITING ASSIGNMENTS

1. You might suggest that students speak with a public relations representative for the organization. Students can find phone numbers at the library.

2. Have students freewrite or cluster before writing on this topic. Small-group discussions would also work well as a prewriting strategy.

3. Use Discussion Question 5 as a prewriting activity.

Smoking Is under Fire in China
Bloomberg Business News

DISCUSSION QUESTIONS

1. You might have students think about cigarette advertisements (i.e., leisure, relaxation). Try to get students to make a connection between these ads and "the leisure class."

2. Students should see the opportunity to develop a Chinese tobacco industry envisioned by some.

3. You might also expand this question to explore the different smoking regulations in U.S. cities (e.g., Los Angeles vs. Chicago).

4. Responses will vary. Encourage students to support their opinions with specific reasons.

WRITING ASSIGNMENTS

1. You might have students give oral summaries of specific articles they have found while doing their research.

2. Students might interview different people to gain a varied perspective (e.g., smokers, nonsmokers, health-care workers, and so on).

3. Students can create interview guides in small-group workshops.

4. Students may need to do some outside research in order to develop their arguments.

If You Can't Lose Weight, You Can at Least Learn to Like Yourself
Daniel Goleman

DISCUSSION QUESTIONS

1. This question will work well in small peer groups. You might have students come up with a specific agenda or program for one therapy session.

2. You might first have students freewrite alone on this question.

3. Encourage students to go beyond simple agreement or disagreement by supporting their views with specific reasons.

4. Responses will vary. Students might look at the connections between emotional well-being and physical well-being.

WRITING ASSIGNMENTS

1. This assignment should produce interesting results. Have students share their narratives with the whole class.

2. You might have students make oral presentations to the class of particular articles they have found interesting.

3. Use Discussion Questions 2 and 3 as prewriting activities.

Can Hormones Turn Back Clock?
Jane E. Brody

DISCUSSION QUESTIONS

1. Encourage students to explore the function and purpose of a question. In what direction does a question lead the mind?

2. This question will hopefully alert students to the questions surrounding hormone replacement. It should also prompt students to know what sorts of questions they need to ask doctors when presented with the possibility of a new or controversial treatment.

3. You might have students consider the connections between this article and the Goleman article.

4. Responses will vary. The issue of universal health insurance may come up.

5. Responses will vary. You might discuss the meaning of *ethical* before tackling this question.

6. Responses will vary. Students might consider questions of population control, care for the elderly, and/or availability of resources.

WRITING ASSIGNMENTS

1. Have students share their logs in small-group workshops. You might also discuss the difference between narration and analysis, depending on how students decide to present their information.

2. If possible, students might want to interview health-care professionals or patients who have knowledge of this treatment.

3. Students will also want to consider ethical implications.

Health Care Once Again
The Washington Post

DISCUSSION QUESTIONS

1. Encourage students to explore the issue from all sides—insurance companies, health-care professionals, patients, hospitals, employers, employees of various income levels, and so on.

2. Students first should explore who is actually helped by these programs.

3. Have students make a chart that outlines the advantages and disadvantages of the approach.

4. Students first might freewrite on this question. Encourage students to support their responses with specific reasons.

WRITING ASSIGNMENTS

1. You might first have students create a cluster on the various problems troubling the U.S. health-care system. From that cluster, students might choose a particular problem to explore in greater detail.

2. Use Discussion Question 1 as a prewriting activity.

3. Encourage students to support their ideas with specific details and examples. They might choose to interview concerned parties on this subject.

4. You might first have students share experiences in small-group discussions or have them freewrite on this topic.

CHAPTER FIVE WRITING ASSIGNMENTS

1. You might have a full-class discussion about other health-care topics that might be covered in the interview and/or the types of questions that might be asked during the interview.

2. Have students explore, either in small groups or with the whole class, the style and format of human-interest stories. You might also brainstorm together for potential human-interest topics.

3. You will probably need to work with students on narrowing the focus of their topics. Have students work on narrowing their topics in small groups.

4. You might first want to explore potential definitions of *human right* and *privilege*.

CHAPTER SIX

Coexisting with Mother Earth

Chapter Introduction

The chapter introduction concludes by asking students to consider what changes may need to occur if we are to create a better environment for ourselves and future generations. You might begin this chapter by discussing with students their values and attitudes toward the environment. Try to get students to see environmental issues from both personal and global vantage points. The following questions are intended to facilitate this discussion:

- What are some of the lifestyle changes people will need to make in order to ensure a better environment?

- Why do you think change is sometimes hard for people to accommodate?

- What values and attitudes will need to be present in order to have a better environment?

A Forgotten Ecological Disaster
Donatella Lorch

DISCUSSION QUESTIONS

1. Students should see the rhetorical strategy of appealing to emotion. Also, you might point out the technique of drawing a reader in by opening an essay with a specific incident or anecdote.

2. You might explore the relationship between educational and environmental issues.

3. Responses will vary. Students might bring up the proliferation of nuclear arms and the toxic waste associated with this type of weapon.

4. Responses will vary. Exploitation of any natural resource is a good starting point for discussion (e.g., timber, oil, water).

5. Responses will vary. Have students focus on the word *forgotten*. Have them think about the connotations of this word.

WRITING ASSIGNMENTS

1. You might get students to create a time line of the changes occurring in the Kibira Forest.

2. Use Discussion Question 2 as a prewriting activity for this assignment.

3. Taking on various roles of people involved in this crisis should help students more clearly see the complexities of the issues.

4. You might first have students in small groups brainstorm for possible solutions.

There Aren't Plenty of Fish in the Sea
Reginald Dale

DISCUSSION QUESTIONS

1. Encourage students to see why this title helps further the author's thesis as opposed to simply identifying the subject matter of the article.

2. You might make a connection to the Burundi's exploitation of the Kibira Forest.

3. Have students brainstorm in small groups for other areas of resource conservation where this philosophy might apply. Have students make a list of potential governmental concerns regarding this policy.

4. Encourage students to consider the long-term goals of conservation when compiling these regulations.

5. You might relate this question to other forms of cheating (e.g., If people think they can cheat and get away with it, many will take that opportunity).

6. In addition to fishing regulations, students might also consider the role of education.

WRITING ASSIGNMENTS

1. You might have students present oral summaries of particular articles on this subject.

2. You might suggest to students that they create a time line of the events leading to the tension.

3. Have students work in cooperative groups to develop a plan for the resolution of this problem.

Europe's Flood of "Sins and Failures"
Rick Atkinson

DISCUSSION QUESTIONS

1. Responses will vary. Help students to see the rhetorical impact of the phrase *Sins and Failures*.

2. Responses will vary. Students might consider the floods that occurred in the American Midwest during the summer of 1993.

3. Encourage students to consider the complexities of this issue. Students should explore the balance between the economy and the environment as it relates to this question.

4. You may first need to discuss the nature of global warming with students. Refer to the article by Epstein and Gelbspan in this chapter.

5. Encourage students to consider emotional as well as ecological costs.

WRITING ASSIGNMENTS

1. You might begin by having students explore what specific routines might need to be changed in order to protect the environment. From that point, they can begin to consider to what extent these routines should be altered.

2. You may need to review with students techniques for synthesizing information.

3. The diversity of the roundtable is intended to help students recognize the complexities of the issue.

4. Use Discussion Question I as a prewriting strategy.

Changing Climate: A Plague upon Us
Paul R. Epstein and Ross Gelbspan

DISCUSSION QUESTIONS

1. Students might want to create a chart or visual representation of the relationship between the specific causes and the greenhouse effect.

2. Students might cite specific weather patterns (e.g., the flooding of Europe).

3. Students might cite heat waves, record-breaking snowfalls, droughts, floods, and so on. Encourage students to be as specific as possible.

4. As a follow-up activity, have students write a narrative to accompany their diagrams.

5. This is a two-part question. The brainstorming students do for the first part of the question is intended to help them answer the second part.

6. Answers will vary. Have students freewrite on the question before discussing it.

WRITING ASSIGNMENTS

1. Emphasize the need for specificity in the essay. General suggestions need to be accompanied by specific advice for implementing them.

2. Use Discussion Questions I and 2 as prewriting activities.

3. As a prewriting strategy, have students create a visual representation of the causes and consequences of ecological ignorance.

4. Encourage students to deal with the complexities of the issues (e.g., the relationship between the economy and the environment).

Q & A: Fading Ecology Movement's Identity Crisis
Ken Shulman

DISCUSSION QUESTIONS

1. The activity is intended to develop students' background knowledge of the ecological movement and to give it historical perspective.

2. You might first have students cluster or freewrite about the term *identity crisis*.

3. Responses will vary. You might want to have students explore the various meanings and connotations associated with the word *power*. Ask students where they think power exists.

4. Responses will vary. You might spend some time discussing what it means to centralize or decentralize. You might then ask students to offer other examples of decentralization.

5. You might have students first freewrite on the terms *sensationalist* and *global consciousness*.

6. You might ask students to think about other acts of civil disobedience and their outcomes.

7. Students should consider the relationship between "a consumer mentality" and conservation. You might have students create a chart detailing the advantages and disadvantages of mounting "a resistance to the consumer mentality."

WRITING ASSIGNMENTS

1. Small-group brainstorming sessions that address this question will help students focus and develop their thoughts.

2. You might want to work first on definitions of *necessary* and *unnecessary* with students. Emphasize the need to support general assertions with specific examples and details.

3. Have students report their secondary-source findings in oral reports to the class or to peer groups.

4. You might suggest that students contact a representative of the organization and interview that person.

5. There may be a tendency on the part of students to write essays in response to this question that lapse into vague generalities. Sufficient prewriting activities should help curtail this problem.

CHAPTER SIX WRITING ASSIGNMENTS

1. As a prewriting exercise, you might have students consider the effectiveness as well as the consequences of civil disobedience efforts in other movements (e.g., civil rights, women's suffrage).

2. Students may want to consider polishing their essays for publication in either the school newspaper or a local paper.

3. Prewriting strategies should get students to consider the complexity of this issue. You may want to review strategies for synthesizing sources.

The Sporting Life

Chapter Introduction

The chapter introduction concludes by asking students to consider why people are so interested in sports-related news. You might begin this chapter by discussing with students their personal views and opinions about sports-related issues. Try to get students to think critically about what makes a sports topic newsworthy. The following questions are intended to facilitate this discussion:

- What are some characteristics of sports that make people so enthusiastic about them?

- Why do you think some people become emotional about sports?

- Why do you think people often are interested in the personal lives of sports figures?

- Why do you think sports figures so often are paid very high salaries?

- What are some positive outcomes of an enthusiasm for sports? Are there any negative consequences of this enthusiasm?

What They Really Need Is a Round Ball
Rob Hughes

DISCUSSION QUESTIONS

1. You will probably want to deal first with the concept and history of apartheid in some depth before attempting to make any connection to sports. Small-group discussion will facilitate a culling of students' collective knowledge on the topic.

2. You might have students consider the nature of teamwork and cooperation. How can teamwork erase racial, ethnic, and national barriers? You might also have students think about how sports could be made exclusionary and/or elitist. Have students think about the aims and goals of the Olympics.

3. You first might want to have students define the nature of pride. Freewriting on pride might facilitate this discussion.

4. Students should support their views with specific references to the article as well as their own experiences.

5. Responses will vary. You might draw upon the experiences of those students who do play soccer.

WRITING ASSIGNMENTS

1. As a prewriting strategy, you might have students freewrite or cluster first on the general topic of racism and prejudice. Then have students do the same for the topic of sports. Finally, have them make connections and associations between the two.

2. This writing assignment probably will require some research. Have students give oral summaries of articles they have researched on this topic.

3. You might have students read biographies of well-known athletes so that they can get a feel for the genre.

A Sport Courting Disaster
Rob Hughes

DISCUSSION QUESTIONS

1. Students should be able to see the multiple meanings of the word *courting*. As a follow-up activity, you might have students write their own headlines for news items.

2. Responses will vary. You might discuss the baseball strike or segregated leagues before the civil rights movement.

3. You might first discuss what rights students think all employees should be entitled to.

WRITING ASSIGNMENTS

1. You may want to have students also critique the effectiveness of the treaty.

2. This assignment could also be presented as an oral debate with teams taking sides.

3. This assignment might be made more manageable if students focus on one particular sport.

Hall of Fame Inductees Sound an Alarm for Baseball
Ira Berkow

DISCUSSION QUESTIONS

1. Responses will vary. You might have students freewrite on this topic before working cooperatively.

2. Responses will vary. Have students explore their own feelings and opinions as well as their experiences at games.

3. Students should explore the value of descriptive language as well as the use of a fragment at the close of the paragraph.

4. This question should provoke heated debate. Try to get students to support their opinions with specific reasons and evidence.

WRITING ASSIGNMENTS

1. You will probably need to stress that the assignment is not to be an opinion paper but a researched essay.

2. You should have students work toward a definition for this phrase with several prewriting activities such as freewriting or clustering. Small-group discussion would also be useful. You might also share with the class some of the works mentioned (e.g., Whitman or Twain).

3. You should probably brainstorm first with students for potential creative works. Students will probably have many suggestions.

From Basketball to Politics
Christopher Clarey

DISCUSSION QUESTIONS

1. Responses will vary. You may need to provide some historical background for students.

2. You might have students consider the first article of this chapter ("What They Really Need Is a Round Ball" by Rob Hughes). In that article, sports are seen as having the potential for a positive effect on a political situation.

3. In addition to having students consider the nature of these problems, you might also have them think about other times when politics interfered with sports (e.g., the 1980 Olympics).

4. You might have students explore the obvious win-lose scenario associated with sports and their effect on the relationship between national rivals.

WRITING ASSIGNMENTS

1. You might want to have students brainstorm cooperatively before beginning their essays.

2. Try to get students to support their opinions with specific reasons by having them create a chart that offers a reason for every opinion.

3. You might have students first conduct the roundtable orally and then have them write up the experience.

When Fashion Moves into the Sports Arena
Mary Blume

DISCUSSION QUESTIONS

1. Responses will vary. Students might look at the rhetorical effect of contrast.

2. You might have students break up the word into two parts—*media* and *-tique*. Have them think about other words that have the suffix *-tique*. Ask them to consider the various connotations of this suffix. What effect does combining *media* with *-tique* have on the reader?

3. Responses will vary. Students should support their opinions with specific examples.

4. Responses will vary. This question might work well in small groups.

5. Try to get students to make connections between the competition of the sports world and that of the fashion world.

WRITING ASSIGNMENTS

1. You might choose to do some advertising analysis as a whole-class activity before giving this assignment.

2. This assignment would work well as a cooperative effort from a small group.

3. Use Discussion Question 2 as a prewriting exercise for this assignment.

CHAPTER SEVEN WRITING ASSIGNMENTS

1. You will probably want to work with students on strategies for synthesizing information. Group brainstorming and discussion of the question will help to facilitate thesis formulation.

2. You might want to do a whole-class clustering activity on this question before having students begin the assignment on their own.

3. You might first have students cluster together for different types of sports. It would be more interesting if students chose sports such as lacrosse and rugby that are not as popular in the United States as they are in other parts of the world.

4. Students might consider the political, physical, emotional, and/or psychological effects of sports on our lives.

Living in a Technological World

Chapter Introduction

The readings in this chapter are intended to get students to think about the ways in which technology has generated change in the way we conduct our lives. At the conclusion of the chapter introduction, students are asked to consider specifically how technology has affected the quality of their lives. In addition, they are asked to think about what computerized technology they may take for granted. You might begin the chapter by asking students to freewrite on the topic "Technology and My Life." You might also have students in small groups create a daily technology chart that illustrates when people use technology and for what purposes in their daily routines. After the initial freewriting and small-group sessions, you might begin a general discussion on some of the questions presented in the chapter introduction. The following questions are intended to facilitate further discussion:

- How have computers changed your lives in the last five years?

- How do you think computers have changed the lives of people in your parents' or grandparents' generations?

- How do you think computer technology might affect future generations?

- What are some positive outcomes of these technological changes?

- Are there any negative outcomes presented by these techno-logical changes?

- Do you think technological change is occurring at a faster rate than it has in previous generations?

The Web: Out of the Lab and Spun around the World
Barry James

DISCUSSION QUESTIONS

1. You might have students form a circle and then toss a ball of yarn back and forth until a web is created. Then have them discuss the qualities and characteristics of a web, especially as it might apply to the World Wide Web.

2. Responses will vary. Hopefully, there will be a variety of innovative uses.

3. You might first want to review traditional top-down and bottom-up management styles with students.

4. You might discuss the concept of monopoly with students. In addition, you might discuss what has occurred with companies such as AT&T and/or Microsoft.

5. Besides pornography and other illegal uses of the Web, students might discuss the issue of intellectual property and copyright. The National Council of Teachers of English has become interested in this concern, so you might consult with NCTE for further information.

WRITING ASSIGNMENTS

1. You might have students first brainstorm about what they perceive to be the specific functions of the U.N. Then they should consider whether or not Caillou's suggestion is appropriate.

2. If you have a computer lab that can accommodate an entire class, you might have students work in groups on this project or share their experiences as they occur in a computer-lab setting.

3. You will want to review the nature and function of a process analysis paper with your class. You also might want to share with your class computer documentation and instruction manuals. Then discuss with students when manuals are useful and how they might be improved.

4. Students might benefit from a whole-class discussion on this topic, using a prewriting strategy such as clustering.

Saving Money on the Web
Laurie Flynn

DISCUSSION QUESTIONS

1. Responses will vary. Try to get students to think about how the Web might benefit them; then they might see potential business uses.

2. Responses will vary. You might see if any students have had firsthand experiences with credit-card fraud.

3. Responses will vary. Students should consider issues of privacy (social security numbers, addresses, and so on).

WRITING ASSIGNMENTS

1. You might have students first cluster or freewrite on the term *customer service*. They might also make brainstorming lists of the functions of customer service. Once they have prewritten on this topic, they can begin to see how the Web might be used to enhance customer service.

2. You might have students in small groups develop interview guides for this assignment.

A Two-Way Virtual Street: Internet Broadcasting Goes Interactive
Peter H. Lewis

DISCUSSION QUESTIONS

1. Students should see how the reader initially thinks of a traditional view from a window but then is surprised to find out the view is on a computer screen. Discuss the rhetorical impact of surprise.

2. You might want to have students write definitions of the term *M-bone*, either on their own or cooperatively.

3. Responses will vary. You also might have students freewrite on this question.

4. Responses will vary. This question also could be tied into Discussion Question 4 (e.g., the reality might present logistical problems).

5. Responses will vary. You might have students think about technology that is presently used in many households but twenty-five years ago would have seemed an impossibility (e.g., personal computers, VCRs).

WRITING ASSIGNMENTS

1. You might have students find other articles on this subject and then present oral summaries of the articles to classmates as a means of supplementing the information on M-bone.

2. This assignment would work well as a cooperative effort among students in small groups.

3. You might want to brainstorm first about possible primary sources of information on M-bone.

4. Use Discussion Questions 3, 4, or 5 as prewriting exercises.

In the War Against Credit-Card Fraud, a Technological Arms Race
Barbara Wall

DISCUSSION QUESTIONS

1. You might have students first freewrite on the term *arms race*. Try to get students to think about the connotations of this term.

2. You might discuss how credit-card fraud has been committed in the past. Try to get students to think of the specific loopholes in credit-card use that make it possible for thieves to abuse the system.

3. This question would probably work best in small cooperative groups with students making brainstorming lists.

WRITING ASSIGNMENTS

1. Alternatively, you might want to have students submit their articles to appropriate community magazines and newspapers.

2. Use Discussion Question 2 as a prewriting activity for this assignment.

3. You might discuss with the students the rhetorical effects of the use of dialogue and primary source quotes in this type of essay.

In the Information Age, a New Set of Have-Nots
Nicholas Negroponte

DISCUSSION QUESTIONS

1. Responses will vary. You may want to discuss the reference to Marie Antoinette's "Let them eat cake."

2. Responses will vary. Try to get students to see computer uses that may be taken for granted (e.g., traffic-light control).

3. You first might want to explore the meaning of the word *literati*.

4. Responses will vary. You might want to ask students about their first-hand experiences with people who fall into the "digitally homeless" category.

5. Try to get students to ground their responses in specific examples.

WRITING ASSIGNMENTS

1. Student papers might be more focused if the essays were narrowed to one or two specific areas (e.g., education, home finances, entertainment).

2. You might want to review writing a process analysis essay with your students.

3. You first might have students brainstorm in small groups about other activities for which this term might apply.

CHAPTER EIGHT WRITING ASSIGNMENTS

1. As part of prewriting, you might have individual students present oral summaries of articles on this topic.

2. You will probably want to spend some time discussing the term *quality of life*. You might want to have students freewrite on the phrase before discussing it in small groups.

3. Before students begin their journals, you might have them make a prediction about how much they come into contact with computer technology. Then they can compare their predictions with the actual journal experience.

4. You might think about moving this assignment beyond a classroom writing exercise by soliciting actual charities or school organizations for a computer donation.

CHAPTER NINE

Understanding the World Economy

Chapter Introduction

The concluding paragraph of the chapter introduction encourages students to make personal connections with what they are reading. Although many of the readings concern economic affairs of foreign countries, encouraging students to personalize or connect the readings to their own lives can make their understanding of the text much richer. You might begin this chapter with a general discussion about students' views of the world economy. The following questions are intended to facilitate this discussion:

- What do you think are some of the most important economic issues facing the world today?

- What do you think are some of the most important economic issues facing young people today?

- What do you think you can learn from other nations about the economy? What do you think other nations can learn from your country about the economy?

- What economic issues would you like to understand better? Why?

- Why do you think it might be important to pay attention to the economy?

Privatization: Lessons of the East
Richard E. Smith

DISCUSSION QUESTIONS

1. You first might explore the various connotations of the word *annex*. Students should perceive the "second-class" or "stepchild" situation many East Germans feel they are in.

2. You might want to have students explore these two concepts in small groups and then share their findings with the whole class.

3. Students should be able to make the connection between this point and Negroponte's contention that "The combination of starting from scratch and having a young population can be a major asset."

4. Responses will vary. You might discuss the Japanese management style that employs similar strategies with employees.

5. Responses will vary. Try to get students to support their opinions with specific examples or reasons.

6. You might turn this question into a freewriting exercise.

WRITING ASSIGNMENTS

1. You might also suggest that students interview people who had some type of connection to this historic event (e.g., former citizens, history scholars, journalists, and so on).

2. Have students brainstorm in small groups about the various sociopolitical ramifications connected to this issue.

3. Use Discussion Questions 4 and 5 as prewriting activities for this assignment.

4. Use Discussion Question 5 as a prewriting activity for this assignment.

Russian Firm Learns to Navigate in a Free Market
Fred Hiatt and Margaret Shapiro

DISCUSSION QUESTIONS

1. Responses will vary. Students will probably see the obvious play on the word *navigate*.

2. You might decide to have students turn their brainstorming into an essay.

3. Students should be able to point to excerpts from the article to support their responses.

4. Responses will vary. Draw on students' personal knowledge of the way businesses are organized and administered.

5. Responses will vary. Try to get students to support their opinions with concrete examples.

WRITING ASSIGNMENTS

1. Students will probably need to consult other sources. You may want to have students present oral summaries of articles they have found on this topic.

2. As a prewriting activity, have students give oral summaries of their research to classmates.

3. Use Discussion Question 5 as a prewriting activity.

Twenty Years After, Vietnam Treads Softly
Clare Hollingworth

DISCUSSION QUESTIONS

1. Responses will vary. The purpose of this exercise is to generate the necessary background knowledge students will find useful as they approach this article.

2. Responses will vary. You will probably first want to discuss more fully the role of language in business affairs before specifically addressing the role of English in the emerging Vietnamese economy. Reviewing "Courses in English Flourish in Vietnam" would be a useful activity.

3. Responses will vary. A clustering activity might work well with this question.

4. Responses will vary. Try to get students to support their opinions with information from either article.

5. You might poll students to see if they think this sort of petty thievery occurs in metropolitan areas with which they are most familiar.

6. Students will need to be familiar with the fall of Saigon in order to respond to this question.

7. Responses will vary. Students can be polled for their own personal opinions as well as what they have heard from others.

WRITING ASSIGNMENTS

1. You may want to have students work on this project in small cooperative groups.

2. Students may want to focus on the economic relationship (or lack of one) between the United States and Vietnam and how this relationship has affected the economic development of Vietnam.

3. You might want to have students review "Privatization: Lessons of the East" and the accompanying discussion questions as a preliminary activity.

The Third World Is Shrinking Fast
Reginald Dale

DISCUSSION QUESTIONS

1. You might need to explore the meaning of the word *anachronism* with students. In addition, you will want to explore the attitudes towards Third-World countries that were prevalent in the 1970s.

2. Responses will vary. Try to get students to root their opinions in specific examples.

3. Responses will vary. You might also have students discuss the political issues involved in this question (i.e., Rwanda and Somalia are war-torn nations).

4. You might want to explore the term *problem children* as a preliminary response to this question.

WRITING ASSIGNMENTS

1. As a prewriting activity, you might want to have students brainstorm in small groups about nations that might be categorized as developing.

2. You might have students make a list of the advantages and disadvantages of providing aid to developing countries.

3. You will probably want to explore what sorts of boundaries might differentiate between "rich" and "poor" countries.

4. You might explore with students the potential of education as it relates to this question.

Real Job Training Sets Plan Apart
Erik Ipsen

DISCUSSION QUESTIONS

1. Responses will vary. Try to get students to support their views with specific reasons and examples.

2. Responses will vary. You might get students to think about the present political climate and voters' reactions to issues such as unemployment and public aid.

3. Responses will vary. You might discuss with students programs such as CETA or certain New Deal initiatives.

4. This question might work well in small-group discussion. You might have students freewrite on the question before they participate in group discussion.

5. Responses will vary. Students might discuss the emotional and psychological benefits of this blurring.

WRITING ASSIGNMENTS

1. You might want to have students interview people at an employment office as part of this assignment.

2. Use Discussion Question 4 as a prewriting activity.

3. You might encourage students to consult secondary sources. You might then ask students to present oral summaries of their research to their classmates.

CHAPTER NINE WRITING ASSIGNMENTS

1. You might suggest to students that they get ideas for their question list by reviewing some of the articles they have read in this chapter.

2. You might suggest to students that they interview business people or business educators about this subject.

3. You might have students brainstorm in small groups about specific aspects of this writing assignment (e.g., various nations, long-term and/or short-term economic consequences, global ramifications).

4. As a prewriting activity, you might have students create a brainstorming map or cluster of the various nations that have received aid from the United States and the effects of this intervention.

5. You might want to focus students' brainstorming by having them explore the causes and consequences of unemployment.

CHAPTER TEN

Fighting for Human Rights

Chapter Introduction

The two questions asked at the close of the introduction should serve as guideposts for reading the articles contained in this chapter. As students read these articles, they not only should begin developing criteria for universal human rights but also should start thinking about ways to protect these basic human rights. You might begin this chapter by having a general discussion about human rights; you might start with a definition of *human rights* and then explore ways of preserving these rights. You might create a definition of human rights by identifying specific incidents considered human-rights violations and then determining what these examples have in common. The following questions are intended to facilitate this discussion:

- What have you heard in the news about human-rights violations?

- Do human-rights violations occur all around the world?

- Do you have any firsthand knowledge of a human-rights violation?

- What do you think are some universal qualities or characteristics of a human right?

- Are human rights universal? Why or why not?

- What are some ways we can preserve human rights?

Rights: A Look at America
The Washington Post

DISCUSSION QUESTIONS

1. Responses will vary. Students might approach this question by looking at many examples and then determining what they have in common.

2. Responses will vary. You first might want to explore the various connotations of the phrase *cutting edge*.

3. Responses will vary. Students might consider the United States's influence around the world in other matters as a possible approach to this question.

4. Responses will vary. You might have students explore this question in small discussion groups.

WRITING ASSIGNMENTS

1. This assignment first might be done in class with students as roundtable participants debating this question.

2. You might have students create a time line of the events leading up to the ratification.

3. Use Discussion Question 1 as a prewriting activity.

Role Reversal for U.S. at Rights Hearing
Julia Preston

DISCUSSION QUESTIONS

1. Students should see characteristics of a traditional editorial in "Rights: A Look at America" and compare and contrast them with this article (e.g., use of quoted material, tone, length, and so on).

2. Responses will vary (e.g., Tiananmen Square).

3. You first might explore the possible meanings of the phrase *a work in progress*.

4. Responses will vary. Try to get students to support their opinions with specific examples.

5. Responses will vary. Students should probably first consider whether or not there are human-rights violations in the United States.

WRITING ASSIGNMENTS

1. Use Discussion Questions 4 and 5 as prewriting activities.

2. You might suggest that students contact human-rights organizations for primary-source information.

3. You might have students brainstorm in small groups for possible topics.

Materialism and Greed Spurring "Dowry Deaths"
Molly Moore

DISCUSSION QUESTIONS

1. You might have students explore the various contexts in which they have heard the word *dowry* used.

2. Responses will vary. You might explore other practices that may or may not have been legitimized by marriage.

3. You might have students consider the role that greed and family honor play in the continuation of this practice.

4. Responses will vary. You might get students first to think about the role of women in their own societies and then have them make comparisons to the society described in this article.

5. Students will hopefully see the illustrative value of these examples and apply the strategy to their own writing.

WRITING ASSIGNMENTS

1. Alternatively, you might have students find their own sources on this subject and write reports on them.

2. As a preliminary activity, you might have students first research the various organizations involved in this sort of work and then report to classmates on what these groups do.

3. Students will be able to gather much support for their argument from the article, but they may also want to consult other sources.

4. You might want to have individual students present oral summaries of particular sources to the class.

In Nigeria, a Scared Silence Reigns
Stephen Buckley

DISCUSSION QUESTIONS

1. Responses will vary. Students might explore the effect of the word *reigns*.

2. Issues such as liberty and self-determination might be discussed in small groups.

3. Responses will vary. You might get students to think about other circumstances in which international intervention has occurred or has been considered.

4. You might have students freewrite about this phrase before they discuss the question.

5. Responses will vary. Try to get students to support their opinions with specific reasons.

6. Responses will vary. Students might contrast safety in silence with loss of liberty in silence.

WRITING ASSIGNMENTS

1. You may want to have students share some of their research in the form of oral summaries with classmates.

2. Alternatively, you might allow students to write about another human-rights abuse.

3. You might want to have students discuss in small groups strategies for developing their arguments.

CIA Ignored Abuses in Guatemala
R. Jeffrey Smith and Dana Priest

DISCUSSION QUESTIONS

1. Student should see the rhetorical benefits of quoted material and primary sources.

2. You might have students freewrite or cluster on the various connotations of the term *rainstorm*.

3. Students should see a connection between the policing of human-rights violations by the United States and the situation discussed in this article.

WRITING ASSIGNMENTS

1. You might also have students brainstorm about particular incidents (other than the one described in this article) when CIA involvement may have resulted in the cover-up of information for security reasons.

2. You might want to have students share their research in the form of oral summaries with the rest of the class.

3. You may also want to have students view the film *Missing*, which is about a similar incident.

CHAPTER TEN WRITING ASSIGNMENTS

1. You may want to share models of film critiques with your students before they begin this project. You will need to stress that the writing assignment requires more than a summary of the plot. Rather, students are to assess how well the film represents a human-rights issue.

2. You might suggest to students that they interview people who have expert knowledge of the issue (e.g., someone who works for a human-rights organization).

3. You might have students brainstorm in small groups for potential issues. Students might consult local papers or community organizations for potential issues (e.g., housing, health care, child abuse).

4. You might suggest to students that they keep daily journals of their experiences so that they will have material readily available for their essays.

5. Student might explore specific strategies with classmates in small-group discussions, or they might consult experts involved with human-rights organizations for advice.